EDUCATION FOR A NATION

CONGRESSIONAL QUARTERLY

1735 K STREET, N. W., WASHINGTON, D. C.

Congressional Quarterly Inc.

Congressional Quarterly Inc., an editorial research service and publishing company, serves clients in the fields of news, education, business and government. It combines specific coverage of Congress, government and politics by Congressional Quarterly with the more general subject range of an affiliated service, Editorial Research Reports.

Congressional Quarterly was founded in 1945 by Nelson and Henrietta Poynter. Its basic periodical publication was and still is the CQ *Weekly Report,* mailed to clients every Saturday. A cumulative index is published quarterly.

The CQ *Almanac,* a compendium of legislation for one session of Congress, is published every spring. *Congress and the Nation* is published every four years as a record of government for one presidential term.

Congressional Quarterly also publishes paperback books on public affairs. These include the twice-yearly *Guide to Current American Government* and such recent titles as *The Power of the Pentagon, Dollar Politics* and *China and U.S. Foreign Policy.*

CQ Direct Research is a consulting service which performs contract research and maintains a reference library and query desk for the convenience of clients.

Editorial Research Reports covers subjects beyond the specialized scope of Congressional Quarterly. It publishes reference material on foreign affairs, business, education, cultural affairs, national security, science and other topics of news interest. Service to clients includes a 6,000-word report four times a month bound and indexed semi-annually. Editorial Research Reports publishes paperback books in its fields of coverage. Founded in 1923, the service merged with Congressional Quarterly in 1956.

Education for a Nation was edited by Book Service Editor Robert A. Diamond and Associate Editor Elder Witt, who was the primary contributor to the book.

Other contributors: Michael A. Carson, Mary Wilson Cohn, Mary Costello, Joan S. Gimlin, Martha A. Gottron, David M. Maxfield, Barry Polsky, Georgiana Rathbun, Helen B. Shaffer and Stanley L. Williams. Researcher: Janice L. Goldstein. Cover and graphics: Art Director Howard Chapman and Sandra Katz.

The modern school facility on the cover was designed by Lamar Kelsey & Associates/Architects, photographer: Guy Burgess. The two other photographs were provided by the National Education Association.

Library of Congress Catalog No. 72-87225
International Standard Book No. 0-87187-035-5

TABLE OF CONTENTS

Charts, Tables, Summaries

Enrollment in Educational Institutions
1899 - 1969

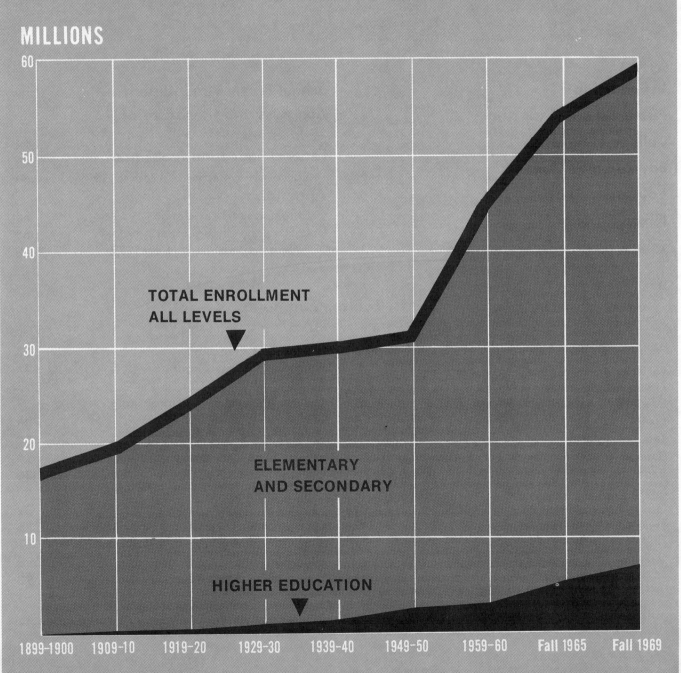

MILLIONS

TOTAL ENROLLMENT
ALL LEVELS
▼

ELEMENTARY
AND SECONDARY

HIGHER EDUCATION
▼

1899-1900   1909-10   1919-20   1929-30   1939-40   1949-50   1959-60   Fall 1965   Fall 1969

SOURCES: Department of Health, Education, and Welfare, Office of Education; Department of Commerce, Bureau of the Census; Department of the Interior, Bureau of Indian Affairs. 1969 is the last year for which complete data is available.

INTRODUCTION

And in the Elementary (public school) bill, they inserted a provision which completely defeated it; for they left it to the court of each county to determine for itself, when this act should be carried into execution, within their county. One provision of the bill was, that the expenses of these schools should be borne by the inhabitants of the county, every one in proportion to his general tax rate. This would throw on wealth the education of the poor; and the justices, being generally of the more wealthy class, were unwilling to incur that burden, and I believe it was not suffered to commence in a single county.
—Thomas Jefferson, *Autobiography*, 1821

Thomas Jefferson's recollections of the political obstacles to establishing publicly financed education in Virginia in the 1780s have a remarkably contemporary ring in the 1970s as the nation once again confronts the problem of financing public education. Jefferson's proposal, introduced in the Virginia House of Delegates in 1779 and enacted in 1796, was part of a group of bills to reform the laws of Virginia he worked on in the three years immediately following the writing of the Declaration of Independence. Public education in Jefferson's view was essential for the realization of the "inalienable rights" of men proclaimed at Philadelphia.

Two centuries later, the nation Jefferson helped establish is still struggling to achieve the principle of equality he enunciated in 1776. And in no area is that struggle more emotionally charged and politically volatile than it is in elementary and secondary education.

Searching for Equality

In 1954, the Supreme Court ruled that a child's constitutional right to equal protection of the laws under the 14th Amendment was denied when a state-supported school system required that child to attend racially segregated schools.

Eighteen years after that historic pronouncement, which overturned the prevailing "separate but equal" doctrine, the problem of segregated education persists; and to it has been added the equally complex issue of financing public schools on a constitutionally equitable basis.

Desegregation. Substantial progress has been achieved in reducing racial imbalances in those school systems (primarily in the South) which prior to 1954 had officially sanctioned segregated education. Most of this progress has occurred since 1968 following more recent Court rulings requiring that segregation resulting from past or present operation of dual school systems must be corrected at once and that busing was a permissible means of achieving racial balance. The result has been a dramatic reduction in the numbers of southern blacks attending racially isolated schools—either by increased busing or continued busing over shorter distances to schools where the majority of the students are white. *(p. 86)*

In other parts of the country where *de facto* school segregation is based on residential housing patterns, particularly in large metropolitan areas, school segregation has actually been increasing as a result of the movement of white families to the suburbs. The Court had set arguments for the fall 1972 term on a Denver case involving the constitutionality of *de facto* school segregation. A related issue which the Court may consider in 1972 involved a federal district Court order (subsequently overruled by the Court of Appeals) requiring the city of Richmond to merge its school system (primarily black) with the school system of two adjoining counties (primarily white).

Both cases involved the highly emotional issue of busing to achieve racial balance. And although it is uncertain how the Court would decide these questions, it is apparent that any further progress toward desegregated education nationwide will require either a redrawing of school attendance zones or busing—and most probably some combination of both, barring dramatic changes in the patterns of residential housing. *(p. 32)*

Hoping to present a major policy alternative to racial integration of the schools by busing, President Nixon proposed in March 1972 a program of "compensatory education" for schools having large proportions of minority group children. The President did not request new funds for the program; he called for redirection of $2.5-billion already authorized under other aid-to-education programs. He proposed a one-year moratorium on all new busing orders and directed the Justice Department to intervene on the side of anti-busing forces in desegregation litigation around the country. *(p. 34)*

By August 1972, only the House had acted on the President's proposals—approving a bill which called for stricter curbs on busing than he requested and earmarking only $1-billion in compensatory aid. Congress cleared a separate piece of legislation in June, dealing primarily with postsecondary education, which included less restrictive curbs on busing than the President requested. In signing the measure, Mr. Nixon described the busing provisions as "inadequate" and "unsatisfactory."

The future of desegregation is unclear; one possibility is that over the longer run, more congressional support will be found for compensatory grants for disadvantaged children and schools having large numbers of minority group children than for busing. But the House decision in August to cut back the President's requests for compensatory education and to go beyond the restrictions he asked on busing would make such a conclusion hasty at the start of the 1972-73 school year.

Finance. Quite apart from the issue of compensatory education as an alternative to integration, the problem of financing public schools has been mounting. The traditional and still the main source of revenue—the local property tax, which supports 54 percent of public school education across the country—has become an object of growing opposition. And this opposition comes at a time of increased financial plight for the schools. *(p. 3)*

State courts have ruled that a child's 14th Amendment rights have been denied by systems of public school finance which allow large inequities in per pupil expenditures to exist from one school district to another when these disparities are based on the wealth of property owners within individual school districts. The Supreme Court will hear arguments on this issue in its fall 1972 term.

Growing nationwide resistance by taxpayers to rising property tax rates has led both major political parties to call in their platforms for reduced reliance on the property tax as a means of financing public schools.

By August 1972 it was unclear what form new methods of financing public elementary and secondary education would take. It was clear, however, that pressures for statewide and federal aid to education would increase. It was also clear that efforts to equalize per pupil expenditures at all levels—among the states, within states and even within school districts—would require the nation's education budget to move sharply upward.

Yet another factor which could add substantially to pressures in the 1970s to increase public spending for education is the financial plight of parochial schools. The nation may be faced with the choice of finding a method of financing parochial school education which can meet constitutional objections or see public school enrollments swollen by spillover from parochial schools having financial problems. In the summer of 1972 Congress began hearings on aid to parochial schools—an issue which has been dormant since the early 1960s.

Postsecondary Education

To speak of "postsecondary education" is to select a more inclusive term to embrace not only college and university education (higher education) but also the rapidly growing volume and variety of programs which prepare people for jobs. It is in these two areas that enrollment is expected to rise most sharply in the 1970s.

The problem of postsecondary institutions and their students is similar to that of elementary and secondary education—one of money. Rising costs have forced some institutions to close their doors and others to curtail their programs. And rising tuitions have forced some students to forego continuing their education. *(p. 12, 20)*

But what does seem hopeful as one surveys the state of postsecondary education and compares it with the state of elementary and secondary education is that at the national level there seems—at least in the summer of 1972—to be a clearer commitment to action. In June Congress enacted the sweeping Educational Amendments of 1972 which authorized $19-billion for postsecondary education. In the act, Congress adopted the hitherto controversial assumption that every qualified student needing aid for postsecondary education could receive it as a matter of right and that for the first time general aid would be granted institutions to help them

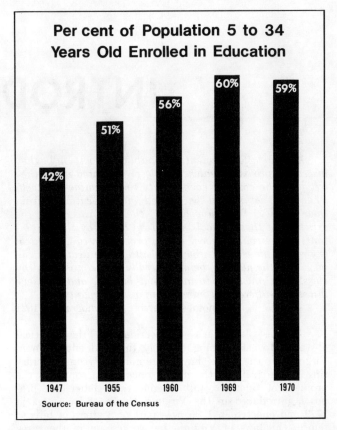

Per cent of Population 5 to 34 Years Old Enrolled in Education

1947	1955	1960	1969	1970
42%	51%	56%	60%	59%

Source: Bureau of the Census

meet the expenses of supporting their federally aided students. In addition, a new program of occupational education was authorized.

Priorities

It is somewhat premature, if not paradoxical, to say that the nation places a higher priority on the education of its adults than its young. But if this is indeed the direction of the 1970s, there may well be serious consequences at a later date.

One thing is clear: at the federal level education is not regarded as a high priority. Until the early 1960s no major federal aid to education program cleared Congress which was unrelated to the consequences of World War II or to possibility of military threats from abroad. Until 1963 the only major federal aid to education programs were the postwar GI bill benefits and the 1958 National Defense Education Act, prompted by the Soviet feat of hurling an object into outer space—"Sputnik" in 1957. For fiscal 1973, the federal budget calls for projected spending of $6.4-billion for education and $76.5-billion for defense. *(Federal programs p. 45)*

With the bicentennial celebrations less than four years away, it is appropriate to recall that the founding fathers, who resorted to arms in defense of their principles, understood other perils facing the young nation. Jefferson regarded education as a prerequisite to freedom: "If a nation expects to be ignorant and free...it expects what never was and never will be."

Robert A. Diamond
Book Service Editor
August 1972

LIMITED REVENUES AND INEQUITABLE DISTRIBUTION

Reforms impending in 1972 in the financing of public schools in the United States rivaled in their social consequences the movement to desegregate the schools that was mandated by the Supreme Court in 1954. In a certain sense one followed inevitably on the other, for both looked to an equalization in the quality of education the government provided to each child in the nation. Court decisions recognized the interlacing of school finance issues with equality of opportunity, the war on poverty and the continuing struggle to eliminate the penalties of racial segregation in American life.

President Nixon and other government leaders across the country responded positively to the implications of those decisions. The President promised in his State of the Union address on Jan. 20 that at some time in 1972 he would propose reforms in taxing for public school support that he described as "revolutionary." School finance reform became a paramount issue in a number of state legislatures, including those in states where courts struck down present methods of public school support. Expert studies of taxation in relation to school support abounded. Academic authorities whose technical studies have long pointed to the deficiencies in the prevailing method of financing public schools believed that the hour for action had come. Virtually no one considering the problem of education finance believed the existing structure of tax support for public schools should be left as it was or could be preserved without serious damage to the schools and ultimately to society itself. The call was for a drastic overhaul.

Problems and Questions

Two major deficiencies in public school financing converged to spur the call for change: (1) the inadequacy of school budgets in many places, especially in the central districts of the big cities, to meet the demands being made on the schools, and (2) the great disparities in the amount of money available for school use from one state to another and from one community to another within the same state. *(Expenditures by states, p. 6)*

The prospect of change raised many questions: Would reform of school financing produce better education for the nation's 51.5 million elementary and secondary school pupils, 46 million of whom were enrolled in public schools? How would the change affect those 5.5 million children, mostly Catholic, who were in financially troubled private schools—schools which President Nixon had promised to help stay open? Could the tradition of local control over schools survive when major support came from larger jurisdictions? Perhaps the overriding questions were: Would taxpayers be willing to pay more for school support? Could the burden of school taxation be more equitably distributed between rich and poor?

In his search for new ways of supporting public education, President Nixon moved with the tide, for the pressures for school tax reform came from every conceivable source—from governors and mayors, education officials, legislators, courts, teachers, tax experts, civil rights groups, taxpayer organizations, and students or their families. Most of the critics agreed that the local property tax was no long suitable as the main source for school support. Few argued with Nixon's 1972 State of the Union statement that the property tax had become "one of the most oppressive and discriminatory of all taxes, hitting most cruelly at the elderly and the retired." Agreeing on a substitute, however, presented some difficulties.

Prospective Nixon Proposals

The President proposed what he called special revenue sharing for six broad purposes, including education. In a special message to Congress on revenue sharing for public education, April 6, 1971, Nixon said revenue sharing offered "a new and more flexible approach to federal aid" and that it "would fundamentally reform the fiscal roles and relationships of American federalism." Congress took no action on the proposal. Nixon also held out his $5-billion general revenue-sharing program as a major means of alleviating state and local financial problems.

Treasury Secretary George P. Schultz, then director of the federal Office of Management and Budget, disclosed on Jan. 6, 1972, that the administration was studying the feasibility of a value-added tax, the returns from which would be used as a partial substitute for the local property tax to finance public education. As employed by several European countries, the value-added tax is placed on manufactured goods at various steps from the purchase of raw material to the point of retail sale. It is, in effect, a national sales tax paid by the ultimate consumer when buying the finished product.

A final decision on whether to recommend a value-added or any other tax was to be made late in 1972 or in early 1973. "We are developing comprehensive proposals" to meet the problems of "soaring property tax rates (which) now threaten both our communities and our schools," the President said in his State of the Union address. He said he was awaiting the recommendations of the President's Commission on School Finance and of the Advisory Commission on Intergovernmental Relations. The presidential commission was named in March 1970 and charged with the task of reviewing the revenue needs and revenue resources of public and private elementary and secondary education. It reported March 3, 1972. *(Commission recommendations, p. 10)*

Among the many documents under study were half a dozen volumes published in 1971 as the result of a

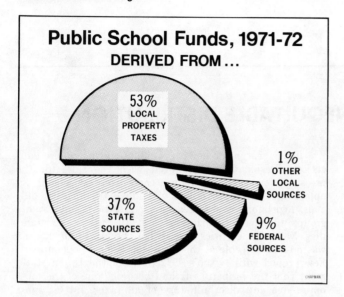

Public School Funds, 1971-72
DERIVED FROM ...

53% LOCAL PROPERTY TAXES

1% OTHER LOCAL SOURCES

37% STATE SOURCES

9% FEDERAL SOURCES

government-financed project which was described as the first comprehensive national study of school finance since 1933. Known as the National Educational Finance Project, initiated in June 1968, the study has engaged the efforts of leading scholars in educational finance under the administrative direction of the University of Florida, Gainesville, in cooperation with the Florida State Department of Education.

The project's publications were critical of existing methods of public school support. "Conventional approaches to financing education are at this time justifiably subject to attack," the authors observed in one of the project's studies. In a summary of its findings on financial equity, the project reported: "The problem of educational equality...will be a major one in what remains of the 1970s and no doubt in the decades beyond." It predicted that "the road to fiscal equality in education may be more tortuous than the one that leads toward racial integration in education."

Courts vs. Property Tax

As in the case of desegregation, the courts were instrumental in moving the nation toward reform in school financing. Courts in five states struck at the traditional method of financing public schools because of the fiscal inequities that resulted. The cases on which the courts acted—in Arizona, California, Minnesota, New Jersey and Texas—were representative of a wave of litigation on school finance. The School Finance Project of the Lawyers' Committee for Civil Rights Under Law, a voluntary group serving as an information clearinghouse for civil rights litigation, noted 44 law suits challenging state school finance systems that were current in mid-1972 and still others on which it lacked information. The cases were filed in 30 states.

The first decision that shook the foundations of the traditional structure of public school financing was rendered on Aug. 30, 1971, by the California Supreme Court in the case of *Serrano v. Priest*. The plaintiffs were school children and parents from several districts of Los Angeles County with large Spanish-speaking and black populations. The suit, seeking injunctive relief from an "inequitable" school taxing system, was

filed August 1968 in the name of one of the parents, John Serrano Jr. It named as defendants a number of state and county officials, including State Treasurer Ivy Baker Priest, who had served as U.S. Treasurer in the Eisenhower administration. The court, by a 6-1 majority, held that the California system of public school financing, "with its substantial dependence on local property taxes and resultant wide disparities in school revenue, violates the equal protection clause of the 14th Amendment (of the U.S. Constitution)." The financing system in California was substantially the same as in all other states except Hawaii, which has a single statewide school district operated by the State Department of Education.

At fault was the traditional plan by which each school district relied on its own tax resources, chiefly the local property tax, to finance the operation of schools within its borders. "We have determined," the California Supreme Court declared, "that this funding scheme invidiously discriminates against the poor because it makes the quality of a child's education a function of the wealth of his parents and neighbors."

Recognizing...that the right to an education in a public school (the court continued) is a fundamental interest which cannot be conditioned on wealth, we can discern no compelling state purpose necessitating the present system of financing. We have concluded therefore that such a system cannot withstand constitutional challenge and must fall before the equal protection clause.

The court also found the California system in violation of the state constitution's equal protection clause. The ruling came on appeal of a demurrer; the case then was returned to the trial court for trial on the merits. Further appeals were possible after judgment in the trial court, including appeal to the Supreme Court on the unconstitutionality of the financing system.

A nearly identical case was filed in federal court in Minnesota. The court, in denying a motion to dismiss the case, set out in a memorandum Oct. 12, 1971, objections to the then-prevailing method of school financing in Minnesota—objections similar to those stated in the California case. The Minnesota plaintiffs, who included students and parents of the White Bear Lake School District in Ramsey County and the Minnesota Federation of Teachers, withdrew their lawsuit after the state legislature on Oct. 30, 1971, revised the school-aid formula to provide more state aid for schools. However, another Minnesota lawsuit of this kind, brought by the Minnesota Real Estate Taxpayers Association along with public school students, was not withdrawn after the legislature acted.

In the Texas case, *Rodriguez v. San Antonio Independent School Board*, a special panel of three federal judges ruled unanimously Dec. 23, 1971, to the same effect as the California and Minnesota courts— that financing schools primarily from the proceeds of the local property tax made per-pupil spending dependent on local wealth and thus violated the 14th Amendment. The Texas court went beyond the California and Minnesota courts by ordering that the state take corrective action within two years. The state's appeal of the decision was scheduled to be heard in the fall 1972 term of the U.S. Supreme Court.

In New Jersey, State Superior Court Judge Theodore I. Botter, in a ruling Jan. 19, 1972, gave the legislature a one-year deadline to devise a new system of

Sources of Funds and
Spending by Educational Institutions

(in $-billions)

	School Years		
	1957-58	1965-66	1971-72
Elementary, Secondary schools			
Sources of funds for public schools:			
Federal	$ 0.7 (4.1%)	$ 2.2 (7.2%)	$ 4.3 (7.9%)
State	4.8 (30.4%)	9.6 (31.7%)	17.9 (33.1%)
Local	8.4 (53.5%)	14.6 (48.2%)	26.5 (49.0%)
Other	.0	0.1 (0.3%)	0.1 (0.2%)
Subtotal	$13.9 (88.0%)	$26.5 (87.4%)	$48.8 (90.2%)
Sources of funds for nonpublic schools:			
Federal	.0	.0	.0
State,	.0	.0	.0
Local	.0	.0	.0
Other	$ 1.9 (12.0%)	$ 3.8 (12.6%)	5.3 (9.9%)
Total: Elementary, secondary schools	$15.8	$30.3	$54.1
Higher Education			
Sources of funds for public institutions:			
Federal	$ 0.4 (7.5%)	$ 1.5 (10.0%)	$ 3.1 (10.0%)
State	1.4 (25.4%)	3.4 (22.4%)	7.3 (23.6%)
Local	0.1 (1.9%)	0.4 (2.6%)	1.0 (3.2%)
Other	1.2 (22.6%)	3.5 (23.0%)	8.7 (28.1%)
Subtotal	$ 3.1 (57.4%)	$ 8.8 (58.0%)	$20.1 (64.9%)
Sources of funds for nonpublic institutions:			
Federal	$ 0.3 (5.7%)	$ 1.4 (9.1%)	$ 2.1 (6.7%)
State-Local	.0	0.1 (0.7%)	0.2 (0.6%)
Other	1.9 (35.8%)	4.9 (32.2%)	8.6 (27.7%)
Subtotal	$ 2.2 (41.5%)	$ 6.4 (42.0%)	$10.9 (35.0%)
Total: higher education	$ 5.3	$15.2	$31.0
TOTAL SPENDING, all levels	$21.1	$45.5	$85.1

SOURCE: Department of Health, Education and Welfare

financing public school education and an additional year to put it into effect. New Jersey has relied, perhaps even more than most other states, on the property tax for school support.

In an Arizona case, *Hollins v. Shofstall,* the court also ruled against the state. It gave the state a similar deadline for action—the end of the 1974 legislative session.

Gov. William T. Cahill, who had already asked the New Jersey legislature to restructure the property tax, said at a news conference in Trenton immediately after the Botter decision that "there is no way of continuing to finance education in New Jersey in the traditional way." Gov. Ronald Reagan told the California legislature Jan. 6, 1972, that he wanted "to revise the funding for local schools in order to achieve a more equitable financing system." The Texas legislature initiated efforts to meet the school financing challenge, and in several states—Massachusetts, Maryland and New York, among others—special commissions were appointed to devise new school-aid formulas.

In Michigan, Gov. William G. Milliken asked the State Supreme Court to hold local school taxes unconstitutional in a suit he brought against three wealthy school districts. His suit was awaiting decision at mid-year. Meanwhile, Milliken proposed a state constitutional amendment to be placed as a referendum question on the November 1972 ballot. The amendment proposed to abolish the school tax on real estate and replace it with an increase in personal income taxes and with a value-added tax on manufactured goods.

Financing and Segregation

A court ruling in January 1972 on school desegregation held out a promise of far-reaching changes in financing and segregation, but it was overturned by an appeals court in June. In the initial decision, Robert R. Merhige Jr., a federal district court judge at Richmond, Va., on Jan. 11, 1972, ordered state authorities to consolidate the city's school district with those of adjoining counties. The intent of his ruling was to break down the pattern of "racially identifiable schools"—through the extensive use of busing. Schools in Richmond were predominantly black and those in the suburbs predominantly white. Breaking down boundaries also would have the the effect of pooling the financial resources of city and suburbs for distribution to all schools in the consolidated district. Judge Merhige told the State Board of Education to submit a plan for financial operations of the new district within 60 days. "This not only offers a means of integrating schools, it also provides a way of equalizing funds between the city and suburbs," commented Jack Greenberg, director-counsel of the NAACP (National Association for the Advancement of Colored People) Legal Defense and Educational Fund, Inc. After the Court of Appeals reversed Merhige, the Richmond school board ordered an appeal to the Supreme Court.

The Supreme Court for the first time agreed Jan. 17, 1972, to review the constitutionality of *de facto,* or "northern style," segregation—that which is based on housing patterns rather than on law. The case, originating in Denver, was to be argued in the court's fall 1972 term.

Congress dealt a setback to integration in the anti-busing provisions it added to the Higher Education Amendments of 1972. The bill cleared Congress June 8, 1972.

The House, at President Nixon's urging, had added severe anti-busing provisions to the bill. The Senate modified the House language. A compromise worked out in conference was narrowly approved in the House.

Nixon, seeking to capitalize on popular anti-busing feeling inflamed by the Democratic presidential primary campaigns, called the compromise "inadequate, misleading and entirely unsatisfactory," but he signed the bill June 23. An aide said if Congress didn't pass Nixon's own more stringent anti-busing proposals the President would make a constitutional amendment against busing a campaign issue in 1972.

As enacted, the bill:

• Postponed until all court appeals had been ruled on, or the time for them had expired, the effective date of all federal district court orders requiring the

Expenditures Per Pupil By States

(all districts, 1969-70)

	High	Low	Average
Alabama	$ 581	$ 344	$ 463
Alaska	1,810	480	1,330
Arizona	2,223	436	775
Arkansas	664	343	549
California	2,414	569	753
Colorado	2,801	444	735
Connecticut	1,311	499	915
Delaware	1,081	633	891
District of Columbia	—	—	971
Florida	1,036	593	717
Georgia	736	365	589
Hawaii	—	—	984
Idaho	1,763	474	595
Illinois	2,295	391	872
Indiana	965	447	675
Iowa	1,167	592	955
Kansas	1,831	454	731
Kentucky	885	358	580
Louisiana	892	499	749
Maine	1,555	229	723
Maryland	1,037	635	893
Massachusetts	1,281	515	691
Michigan	1,364	491	858
Minnesota	903	370	818
Mississippi	825	283	495
Missouri	1,699	213	720
Montana	1,716	539	802
Nebraska	1,175	623	653
Nevada	1,679	746	753
New Hampshire	1,191	311	687
New Jersey	1,485	400	1,016
New Mexico	1,183	477	690
New York	1,889	669	1,245
North Carolina	733	467	607
North Dakota	1,623	686	665
Ohio	1,685		729
Oklahoma	2,566	342	560
Oregon	1,439	399	875
Pennsylvania	1,401	484	892
Rhode Island	1,206	531	885
South Carolina	610	397	615
South Dakota	1,741	350	667
Tennessee	766	315	561
Texas	5,334	264	608
Utah	1,515	533	611
Vermont	1,517	357	1,034
Virginia	1,126	441	753
Washington	3,405	434	873
West Virginia	722	502	646
Wisconsin	1,432	344	941
Wyoming	14,554	618	884

Source: Senate Select Committee on Equal Educational Opportunity.

• Barred busing where it would risk the health of the pupils or require that pupils attend schools educationally inferior to the schools they previously had attended.

• Prohibited federal pressure on local school boards to induce them to undertake busing "unless constitutionally required."

Integration *per se* is a dead issue in the black community, according to Julius W. Hobson, a black leader whose suits against inequities in the District of Columbia school system resulted in extensive busing of pupils from poor areas. The real issue, he told the Senate Select Committee on Equal Educational Opportunity, Sept. 23, 1971, is inequality in the distribution of public resources. "The point of integration was to go where the gravy was, the resources," he said. "The resources—good schools— were in the white community.... Integration was only a temporary and expedient ploy to postpone the more important and revolutionary issues related to the equal distribution of public funds in public programs."

A suit filed by Hobson resulted in a landmark decision by Judge J. Skelly Wright of the U.S. Court of Appeals in the nation's capital. Wright ruled June 19, 1967, that racial separation in the school system resulting from racial separation in housing was unconstitutional. Hobson sucessfully pleaded in the 1967 case that the separation had resulted in marked differentials in the financing of black and white schools. Wright ordered the busing of children from poor and crowded schools to better schools in well-to-do neighborhoods. He also ordered that the so-called track system be abolished because it tended to concentrate large numbers of poor Negro students in classes for slow learners—in effect, re-establishing segregation. Hobson went to court again three years later, claiming that the inequities in financing still existed. He won another decision from Judge Wright, who on May 23, 1971, ordered local authorities to equalize expenditures among the city's schools.

Taxpayer Resistance

Other pressures for reform of school financing were mounting. One was the "taxpayer revolt" which emerged in the late 1960s and included the property tax high among its targets. In a Nov. 19, 1971, speech, Caspar W. Weinberger, director of the federal Office of Management and Budget, then serving as deputy director, said the proportion of bond referendums approved by voters dropped from 89 per cent in 1960 to 48 per cent in 1970. "The public knows that the only way these bonds can be financed is through an increase in the property tax," he said, "and they will not have it." Taxpayer resistance to higher property taxes sharpened academic criticism of the schools' dependence on this source of funding. Local tax sources provided 54 percent of all the money spent on public schools in the 1971-72 school year; 98 per cent of the local share came from the property tax. *(Graph, p. 4)*

More pressure arose from the growing militancy of the teaching profession, which was generally critical of the uncertainties that result from dependence on local financing decisions. Teacher unions would prefer negotiating on a statewide basis. They believe that in this way they may bring teacher pay rates up to the highest levels within the state.

transfer or transportation of school pupils to achieve racial balance (the provision was to expire Jan. 1, 1974).

• Limited the use of federal funds for busing intended to overcome racial imbalance or to desegregate a school system to those instances in which local officials requested federal funds for that use.

Recognition of the political force represented by the education lobby was indicated when President Nixon met on Sept. 30, 1971, with representatives of nine elementary and secondary school organizations. Several months earlier, in June 1971, the president of the National Education Association (NEA) had attacked the administration as "the most anti-education administration this country has had for years" because Nixon had vetoed a school aid appropriations bill as inflationary.

Perhaps the most pressing reason for restricting the public school financing system was the plight of the schools themselves. This was not a new condition, but it was growing worse. In some places it had reached a critical stage. The need for more money was evident, especially in the big cities. On the other hand, there were those who argued that there was money enough if only it were fairly distributed and properly used.

Financial Plight

Public schools in all parts of the country in 1972 were in serious financial trouble. According to the U.S. Commissioner of Education's Ad Hoc Group on School Finance, most of the nation's 17,000 school districts were finding it increasingly difficult to obtain adequate funds from resources available to them. They were in trouble despite very substantial growth in the amount of tax money devoted to school support.

PUBLIC TEACHER SALARIES

Public schools today are a $48.8-billion enterprise; that amount was the estimate of total revenues the schools received in the 1971-72 year. Of that, $46-billion was cash revenue, $21-billion more than in 1965-66 and $29-billion more than a decade previously. The average expenditure for operating the public schools was $929 per pupil, more than twice what it was ($419) in 1961-62.

In the intervening time, teachers' salaries doubled and enrollment rose by eight million. But much of the revenue increase constituted a real gain in educational purchasing power. The rise in school expenditures has averaged 9.7 percent a year, more than the 6.8 percent average annual growth in gross national product. A 1971 National Education Association study of the increase in state and local expenditures for schools between 1965 and 1969 indicated that 57.6 percent of the increase was due to the rise in prices, 14.5 percent to an increase in the workload, and only 27.6 percent was due to the improved quality and scope of the educational program. *(Table of average teacher salaries, this page)*

The paradox of higher revenues for schools coinciding with their deepening financial crisis led some observers to suspect that the fault lay not with a lack of funds but with improper management. The taxpayer revolt on school support issues has been attributed in part to a "crisis of confidence" in the ability of schools to make good use of the money they already were getting.

BIG CITY SCHOOLS

"How, the public might ask, can education be in straitened circumstances when (1) it receives the largest proportion of public support of all domestic governmental services, more than twice as high a percentage as either

Public Teacher Salaries

Year	Amount	Year	Amount
1960-61	$ 5,449	1966-67	$ 7,129
1961-62	5,700	1967-68	7,709
1962-63	5,921	1968-69	8,272
1963-64	6,240	1969-70	9,047
1964-65	6,465	1970-71	9,698
1965-66	6,935	1971-72	10,146

Source: National Education Association.

highways or public welfare, or (2) when state and local governments devote nearly 35 percent of their expenditures to education or (3) when the richest nation on earth allocates a larger proportion of its income to education than any of the other large industrialized states of the world?"

The education finance specialist who posed that question in 1971, Joel S. Berke of Syracuse University, also suggested an answer. The financial difficulty, he said, was most acute for two kinds of schools, those in rural areas and those in large central-city districts. "The former suffer from the effects of low population density and heavy public service demands on deteriorating tax bases." Attention has centered mainly on urban schools because so many children are involved. The point made by Berke was developed in a report of the U.S. Commissioner of Education's Ad Hoc Group on School Finance, which stated:

Many of the roots of the crisis in financing large city educational programs may be found in the redistribution of population and various economic developments that have taken place during recent years. These changes have left the poor, under-educated, aged and non-white in the central cities and have taken heavy manufacturing, many retail establishments and other kinds of business activity to the suburbs along with middle and upper income families.

The obvious result has been the inability of the tax base of the cities and income level of its residents to meet the high-cost educational and other needs of the population in the city.... For the nation as a whole, the suburban property growth rate in recent years has been more than two and one-half times that of the central cities.

On the other hand, a 10-state study conducted on behalf of the National Educational Finance Project showed that in eight of the states the central-city districts had higher average property valuations per pupil than the suburbs. The eight states in which assessed valuation per pupil was higher in the cities than in the suburbs in 1968-69 were Colorado, Georgia, Missouri, New York, Ohio, Oregon, Texas and Wisconsin. The other two states covered by the study were Alabama and Michigan. The amount of wealth available for tax purposes was found to vary greatly from suburb to suburb. In five of the 10 states, the suburban district with the highest valuation per pupil was three times as wealthy for tax purposes as the suburb with the lowest valuation.

The value of taxable property in a district, however, did not tell the whole story of the availability of funds for schools. The competition for the tax dollar was usually greater in the city than in the newer suburbs. Cities bore heavy burdens for other government services—for health, public safety, sanitation, public works, transportation, public welfare, housing and recreation. "Central cities devote nearly 65 percent of their budgets to non-educational services," the Ad Hoc Group reported, "while their suburbs...devote less than 45 percent." Moreover, city school budgets bore higher costs of land for school sites, higher construction costs and higher teacher salaries. The cities also had relatively high proportions of disadvantaged students who needed special educational services that add to school costs.

Still another handicap suffered by many city school districts was a restriction on the level of taxation they were permitted to impose. According to James A. Kelly, the Ford Foundation's "program officer in public education," school districts in about half of the nation's largest cities were more restricted in their access to property tax resources than other school districts in their states. For instance, Kelly said, in Missouri the restriction applied only to St. Louis; in Wisconsin only to Milwaukee; in Michigan only to Detroit. "These...laws...were passed 30 or 40 years ago," Kelly told the Senate Select Committee on Equal Educational Opportunity, Sept. 27, 1971, "when it was widely perceived that city schools were in a favored position and should be controlled by the state for the benefit of the rural and out-of-state interests."

Not only did states impose ceilings on tax rates, Kelly noted, but also some cities had let their assessment ratios slide "down and down over a period of time, thus concealing from the school district a portion of the real tax base...that it otherwise would have access to." He added: "When the city government drops the assessment ratio over two or three decades from say 80 to 40 percent, which is not untypical from the mid-1930s to mid-1960s, you see the bind these schools are in."

BUDGET CUTBACKS

At the request of Sen. Walter F. Mondale (D Minn.), chairman of the Select Committee on Equal Educational Opportunity, the National Education Association sought to obtain quick first-hand information at the beginning of the September 1971 term on how serious the financial crisis was in the schools. Telegrams were sent to 103 school systems, including all that enrolled at least 50,000 pupils, asking if they were experiencing cutbacks made necessary by financial shortages. Within four days 63 systems responded. Forty-one reported cutbacks of some kind for financial reasons. Of the others, 13 reported a "hold-the-line" budget of no cutbacks but no improvements and the possibility of cutbacks later if additional revenues were not obtained.

Schools were meeting the financial crisis in various ways. Pinellas County, Fla., was dropping art, music and social work. Anchorage, Alaska, reduced its reading and speech programs; Portland, Ore., its vocational and physical education courses; Boston its bilingual teaching and field trips; Columbus, Ohio, its advanced language instruction, eighth-grade typing classes, and counseling programs; Seattle its language instruction in elementary schools. Some schools stopped serving hot lunches while others cut out extra-curricular activities. Building maintenance suffered. Textbook purchases were suspended. Some schools shortened the school day, reduced the number of school days in the year, or boarded up some buildings and put children on double shifts at others.

Perhaps the most serious consequence of all was the reduction of—or failure to expand—the teaching staff.

Of the systems polled, 23 had eliminated a total of 4,388 regular teaching positions. Other systems said a job freeze was in effect. Some schools eliminated teacher aides and substitutes. NEA President Catharine Barrett told the Select Committee Sept. 23, 1971, the cutbacks meant "larger classes, less individualized instruction, less time to meet the pupils' needs." For the ghetto child, she said, the most important instructional element was the time a teacher gave him as an individual.

Losses of what some considered "frills" resulted in serious deprivation of educational opportunity, she said. Without their aides, teachers had less time for individual instruction. Elimination of special programs in art, music, drama, industrial arts and physical education—often the first to go when money runs short—might not only deprive gifted children of a chance to develop their talents but close the door to educational achievement of slow learners as well. "Pupils who do not achieve quickly in basic subjects frequently achieve remarkably well here, and this success is a key to faster learning in other subjects," Mrs. Barrett said.

State Equalization Aid

The plight of public education may be viewed as the end product of a historical process by which the schools were called on increasingly to do more and more while remaining locked in an obsolete funding system. The public schools began as modest enterprises for teaching the Three R's and a few other basic subjects to children of working-class families. School facilities and teacher qualifications were minimal and costs low. The founding fathers made no provision for education in the Constitution; hence responsibility for tax support of education fell to the states. As the public school movement gained momentum during the 19th century, the states followed the practice of delegating responsibility to local school districts, granting them authority to tax within their boundaries for school support. In time, states began to provide additional aid, but in small amounts and on the basis of a school census. By 1890, when tax-supported public schools had been established in all states, only one-fourth of the states—nearly all in the South—were contributing more than one-half the costs of school support. There was little consideration for equalization of opportunity or provision of a minimum program for all children.

With the growth of school attendance and rise of educational standards in the early part of the 20th century, state aid grew, as did local taxes for schools. From 1900 to 1915 state aid increased one and one-half times, while local support nearly doubled. From 1915 to 1930 state aid increased two and one half times, but local support increased even more. From 1948 to 1956 gross state aid increased in all but one of the states but local support outran state support in 27 states. In the 20 years between 1950 and 1970, both state and local funds for public schools grew sevenfold. *(Table of sources of public school revenues, p. 9)*

State grants may be general funds, to be used as the locality sees fit, or categorical, for specified uses. Some are so-called "flat grants," distributed uniformly on the basis of the number of pupils or some other numerical guideline; others are equalizing grants that take into consideration the fiscal ability of the locality.

Proportion of School Revenues

Year	From federal sources	From state sources	From local sources
1919-20	0.3%	13.8%	85.9%
1929-30	0.4	16.9	82.7
1939-40	1.8	30.3	68.0
1959-50	2.9	39.8	57.3
1960-61	3.8	39.8	56.4
1961-62	4.3	38.7	56.9
1962-63	3.6	39.3	57.1
1963-64	4.4	39.3	56.4
1964-65	3.8	39.7	56.5
1965-66	7.9	39.1	53.0
1966-67	7.9	39.1	53.0
1967-68	8.8	38.5	52.3
1968-69	7.4	40.0	52.6
1969-70	7.2	40.9	51.8
1970-71	7.2	40.0	52.8
1971-72	9.0	37.0	54.0

Sources: National Education Association and U.S. Office of Education.

The trend in the past two decades has been toward equalizing grants. More than three-fourths of all state money provided for schools is of that type; 20 years ago it was less than one-half.

Federal Role

The federal government was drawn increasingly into public school financing, chiefly by way of categorical grants for purposes considered to bear on the national interest. From approximately $2.5-million in 1919-20, the amount of federal aid grew to $3.3-billion in 1971-72. Despite the larger percentage increase, federal aid has remained a minor factor in school finance. Major federal enactments providing money for schools include the National Defense Education Act of 1958 and the Elementary and Secondary Education Act of 1965. The 1958 act authorized funds to improve the availability and quality of courses in science, mathematics and foreign languages. It was enacted the year after the Soviet Union launched Sputnik, the first earth satellite, and reflected a national desire to catch up with Russia in the space race. The 1965 act was intended primarily to help schools meet special instructional problems of children in poverty areas.

Neither federal nor state aid, however, has been sufficient to forestall the growing crisis. Nor have equalization formulas succeeded in their goals. Studies and briefs presented to the courts in school finance cases were replete with data showing great discrepancies in expenditures per pupil from one district to another as well as differences in their taxable resources. There were wide ranges between extremes within each of the states and marked differences among the states. Ironically, districts that taxed themselves most heavily were often the least able to educate their children.

In its *Serrano* decision, the California Supreme Court cited differences in tax rates and tax yields between Beverly Hills and Baldwin Park, two communities in the same county. Property owners in Beverly Hills paid a school tax of $2.38 per $100 of assessed valuation while in Baldwin Park they paid $5.48, yet Beverly Hills had $1,231.72 to spend on each pupil and Baldwin Park only $577.49. The main source of the difference was in assessed property valuation per child—$3,706 in Baldwin Park and $50,885 in Beverly Hills. "The poor district," the court said, "cannot freely choose to tax itself into an excellence which its tax rolls cannot provide."

Challenges in School Finance

The money crisis in the schools has inspired a number of proposals for putting the financing of public education on a sounder course. Nearly all would be expensive. How expensive would depend on how great a demand the nation made on its public schools in the years ahead. Expansion of school offerings was popular during the 1950s, especially after the Russians launched Sputnik, and new money was forthcoming. The schools in 1972 were under a barrage of criticism and the flow of money, if not decreasing, was rising at a slower rate. If there was indeed a widespread loss of faith in the benefits to be gained by giving the schools more money, the bonanza days for public education might be over for some time to come.

Much depended on what happened to private education. "We are all familiar with the problem faced by a public school system once it deteriorates to a point where wealthier parents are willing to send their children to private schools and then are unwilling to vote for adequate school taxes," economist Kenneth E. Boulding wrote in a section of the National Educational Finance Project report. On the other hand, most of the private schools are Catholic, and these are having financial difficulties too. Catholic school enrollment dropped by 1.2 million from its 1967 level to a total of 3.9 million in 1971-72. The number of Catholic schools in that period fell from 12,600 to 10,900.

If this trend continues, the spillover of Catholic children may keep public school enrollment up despite a prospective decline in the school age population during the 1970s. A drop in the birth rate during the 1960s has already showed up in public school enrollment. There was a scant increase of 0.7 percent in 1971-72. The number of children of school age actually declined slightly, but an increase in kindergarten enrollment, the closing of many parochial schools and the return of pupils who had gone to integration-dodging private schools apparently took up the slack.

A number of states sought to prevent an outpouring of parochial school pupils into the public schools by paying part of the cost of secular instruction in the church schools. But the Supreme Court on June 28, 1971, struck down laws in Pennsylvania and Rhode Island that provided public funds to pay part of the teachers' salaries and purchase educational material in church schools. Connecticut, Louisiana, New Jersey, New York and Ohio had enacted similar laws, and at least nine additional states were reported to be considering similar legislation before the decision.

When a federal Court of Appeals panel in January 1972 found the New York law unconstitutional, Gov.

Expenditures of Public and Private Schools

(in billions of dollars)

Year	Including college	Primary and secondary
1959-60:		
Total	32.8	23.9
Public	26.1	21.1
Private	6.7	2.8
1964-65:		
Total	49.2	33.3
Public	38.1	29.2
Private	11.1	4.1
1970-71:		
Total	77.6	49.6
Public	62.7	44.6
Private	14.9	5.0

Future Projections

Year	Including college	Primary and secondary
1974-75:		
Total	84.1	50.1
Public	67.6	45.2
Private	16.5	4.9
1979-80:		
Total	97.4	55.2
Public	78.4	49.7
Private	19.0	5.5

Source: U.S. Office of Education.

Nelson A. Rockefeller said he would continue to seek an "appropriate" means of helping the parochial schools. President Nixon, in a speech at a Knights of Columbus dinner in New York, Aug. 19, 1971, pledged support for the Catholic Church effort to keep its schools operating. Responding extemporaneously to a charge made earlier in the evening by Terence Cardinal Cooke—that denial of public funds to church schools was "discriminatory"—Nixon noted that private schools were closing at the rate of one a day. "You must resolve to stop that trend and turn it around—and you can count on my support to that," he said.

Nixon's Commission on School Finance recommended a program of emergency aid to private school systems for at least five years. It also recommended consideration of new federal assistance to private and parochial schools in the form of tax credits and deductions, tuition reimbursement and scholarship aid. The commission further urged equitable sharing for public and parochial schools in any new federal education aid programs. By mid-1972 Nixon had taken no action to carry out his promise of support, and no action had been taken to implement the commission's recommendations.

School Expenses in 1970s

In its projections, based on current trends, the U.S. Office of Education has forecast a relatively static enrollment in public schools and a 5-percent decline in private school enrollment during the 1970s. Nevertheless, public school expenditures (including college) were expected to be almost 25 percent higher by 1979-80 than they were at the beginning of the decade. These projections did not take into account a proposal by the National Education Association to provide full-scale nursery and kindergarten programs for four- and five-year-olds in the public schools and to improve the quality of education offered. The NEA plan called for special programs for all pupils with physical and mental handicaps and emotional problems, intensive vocational training in high schools and extensive summer and adult education programs. It was estimated that by 1970 the plan, if implemented, would cost $76-billion in current prices.

To bring all schools up to a minimum standard immediately, according to the NEA, would require the hiring of at least half a million teachers in addition to the two million already employed in the public schools. At prevailing salary levels, the new teachers would add approximately $5-billion to the nation's public school budgets. Where would the additional money come from? Most would-be reformers believed there was no solution to school financing problems without considerably more federal and state aid. The NEA suggested that the federal share should be at least one-third of the total. Some others favored a 40-40-20 ratio of federal, state and local funds.

Statewide Financing

Pressure was increasing on state governments to take more of the fiscal responsibility for the schools. The Advisory Commission on Intergovernmental Relations recommended that the states assume substantially all of this responsibility. Gov. William G. Millikin of Michigan and Dr. James B. Conant, a former president of Harvard and a leading critic of public schools, were among those who favored statewide financing. After making an intensive study of school fiscal problems in Washington state, an NEA panel observed in 1971 that "informed opinion is rapidly moving toward the proposal that state governments assume substantially the total cost of operating local schools."

State assumption of the cost of financing public education was the principal recommendation of the President's Commission on School Finance. The recommendation was in three parts, bearing on the states, local school districts and the federal government:

● The states should determine the amount and raise the funds required for public education, allocate the funds among school districts and evaluate their use.

● Local boards of education should be given wide latitude, within state guidelines, to use the funds provided.

● The federal government should provide general purpose incentive grants to reimburse the states for part of the cost of increasing the state share above the previous year's proportion of total state and local education costs; further, the federal government should provide incentives and mechanisms to more nearly equalize resources among the states.

The commission urged that the federal government recognize the primary role of the states by distributing federal aid for education primarily through the states. It recommended a program of emergency aid, on a matching basis over at least five years, to large urban school systems and to non-public schools.

How the states could raise additional funds posed a problem. State and local taxes together more than doubled in 32 of the 50 states between 1960 and 1970, according to the Tax Foundation, Inc. The range was from 159 percent in Alaska to 73 percent in Oklahoma. A consultant in government finance, Allen D. Manvel, in 1971 estimated that "if all state governments had carried the school financing load being borne by local governments (in 1969), they would have had to increase total state government expenditures by about 30 percent—a sum amounting to nearly half their total tax revenue that year."

Some persons wanted the state to take over the property tax; others wanted to make less use of the property tax in school finance. Contrary to a widespread impression, the recent court decisions did not outlaw the use of the property tax for school support—the judges declared that school resources could not be limited to the tax return within a district's boundaries. If a state devised a formula for pooling the revenues from the property tax there was no constitutional bar to its continued use.

Some reformers believed the property tax could produce an appreciable increase in revenue if it were applied more vigorously to business and industrial holdings. "There are literally billions of dollars in potential property tax revenues that state and local governments have not begun to tap, and much of which they can tap simply by enforcing the laws as they are already written," Ralph Nader, the consumer advocate, told the Senate Select Committee on Sept. 30, 1971. Nader's Public Interest Research Group estimated that at least $7-billion of property tax revenues was foregone each year. Under-assessment of industry was seen as a major cause of the tax loss. In come states, under-assessment originated as tax concessions to lure industry to a particular area.

Local Control and Equity

Enlarging the state's function as financier of public schools raised the question of preserving local control. But proponents of centralized funding did not regard that as a serious problem. States already exercised a certain amount of control over public education. Further, there was nothing to prevent a legislature from providing all the money and still permitting the local districts to exercise their discretion in using the funds, especially in such matters as curriculum and teacher hiring.

"Though a state provides all funds from the state level it may yet encourage very substantial decentralization by delivering the money directly to the school rather than to the district," according to John E. Coons, a law professor at Berkeley who helped argue against California local school financing in the *Serrano* case. "To go the final step (the state) could even deliver the funds directly to the family unit in the form of vouchers or school stamps." Under the voucher system, the parents could "purchase" education for their children from the school, public or private, of their choice. The American Federation of Teachers, the NEA and organizations fighting aid to parochial schools have expressed strong opposition to the voucher plan.

Much interest has been shown in another Coons proposal: to establish a state schedule of minimum funding per pupil, with each level of funding based on a specified tax rate. If the rate a locality levied fell short of meeting the corresponding level of support, then the state would make up the difference. If a community decided to tax itself at the rate of $1 for every $100 valuation, and if, according to the state schedule, this tax rate entitled the local district to $900 per pupil but the rate actually yielded only $500, the $400 difference would be the state's share. On the other hand, if the community had greater property wealth, and the tax yield turned out to be $1,000, the $100 extra would be turned over to the state. Thus a rich and a poor district that taxed themselves at the same rate would have equal amounts to spend per pupil. Dr. Coons developed this "power-equalizing" proposal in full in a book entitled *Private Wealth and Public Education* (1970), co-authored with William H. Clune III and Stephen Sugarman.

A major problem reformers faced was how to assure equitable rather than equal financing per child. A mathematically equal distribution of school funds would not result in equity. Costs and needs differ from district to district, from school to school within a district, and from child to child within a school. The litigation challenging existing systems of school finance involved certain hazards. The courts have upheld only the principle of "fiscal neutrality." Earlier litigation—McGinnis v. Ogilvie, for example, in which the advocates of equity sought to develop a constitutional principle that each child was entitled to an education sufficient to meet his individual "need"—failed to win judicial approval. In the *McGinnis* case, a panel of three federal judges in Chicago heard the plaintiffs argue for a redistribution of resources based on educational need. But the court in 1969 dismissed the case for lack of a cause of action and for nonjusticiability. The Supreme Court summarily affirmed the decision in 1970.

Particular concern centered on the disadvantaged pupils in big city schools, many of which already spent more per pupil than schools in less troubled areas. Some of the city schools were in districts where property values were high even though family incomes were low. These schools were therefore already low in eligibility for state aid. They would continue to be low under any plan for additional state equalizing funds that did not take into consideration their peculiar handicap.

What seemed needed was an acceptable formula to measure the educational "need" of each child and translate that into its money cost in his school and in his area. Without such a formula, the "fiscal neutrality" dictated by the courts left the city schools no better off, and possibly worse off, than before. The Lawyers' Committee for Civil Rights Under Law, after sponsoring a strategy meeting on the question in October 1971 in Washington, prepared an analysis, published by the National Legislative Conference, of four different state programs designed to achieve equity in school finance. Nearly every state had a commission studying the question in 1972.

In the *McGinnis* ruling, the judges agreed that there were inequities. But they said these were problems for the legislature, not the judiciary, to decide. That seemed to be true in regard to problems of school financing generally. The effort to devise new means of financing schools to replace the old was essentially a matter to be grappled with in the state capitals and in Washington. It promised to command much of the nation's energies in the coming months and years.

INSTITUTIONS AND STUDENTS SHORT ON FUNDS

The great money problem looms over the American campus. It has, for the moment at least, replaced issues of war and peace, riots and drugs as the preoccupation of the college community. Emphasizing the extent of the problem, the president of Harvard, Derek Bok, announced at a press conference that the nation's oldest and most lavishly endowed university (over $1-billion) is "heading toward a period of financial stringency. There will," he said, "be a great deal of attention paid toward cost-consciousness." In 1970, the university ran a deficit of $760,000 for the first time in 25 years.

Bok's remarks appeared in the midst of a growing stream of announcements and reports issuing from colleges, universities, and educational foundations and associations—all of them testifying that most institutions of higher education are headed for serious financial trouble. In fact, many of them are already suffering the pangs of financial starvation. And the list is headed by some of the country's most prestigious institutions. In 1970, Yale University ordered a freeze on hiring in the face of an anticipated budget deficit of $1.5-million to $2-million. Columbia University has announced plans to curtail services and programs by 8.5 percent in 1972 and by 15 percent in 1973 in an attempt to end a budget deficit. Cornell University will reduce its budget for 1972 and 1973 in an effort to avoid depleting the school's unrestricted endowment.

Many small institutions have already disappeared—21 of them in 1971—while many others are firing faculty and dismantling entire departments. Hiram Scott College in Scottsbluff, Neb., dismissed one-third of its faculty and operated under the supervision of a bankruptcy court before finally closing its doors on July 28, 1971. John J. Pershing College in Beatrice, Neb., closed for lack of funds on Jan. 29, 1971, shortly after its students began the second semester. The Nebraska Office of Education reported that other colleges interviewed students enrolled at the closed schools and that most of them were placed elsewhere.

Surveys Into Depths of Campus Financial Woes

Details of the financial crisis have been set forth within the past year in reports issued by the Carnegie Commission on Higher Education and the Association of American Colleges.[1] The association gathered data from 554 out of 733 private four-year accredited institutions throughout the country. Starting with the 1967-68 academic year, the association found that although the 554 institutions had an average net surplus of $39,000, schools

with 500 or fewer students were already showing an average deficit of $2,000. The following year the average institutional deficit was $20,000, and the average for 1970-71 was projected at $115,000.

While the average deficit of small schools has grown, the most startling change has taken place in schools that enroll more than 4,000 students. Within four years the picture changed from one of surpluses averaging $147,000 to deficits averaging $558,000. The report concluded: "Private colleges and universities are apprehensive and they have reason to be. Most colleges in the red are staying in the red and many are getting redder, while colleges in the black are generally growing grayer."

Findings of the Carnegie Commission on Higher Education indicate that many public as well as private institutions are in financial trouble. Basing its projections on a study of 41 representative colleges and universities, the commission estimates that two-thirds of the nation's 2,340 institutions of higher education are either "in financial difficulty" or "headed for trouble." Among the giant public universities judged to be in financial difficulty already are the University of California and the State University of New York. The reports are agreed that unless significant aid is forthcoming soon, colleges will not be able to serve higher education and the nation with strength.

One of the ironies of the situation is that Negro colleges, a particularly hard-pressed group, are too poor even to take advantage of some $30-million released in September 1970 by the Nixon administration in response to their plea for aid. Twenty million dollars of the federal funds were allocated for construction, with the stipulation that Negro schools provide 30 percent in matching funds for every construction project. Dr. Herman Long, vice president of the National Association for Equal Opportunity in Higher Education, an organization of Negro schools, and president of Talladega (Ala.) College, termed the grant "entirely unrealistic in terms of our needs." To construct a $1 million building, a school would need $300,000 of its own. "So some schools just didn't even bother to apply under the circumstances." The $10-million in nonconstruction funds was spent for work-study programs and for teaching, administrative and student services.

The Carnegie Commission, in a report dealing with Negro colleges (*From Isolation to Mainstream*), has recommended a tripling of federal support for these schools in preparation for a doubling of their enrollment by the end of this decade. It found Negro colleges facing especially heavy burdens in providing student financial assistance. An analysis of the most recent survey on freshmen students made by the American Council on Education indicated that the median family income for freshmen at all colleges and universities in the United States was $11,000 a year, while at colleges for Negroes it was only $7,300. Among other burdens of Negro colleges,

1 See Earl F. Cheit. The New Depression in Higher Education (1971. the Carnegie Commission on Higher Education) and William W. Jellema. The Red and the Black: Special Preliminary Report on the Financial Status, Present and Projected of Private Institutions of Higher Learning (1971. Association of American Colleges).

Where Colleges Get Their Money*

	Public institutions	Private institutions	Combined
	(in millions of dollars; percentages in parentheses)		
Tuition and student fees	$ 1,399 (11.8)	$ 2,431 (34.1)	$ 3,830 (20.2)
Federal government	1,566 (13.3)	954 (13.4)	2,520 (13.3)
State governments	4,783 (40.3)	79 (1.1)	4,861 (25.6)
Local governments	580 (4.9)	34 (0.5)	614 (3.2)
Endowment earnings	49 (0.4)	365 (5.1)	413 (2.2)
Private gifts	54 (0.4)	552 (7.8)	606 (3.2)
Other general revenues	888 (7.5)	684 (9.6)	1,572 (8.3)
Auxiliary revenue	1,561 (13.2)	1,135 (15.9)	2,696 (14.2)
Student aid grants	299 (2.5)	279 (3.9)	579 (3.0)
Public service programs	672 (5.7)	610 (8.6)	1,282 (6.8)
Totals	$ 11,851(100.0)	$ 7,123(100.0)	$ 18,973(100.0)

* *Current-fund revenues only.*

SOURCE: U.S. Office of Education for fiscal year 1968-69, latest statistics compiled.

according to the commission, were low pay for faculty members, small or negligible endowments, and academic programs weak from chronic underfinancing.

Hostility of Alumni

Colleges are hurting from inflationary pressures that drive up salaries and other expenses, and from a general lag in the funding of federal projects. Moreover, many colleges are being punished by alumni who disapprove of the way they have handled student unrest. According to the acting president of Brandeis University, Charles I. Schottland: "Contributors ask very blunt questions. They say, 'Why should I give money to support a bunch of radicals who are trying to destroy us?' " One disgruntled Amherst College graduate wrote to his *Alumni News* last fall, "I abhor and reject what Amherst now condones or even encourages.... I will not contribute anything but criticism and dissent from what Amherst now is and stands for...." Although these attitudes may not reflect majority opinion of alumni, they have been prevalent enough within the past two years to cause significant losses in contributions at such universities as Wisconsin, Indiana, Colorado, Rutgers, Duke, Michigan State, and California at Berkeley.

Hostility has been reflected to an ever greater degree by the general public. And this attitude threatens the support of public institutions in state legislatures. The president of Ohio University, Claude R. Sowle, acknowledged that order on Ohio's state university campuses would be the determining factor in obtaining adequate funds for higher education from the Ohio General Assembly. "If we are to have any real hope of winning the substantial additional support we need, we must, in the few months remaining, transform the public's growing mood of

2 Calculated by Dr. M. M. Chambers in a publication of the National Association of State Universities and Land-Grant Colleges, *Appropriations of State Tax Funds for Operating Expenses of Higher Education 1970-71.* The association contends that state tax funds for operating expenses are a more valid measure of state support of higher education than total appropriations made by state legislatures for that purpose since the latter may include re-appropriated income received from student fees and other non-tax sources.

hostility toward higher education into one of understanding, and hopefully, friendship."

Even if the legislatures of the 50 states are imbued with good will toward the colleges, there is some doubt that they will have the resources to keep pace with rising campus costs. State tax funds for college operating expenses of higher education have risen from $1.6-billion in 1960-61 to more than $7-billion in 1970-71.[2] This increase includes costs of the growing system of community junior colleges, which have to some degree diverted funds from existing four-year colleges and universities. These funds, however, deal only with operating expenses. They do not reflect expenditures for capital improvements, an area of growing need.

Cost Problems for Students and Their Parents

Colleges are suffering from the cost squeeze, but students and their parents are feeling the pressure too. For many students rising costs mean either no college or a search for a cheaper school. Average basic costs at private colleges and universities run twice as high or more as at public institutions. Among junior colleges, the private-public ratio is even greater, as is shown in the following table:

	Private	Public
Two-year colleges	$2,121	$ 827
Four-year colleges	2,423	1,117
Universities	2,993	1,390

To these basic costs—room, board and tuition—at least $500 must be added for such items as transportation, books, laundry and cleaning. The total outlay for an Ivy League student can easily reach $4,500 or $5,000 a year.

Contrary to some popular images, it is not the rich but the middle class which has been the backbone of the prestige institutions for a long time, and this group is finding it difficult to support education at these levels. A Yale alumnus noted that the cost of attending the university has doubled in the 17 years since his graduation. "Projecting this forward to when the youngest of my three children would finish college...it will cost me approximately $100,-000 for their 12 years at Yale. This kind of tab effectively cuts the middle class out, leaving Yale for only the very rich and the very poor."[3]

Scores of colleges have fewer freshmen and fewer applicants. At New York University, the freshman class in 1970-71 shrank 4.8 percent, a decline which the school's director of admissions, Herbert B. Livesey, attributed to "fear of the city and the prospects of higher tuition every year." The number of youths seeking admission to many of the prestige—and expensive—colleges has dropped off while it has increased at some of the relatively inexpensive state universities. As reported by *Time*, Feb. 22, 1971, Ivy League applications were down by 6 percent while they have risen 10 percent at the state universities of Maine and Massachusetts.

Students who need help may apply for loans guaranteed by the federal government. For a National Defense Student Loan, the student applies to his college. The government provides 90 per cent and the college 10 per cent of these funds; the college decides who receives them. The maximum amount is a cumulative total of $5,000 for an undergraduate or $10,000 for a graduate student. Repayment begins nine months after graduation at 3 per cent interest. The student has 10 years to repay the loan but repayment may be deferred or partially cancelled if he goes into community or national service.

Other government loans are provided by the Higher Education Act of 1965. Under the terms of this act the state, a private agency or the federal government guarantees a student loan from a bank up to $2,500 a year, and the federal government pays the loan interest if the family's adjusted annual income is less than $15,000. Repayment begins one year after graduation and is to be completed within 10 years. Originally the interest rate on these loans was set at 7 per cent, but many banks refused to make them when their money could earn more elsewhere. Response from lending institutions was so poor that the 91st Congress passed new legislation in 1969 (PL 91-95) to raise the effective interest rates on guaranteed loans to 10 per cent by adding adjustable special allowances of up to 3 per cent on top of the initial 7 per cent.

Questions of Federal Help and Open Admissions

In his 1970 message on higher education, President Nixon told Congress that as a national goal "no qualified student who wants to go to college should be barred by lack of money." The government, the colleges and universities, the foundations and various segments of the public disagree over what combination of loans and grants to students and to institutions will be both fair and feasible. Until now, the federal government has put the bulk of its financial support into loans and grants for students, and into grants to educational institutions for specific projects. Federal money for building construction has required matching funds from participating schools. Within the

3 Quoted in Yale Alumni Magazine, *November 1970, p. 30.*

Government-Assisted Student Loans				
	Government-guaranteed (private funds)		National defense loans (90% federal funds)	
Fiscal Year	Number of loans	Millions of dollars	Number of loans	Millions of dollars
1971	1,081,286	1,043	560,400*	236
1972	1,253,577*	1,297*	648,900*	286

* Estimated.

SOURCE: U.S. Office of Education

past few years federal funding for on-campus projects has lagged behind the rising cost of education at a time when most institutions could not afford the loss. The most recent administration proposals have favored long-term federally-backed loans from the private money market to students as the way to funnel money onto university campuses.

President Nixon renewed his plea to Congress on Feb. 22, 1971, in another message. He proposed a two-part program similar to the one he offered a year earlier. It would: (1) provide a combination of grants, work-study payments and subsidized loans for full-time undergraduate students from families with low and middle incomes, and (2) create a National Student Loan Association to raise money privately and make it available to students at all income levels. The association would be established and chartered by the federal government but it would be a private operation, raising funds by issuing its own obligations for sale in the nation's money markets. Higher-education groups were critical of the Nixon proposals on the ground that they did not help the colleges accommodate the new influx.

Major higher education organizations favor direct grants to institutions. They maintain that tuition dollars alone cannot keep colleges and universities in good operating condition. And they are afraid that the educational supermarket approach, which they say would put all the power in the hands of consumer-students, would destroy some of the most important qualities of the university.

There was a second source of argument embedded in the President's educational policy statement. The key word was "qualified." It is obvious that many of the students who most need financial aid are also members of minority groups—mostly blacks—who also require academic help to qualify them to do work at the college level successfully. How much should be done to help students qualify academically, and what group will absorb the additional cost of this aid? There is a point of view, growing more vocal as education costs grow, that it is time to consider whether college is really a suitable goal for the majority of young people.

If the open-admissions policy, now operating in California junior colleges and at the City University of New York, spreads to more states, colleges will need space for at least 50 per cent more students. Critics of the move toward mass higher education maintain that when two years of college become "mandatory," deterioration of academic standards is almost certain to take place, reducing college studies to the level of the high school. In a recent issue of the *Bulletin* of the Association of

American University Professors, Louis and Helen Geiger maintain that minority students will not benefit from lowered standards because "the alternative of requiring less of the black or chicano than of his better-prepared white classmates is patronization of the most flagrant variety, recognized and despised for what it is by the very students their patrons seek to help." According to *Fortune* writer Edmund K. Faltermayer:

> The urge to go to college has been so intimately woven into the American Dream that the mere issuance of ukases limiting total admissions will not work. What might work is a series of steps to dispel the fantasies about higher education, to provide alternatives to entering college at eighteen, and to remove the subsidies that artificially stimulate going to college.[4]

Ivar Berg, a sociologist at Columbia University, has written in *Education and Jobs: The Great Training Robbery* that more people are receiving bachelor of arts degrees than the country needs. As a consequence, many jobs that formerly did not require a B.A. are now being defined in such terms that they appear to require one. He predicted that many college graduates who have high expectations thus will experience great frustration in jobs that do not have possibilities for promotion and responsibility.

Those who oppose the college-for-everyone approach suggest that college vocational training is the great need for the majority of youths beyond high school. The National Advisory Council on Vocational Education, in a report in 1969, decried the idea that "the only good education is an education capped by four years of college;" it is "snobbish and undemocratic, and a revelation of why schools fail so many students." The report concluded that the federal government has been "infected" with this attitude, as reflected by the fact that for every 14 dollars invested in the nation's universities only one dollar is invested in vocational-technical education. *(p.20)*

Within the past seven years, the number of students enrolled in full-time vocational or technical schools has risen from 150,000 to nearly two million. Many students who attend such schools have had to reject the advice of parents and high school counselors. The Office of Education estimates that 50 per cent of all job openings in the 1970s will require training beyond high school, but less than a four-year degree. Proponents of high-level vocational education suggest that dollars spent on these programs will profit the nation and students more than equivalent sums spent on traditional academic institutions.

In response to this new interest in alternative modes of post-secondary education, Congress in 1972 authorized a new program of federal aid for vocational education— through which up to $850-million could be spent in fiscal years 1973-1975. *(1972 legislation p. 90)*

Patterns of College Support

During colonial times and the early days of the Republic, higher education was considered to be the responsibility of private citizens and of the church. Harvard, the first college (1636), and most other early institutions were established with a view to ensuring a supply of educated men for the ministry, and secondarily for other professions. Even in the fields of primary and secondary education, responsibility for establishing and funding schools was essentially a local and not a state matter. A historian has observed that a proposal for federal or state responsibility for education would have elicited a question as to which church should control it.

Although the Constitution makes no reference to education, many leaders in the government were interested in establishing a national university to provide American youth with an education the equal of any in Europe. The idea came early and is closely associated with George Washington, who recommended it to Congress, selected a site in the District of Columbia, and left an endowment in his will. Several succeeding Presidents urged Congress to found the university but the lawmakers balked. There were those who viewed higher education as undemocratic and tending to the growth of privileged classes. One writer at that time, Robert Coram, thought it a shame that youth would be sent to college where they would merely "learn to cheat the rest."

But the founding and funding of colleges soon became part of a general wave of boosterism which spread across the land. Almost every frontier hamlet was eager to style itself a city, and "an easy way to prove that one's 'city' was destined to be a great metropolis was to provide it as quickly as possible with all the metropolitan hallmarks, which included not only a newspaper and a hotel, but an institution of higher learning," wrote historian Daniel J. Boorstin.

Congress first supported the founding of colleges when, in the Northwest Ordinance of 1787, it provided in the sale of two million acres to the Ohio Company that two townships of good land near the center of the purchase be used "for the support of a literary institution, to be applied to the intended object by the legislature of the State." This first federal grant eventually provided an endowment for Ohio University at Athens. Public funds were used to found five state universities before 1815 and a total of 20 before 1860.

Private and church-supported institutions were jealous of their autonomy, however. Efforts by various states to take over existing private schools were deterred by the famous Dartmouth College case. The Supreme Court held that a college charter was a contract which could not be impaired. After that the mixed nature of American higher education was an accepted fact. "No community could be complete without its college or university," Boorstin wrote. "Usually the denominations gave the initial push and provided a plan, but the whole community, regardless of sect, then built and maintained the college."

The federal government established the U.S. Military Academy at West Point, N.Y., to provide the nation with a pool of trained manpower which was not forthcoming from other institutions. The academy graduates proved their worth in peace as well as in war; they were the engineers who planned and supervised much of the highway- and bridge-building in the last century.

Educational historians agree that the Land-Grant College Act of 1862, known as the Morrill Act, brought about significant change in higher education in the latter half of the 19th century. The act granted public lands for specific educational purposes to the states; income from the sale or use of these public lands was to constitute an endowment of a college of agriculture and the

4 Edmund K. Faltermayer, "Let's Break the Go-to-College Lockstep," *Fortune,* November 1970, p. 101.

mechanic arts. The grant was particularly significant in that it was made not only to new states but to all states in the Union.

Land Grants and Private Funds

Moreover, the act did not require that institutions which benefited or which were created as a result of the act had to be publicly supported or controlled. Private institutions such as Cornell University and the Massachusetts Institute of Technology continue to receive funds under the original legislation and its subsequent amendments. While emphasis was originally on agriculture and practical application of engineering and the sciences, the terms of the act were loose enough to allow for expansion into all fields of study.

The success of the initial act was such that Congress enacted further legislation in 1890 providing annual payments to the states for the support of the land-grant colleges. Although "these federal subsidies were of considerable help to the land-grant colleges at the time they were instituted...their recent significance lies more in their continued existence than in size." These laws of 1862 and 1890 established principles which have guided subsequent federal involvement with higher education; when the government needs trained manpower it must often subsidize this training, and second, both public and private institutions can supply this need.

Historians Richard Hofstadter and Wilson Smith characterize the latter part of the 19th century as a period of "revolutionary change." One major change had to do with finances. Money available for higher education "dwarf(ed) the means available to previous enterprises" in the field. Aside from federal help, some of the nation's growing wealth was being funneled into higher education by private philanthropy. Men of wealth established such universities as Vanderbilt, Cornell, Johns Hopkins, Leland Stanford and Chicago, and contributed heavily to state universities and to older private universities.

A second great change involved "the growing importance of science, itself one of the things that attracted the attention of men of great wealth to the importance of the university. When Charles William Eliot (president of Harvard) wrote in 1869 about what he called 'The New Education,' it was the demand for the applied sciences and the stimulating work of the scientific schools that he mainly had in mind." Not only were the new land-grant colleges oriented toward a greater "practicality" in courses of study, but colleges as a group broke the old molds of the classical curriculum in an effort to prepare graduates for careers in science, medicine, law and business.

Federal Role Since 1945

The need for manpower trained along "practical" lines had brought the federal government into higher education, but government involvement did not become truly extensive until World War II. Before the war almost all funds spent by the federal government on research had gone into agriculture. During the war the government sponsored a massive research effort in other fields. Some of the research was conducted in government laboratories, but much of it was carried on in universities, where the government paid the salaries of professors who did the research and contributed a portion of other costs. This policy of government-funded research continues to the present time and has become a regular source of income for larger universities, both public and private.

Unlike federal grants to colleges and universities, federal aid to students is largely a postwar development. During the Thirties a federally supported student work program was provided as an emergency relief measure, and during World War II students in fields where manpower was short received war loans to help complete their training. But it was the Servicemen's Readjustment Act of 1944, the famous "GI Bill," which opened a new era of federal support for higher education. Public Law 78-346 provided educational and training allowances for World War II veterans for periods up to 48 months, depending on their length of service. Similar benefits were extended to veterans of the Korean War and, in 1966, to veterans of Vietnam and other cold war veterans.

The impact on colleges was tremendous. Male enrollment jumped from 928,000 in 1945-46 to 1,836,000 in 1947-48, creating a critical shortage of instructors, classrooms and housing. Prefabricated Army barracks became a familiar sight on American campuses and government payments became an important part of college income during the period; private institutions obtained 29 per cent of their educational and general income from this source while public institutions received 20 per cent.

In 1946 President Truman appointed a Commission on Higher Education and its investigation resulted in a six-volume series of recommendations on *Higher Education for American Democracy*. Opening a debate which still rages a quarter-century later, the commission recommended that state and local governments provide free public education through the first two years of college. To help the states pay for this program the commission suggested federal grants-in-aid to the states both for operating expenses and capital outlays of public institutions. The commission also proposed a substantial federal scholarship program under which scholarships would be provided for 20 per cent of all non-veteran college students. In addition, the commission recommended federal fellowships for up to 30,000 graduates a year. Although it aroused intense discussion, the report did not result in comprehensive legislation.

It took Russia's early successes in space to set the federal government on a new wave of financial support for higher education. The shock to Americans of Sputnik's launching in 1957 led to anguished warnings that the United States was falling behind in scientific fields. Congressional committees on education heard a parade of witnesses offer myriad proposals for improving American higher education. The legislation that emerged was entitled the National Defense Education Act of 1958— "a hodgepodge piece of legislation, representing deliberate compromises, and...labeled an emergency defense measure, not a permanent program of federal aid to education as such." Among other things, the act provided for student loans and graduate fellowships. This legislation was followed in 1965 by the Higher Education Act which featured extensive aid for needy students and new programs of graduate study for public school teachers. The various provisions of these acts were expanded and extended by the Higher Education Amendments of 1972.

The 1972 law also provided a new program of basic federal grants to which every qualified and needy student was entitled, and for a new program of federal aid directly to the institutions attended by federally-aided students.

Innovation and Reform

Universities are notoriously inefficient in their accounting procedures. In an effort to help them make necessary financial reforms, the Ford Foundation has made grants to several institutions around the country, including a grant of $163,000 to George Washington University. It is a large urban university enrolling 15,000 students and embracing a complex of buildings in downtown Washington that includes a college of liberal arts, schools of law, engineering and medicine, plus a hospital and clinics. As recently as 1967-68, the university was able to live within its budget, then based on the collection of $16.7-million in student fees. But in 1970-71, in spite of enrollment growth and a rise in tuition, George Washington exists, in common with most other schools, on the borders of financial panic.

As director of the university budget, William D. Johnson is relying heavily on detailed cost accounting procedures to lead the school out of the financial wilderness. "As far as I know," Johnson told Editorial Research Reports, "we are unique in that we are concentrating on allocating the tuition dollar. We cannot run a deficit because we have no endowment to fall back on." The university has been able to keep its hospital, medical school and clinics open only with the aid of emergency federal funds. "Whether we considered the good of the community or the national shortage of medical personnel, it was not feasible to close the doors of the hospital, the medical school and the clinics," Johnson said. "Yet we had no money to operate, and it is impossible to finance this complex out of the tuition of the average student."

Apart from the problem of the medical center, the university is trying to survive by finding out just which academic departments are financially productive. "We can tell each department how much it 'earns'," Johnson said. "We are providing the faculty with the necessary information. They will have to make decisions about where to allocate funds." The university's budget office uses a formula to show an income-cost comparison and cost-per-credit-hour for each department.

By comparing a department's tuition and fee income with its direct expenses, it was discovered that in 1969-70, anthropology spent less than 20 percent of its "earnings" while chemistry spent 122 per cent. Costs to the university per credit hour ranged from $12.32 for anthropology and $14.16 for political science up to $63.22 for physics and $83.11 for chemistry. Departments such as English are consistent money makers while those in the hard sciences are consistent losers. Accounting disclosures such as these will invariably raise questions of whether a university is willing to lop off some of its uneconomical courses —and to what extent it can do so without impairing its service to students and the community.

Administrators are frequently accused of viewing education through a haze of dollar signs. Yet many faculty members acknowledge that survival of the university depends on judgments about which departments and programs deserve subsidies and which do not. The president of George Washington University, Lloyd Elliott, is enthusiastic about the new budget procedures. "I think," he said, "that we will know more about our actual costs and, on the other side, our income, than 90 per cent of the colleges and universities in the country." Not "all our decisions, or even half our decisions, ought to follow the financial lines revealed by this information. But, without this information, you're still flying by the seat of your pants."

Strict cost accounting has paid off for the University of Southern California at Los Angeles, a private university which enrolls more than 20,000 full-time and part-time students. USC has actually managed to run modest surpluses within the past few years, a remarkable feat which is only partly attributable to its cost consciousness. Another part of its success depends on the fact that only 2,000 of its students live in campus residential halls. Basically a commuter school, it has few duties as foster parent and hotelkeeper—duties which are expensive. In addition, it has been highly selective in its programs— attempting to avoid duplicating those that exist at neighboring schools—and "until quite recently it has done little to build up its undergraduate College of Letters, Arts and Sciences."

Nevertheless, the university is proud of its efficient business procedures. Each school and department is expected to be largely self-supporting and to live within its budget, which includes a regular assessment for university overhead. According to the USC business office, operation and maintenance costs have declined from 11 per cent of the operating budget in 1949 to 5 per cent at present. The internal auditing system checks any department which veers away from its budget; each department gets a monthly balance slip which indicates what funds are left for the remainder of the year. Critics of this business approach are pressuring the administration to improve the school's liberal arts program. But in the face of rising costs it seems unlikely that USC will relax the efficient business procedures which have made it solvent in an academic world filled with red ink.

Deferred Payment Plan

Yale University, with an endowment (almost $500 million) second only to Harvard, is pioneering in an area of student "deferral" of tuition payments, in effect long-term student loans. While most student loans are to be repaid within 10 years, Yale will permit up to 35. But more than that, repayment will be pegged to the graduate's income—the more he earns during his business or professional career, the more he will repay. [6] Major provisions of the plan are as follows:

Amount of student borrowing. Up to $800 the first year of the plan's operation. The ceiling will be raised each year by the amount which tuition increases.

Terms of repayment. The usual annual repayment will be four-tenths of one per cent of the borrower's adjusted gross income after graduation—in no case less than $29 for each $1,000 owed.

---

6 Assuming that a graduate's average earnings were $20,000 a year during a 26-year repayment period, he would have repaid $8,320 on a $4,000 loan—the equivalent of 6.5 per cent annual interest. If his average earnings were only $10,000 a year, the total repayment would amount to $4,160—in effect, a virtually interest-free loan. See *U.S. News & World Report* Feb. 22, 1971, p. 28.

Length of repayment. The debt is expected to be paid in 26 years, or 35 in exceptional cases. Debts unpaid after 35 years will be cancelled and the university will assume the loss.

Yale may seem an unlikely candidate to lead a revolution in traditional payment policies since, as *Fortune* writer Ernest Holsendolph noted, it "still does things with style." In spite of its enormous endowment the school has been operating in the red since 1966-67 and expects an operating deficit of at least $3-million in 1971-72. Since admission for the past several years has been based on personal and academic merit rather than ability to pay, almost 50 per cent of the Yale student body is receiving some form of financial aid. Although the university will raise tuition fees in September 1971, there are no funds for students who will need more aid. So the deferred tuition plan has been formed to fill the gap.

The Yale plan is being eyed with interest by Harvard and some other institutions, as well as by the U.S. Office of Education. Harvard President Bok has characterized the new approach as "a novel idea, which is attracting a lot of student interest." "Obviously," he added, "such a plan could change the whole relationship of the student to the university. If he himself were paying for his education, rather than his parents, he might become far more deeply concerned with the quality of his education." A panel of presidential advisers in 1967, headed by Dr. Jerrold R. Zacharias, recommended a similar "equal opportunity bank" which would enable students to "sell participation shares in their future income."

"Consider what would happen if the plan went national and any student accepted by a college could borrow up to the total cost of his education," *The New Republic* of Feb. 20, 1971, theorized. "Operating costs of a college would no longer need to be financed through public funds, as they are at present in state and municipal colleges and universities. The burden for paying a large part of these costs would be removed from the taxpayers and placed on the beneficiaries of higher education.... With financial barriers to college attendance removed, students as consumers could be more selective in their college choice.... The quality of education would be enhanced, since the colleges to which students did not seek entrance would suffer and perhaps be forced out of business."

Most public institutions object to basing higher education costs on long-term loans on the ground that society would, in effect, be abandoning responsibility for the higher education of its young people. The president of the University of Wisconsin, Fred H. Harrington, told a Senate subcommittee, "We are unalterably opposed to the concept implicit in such an arrangement...that universities should transform themselves into private institutions selling services for what the traffic will bear." According to this view, those who would suffer most from loan plans are precisely those disadvantaged students whom the administration has declared most in need of aid. "No one has any evidence to support the notion that a ghetto student would be willing to assume a heavy load of debt," Harrington added. "Common sense suggests the opposite; with no family experience of home mortgages and other borrowing, with little confidence in his own earning capacity, he probably would not be attracted at all by a loan."

Pleas for Federal Grants to All Colleges

Major educational associations asked the federal government to make operating grants directly to all institutions of higher learning, private as well as public. Two of the leading associations[7] stated in a 1970 position paper that eligible institutions spend $10-billion to $12-billion annually on general educational expenses. If federal grants offset 4.5 to 5 per cent of these costs—a level which the associations considered "reasonable"— they would amount to $450-million to $600-million a year. The position paper emphasized that while government loans and grants to students are valuable, they do not provide the colleges with money to function properly. "No institution charges all its students the full cost of their instruction," the paper continued. "An additional student, therefore, is no financial boon to a college; instead he represents an additional cost which, somehow, must be met."

Christian K. Arnold, associate director of the National Association of State Universities and Land-Grant Colleges, said that his organization "reluctantly supported" the institutional aid provisions of the Higher Education Amendments of 1972. The association favored federal grants to universities based upon the number of full-time students or graduates rather than aid based upon the number of students receiving federal assistance as the education bill provided.

Under the expanded federal assistance programs for students it is expected that a million more students will enter college in the next five years—an increase of 16 new students for every 100 now enrolled full-time. At the same time that enrollment, particularly of disadvantaged students, has been rising, the increase in federal support of institutions of higher education has not kept pace with inflation.

A Princeton alumnus wrote in his *Alumni Weekly,* "We can muddle through, pulling in belts, trimming

Federal Outlays for Higher Education

(in millions of dollars)

Agencies	Fiscal 1971 actual	Fiscal 1972 estimate	Fiscal 1973 estimate
Department of Defense	516	535	543
Office of Education	1,388	1,469	1,394
Other HEW agencies	2,055	2,339	2,624
Housing and Urban Development	118	69	64
Veterans Administration	1,252	1,706	1,828
National Science Foundation	353	413	432
Others	472	519	560
TOTAL	6,154	7,050	7,445

SOURCE: Bureau of the Budget

7 The National Association of State Universities and Land-Grant Colleges, and the American Association of State Colleges and Universities. Their position paper was submitted to Elliot L. Richardson, the secretary of health, education and welfare, Jan. 4, 1970.

sails, cutting frills, gritting teeth, speeding degrees, freezing out faculty, squeezing in students. We have started...." But he added, "Let's not equate thrift with progress.... Palatable or not, possible or not, federal support seems the only alternative to atrophy."

Considering the future of both private and public higher education, Alan Pifer, president of the Carnegie Corporation of New York, has said, "It is conceivable that private higher education as we have known it in the past will gradually disappear and we will end up with a system in which some institutions historically have their roots in the government sector and some in the private sector but all (will be)...public institutions, responsive to the public need."

Resources Sharing: Proposals for Basic Changes

Will survival at subsistence level be the only goal for higher education in the Seventies? Those who believe that an activity which engages one-third of the nation's youth ought to be more than a holding action are proposing a number of reforms. Educators and legislators seem agreed on at least one point—that the preoccupation with adding students and putting up buildings must give way to a fresh consideration of the purposes behind all this educational activity.

The 1972 federal budget proposed that a National Foundation for Higher Education be established to provide funds for colleges and universities that want to experiment with new educational forms. The foundation, moreover, would engage in development of long-range national policy on higher education. Congress refused in 1972 to authorize establishment of the foundation.

The "common market" approach to saving money and improving quality is being tried by many colleges and universities. These cooperative arrangements, formally called consortia, multiplied during the past decade. Sixty-one were counted in 1970, involving more than 550 private and public colleges and universities. Perhaps more than twice that number of schools have made informal arrangements for sharing.

"While mounting costs of operation have been a chief stimulant for colleges adopting the consortium approach, it turns out that cutting operational expenses is neither sought nor achieved as a primary goal once a consortium is under way," according to Dr. Herbert H. Wood, president of the Kansas City Regional Council for Higher Education. He added in a guest article in *The New York Times*, Jan. 11, 1971, that "joint purchasing of goods and services provides certain economies, of course, but the resulting qualitative improvements are viewed as being of greater significance."

A number of reform-minded persons and groups question the value of college education, as now constituted, for everyone. These groups have proposed basic changes in the character and structure of education—changes which would have a profound effect on college financing. A study group of the American Academy of Arts and Sciences has spoken of the "involuntary servitude" of students who are pushed into college by parents or society. Calling for a release from "lockstep" higher education, the group notes that "there is no rhythm or pattern of intellectual curiosity or social maturity common to all....

High School Graduates Who Go To College*

	Total high school graduates *(in thousands)*		Completed 1 year or more of college *(in percentages)*	
Year	Male	Female	Male	Female
1970	5,774	6,777	52.4	41.7
1969	5,267	6,310	52.0	40.3
1968	5,080	5,990	52.8	41.7
1965	4,413	4,933	45.7	33.5
1960	3,269	3,598	42.2	32.8

*Among persons of ages 20 to 24.

SOURCE: Bureau of the Census.

What a young person may not wish to do at 18 or 22 he or she may be very interested in pursuing at 30 or 40."

The same report advocates reserving places in college for persons who want to enter after age 21; making it possible to take a degree in one, two or three years instead of four; setting up a system of waiver exams so students could go directly into graduate or professional study without a bachelor's degree; and, as an experiment, giving credit for important work experience or independent study done off campus. New York State will soon grant some college degrees on the basis of equivalency tests—an idea similar in concept to the long-accepted high school equivalency tests.

Proposals have been made for work-study programs for both college students and for the two-thirds of the nation's youth who do not go on to college. According to Jerome M. Rosow, an assistant secretary of labor, Americans are faced with the "question of whether the inordinate postponement of adulthood that is increasingly the reality for our youth is a factor in their present rebellious state of mind." Rosow believes that "the world of work and the world of education must be joined together —I mean a radical reform of the American educational and labor-force entry system."

In a study of American higher education commissioned by the U.S. Office of Education, professor Amitai Etzioni of Columbia University advocates the introduction of one year's national service, preferably voluntary, for students between high school and college. He recommends the reduction of undergraduate training by one or two years and open enrollment for all high school graduates to two years of college. "At present, the American college and university system is best at preparing students for a society which is committed primarily to the production of commodities, while the society is reorienting toward a growing concern with the Good Life," he said.

British Open University

The Carnegie Commission claims that its suggested list of reforms would reduce college operating expenditures by 10 to 15 per cent a year by 1980 and cut construction costs by one-third, or $5 billion, in the Seventies. But the commission is interested primarily in improving educational values; savings would be a side benefit. The report concludes that it would seem wise to space formal

(Continued on p. 36)

VOCATIONAL EDUCATION GAINS NEW RESPECTABILITY

Vocational Education—training for the world of work that does not require a bachelor's degree—has long been considered the stepchild of American education. The stepchild has emerged during the past few years to become a subject of increasing public concern. Sidney P. Marland Jr., U.S. Commissioner of Education, had good reason to call vocational training the No. 1 priority in education. A recent study by the Department of Labor indicates that by 1980 about 80 per cent of all jobs will require less than a bachelor's degree but very few will be available to the unskilled. It is estimated that over 40 million of the 46 million students now in school will not graduate from college. Without some kind of vocational training, many of these young people will be unable to find work.

Even a college degree offered no assurance of a job in the early 1970's and, according to numerous forecasts, job prospects would remain dim in several professions for years to come. Professional journals and the popular press told of overcrowding in many fields and of large numbers of new graduates being left unemployed. Even holders of advanced degrees were not immune from these conditions. The Ph.D was no longer a meal ticket, especially in teaching and engineering, two of the professions hardest hit by changes in the job market. These changes were being wrought by such diverse factors as uncertainty in the national economy, a slippage in the rate of population growth, and a large outpouring of college and university graduates in the past decade.[1]

"At a time when there is a glut of Ph.D.'s, and perhaps 65,000 engineers are out of work," *Business Week* observed, "many jobs cannot find people." "This year... only about 38 per cent of the jobs for sub-professional health workers will be filled by trained people. By 1980 the nation is expected to be short 400,000 such workers, trained or not. In the next four years, some 1.5 million more secretaries will be needed, the number of people employed in certain computer fields should double, and such comparatively new areas as pollution control will increase the need for technicians."

Fading Stigma of Trade Schools

Despite the opportunities for vocationally educated students, there remains a deep prejudice in many quarters against such training. The first annual report of the National Advisory Council on Vocational Education in 1968 stated:

At the very heart of our problem is a national attitude that says vocational education is for somebody else's children.... We (Americans) have promoted the idea that the only good education is an education capped by four years of college. This idea...is snobbish, undemocratic, and a revelation of why schools fail so many students.

Dr. Bruno Bettelheim, professor of psychology at the University of Chicago told the House Special Education Subcommittee in 1969: "In my opinion, there are today far too many students in the colleges who have no business to be there.... Many would be better off in a high-level program of vocational education which is closely linked to a work program...."

The stigma of vocational education is fading, though slowly, as student disillusionment with college education increases. The scarcity of jobs for graduates, especially those in the liberal arts, is encouraging many young people to forego four years of college for vocational training after they finish high school. A trend is already apparent. The nation's college enrollment in the fall of 1971, as estimated by the U.S. Office of Education, showed the smallest rate of growth (6 per cent) in a decade. *(table, p. 22)*

The total number of trainees in vocational programs of all types, including those in high school, stood at 10.5 million in 1971.

One expert has projected that the total will exceed 17 million in 1975.

Despite the gains made by vocational education in attracting youth, it does not offer full assurance that a job lies ahead. According to statistics compiled by the U.S. Office of Education, in 1970 some 76 per cent of the high school graduates who completed vocational training and were available for jobs were able to find them in their field or related fields. The pre-1970 figure for job placement was higher—about 85 per cent. A spokesman at the Office of Education—attributed the decline to general economic conditions.

Occupational Training

Vocational education at the high school level accounts for about two-thirds of all persons enrolled in job-training programs. Vocational courses may be offered in either regular or vocational-technical high schools. Educators have been debating the relative merits of the two types of high schools for years. Those favoring separate vocational-technical schools argue that these institutions are able to provide more specialized training and have better equipment and facilities. They also say that removing vocational students from the academic environment of a regular high school tends to eliminate any feeling of inferiority on their part. Others argue that it is costly to maintain separate vocational schools, that these schools have high dropout rates, and that they foster socioeconomic segregation.

---

1 "From 1861, when Yale became the First American university to grant the Ph. D., through 1970, American universities awarded 340,000 doctor's degrees. Half of these degrees were awarded in the last nine years of that period. If current projections...are borne out, another 340,000 (and probably more) will be awarded in the 1971-80 decade," Dael Wolfle and Charles V. Kidd, "The Future Market for Ph.D.'s," *Science,* Aug. 27, 1971, p. 784.

Vocational Education Financing and Enrollment

	Funds Expended			Enrollments			
Fiscal year	State and local	State, local and federal		High school	Post-high school	Adult	Special needs
	(in thousands)				*(in thousands)*		
1961	$206,063	$254,073		——	not available	——	—
1965	477,709	604,645		2,819	207	2,379	26
1966	566,100	799,894		3,048	442	2,531	49
1967	743,812	1,004,133		3,533	500	2,941	74
1968	939,479	1,192,862		3,843	593	2,987	111
1969	1,114,080	1,368,756		4,079	706	3,050	143
1970	1,405,651	1,784,515		5,075*	997*	2,650*	769*

*New Hampshire and North Carolina figures not available; 1969 state totals submitted.

SOURCE: American Vocational Association, Washington, D.C.

Increasing numbers of students exposed to vocational education in high school are entering community colleges. More than 1,000 community colleges are in existence, twice as many as 10 years ago. Their enrollment has more than tripled since 1960, reaching two million, a figure that is expected to double by 1980. "The community college has proved its great worth to American society," the Carnegie Commission on Higher Education said in June 1970. "Occupational programs should be given the fullest support and status within community colleges. These programs need to be flexibly geared to the changing requirements of society.

One of the problems facing community colleges is the relationship between liberal arts and career curricula. A frequent criticism is that teachers are geared to academic rather than vocational instruction and are primarily interested in students who plan to transfer to four-year colleges. Vocational students are often forced to take traditional college courses in which they are not interested. Kenneth B. Holt of the University of Maryland College of Education has recommended that community colleges "eliminate the artificial requirements of liberal arts courses for those who wish vocational education." To do so, he wrote, "would immediately draw many more vocational education students to the campus and would reduce the dropout rate among those now in attendance."

Dropout rates in community colleges are high; 60 to 70 per cent of all students who enter and 90 per cent of students from low-income homes drop out before completion of the two-year program. Despite these problems, Dr. Holt believes that "the community college movement itself holds great potential for combatting the prevalent biased view of vocational education." The American Vocational Association and the American Association of Junior Colleges have begun working together toward this goal.

"The student in a vocational education program must be taught skills and content relevant to the entry-level job he is aiming at," according to Lowell A. Burkett, executive-director of the American Vocational Association. "Linkage with manpower trainees are required to insure the relevance.... The most effective and immediate linkage—one which can scarcely be improved—is the cooperative vocational program. Cooperative education contains elements of apprenticeship training; it is on-the-job experience coupled with related subject matter and is perhaps the best example of linkage between vocational educator and manpower trainer."[2]

Interest of Businesses

Students in cooperative programs are able to apply what they have learned in the classroom to actual job conditions. And because training in these programs is closely related to full-time employment, cooperative programs are far more responsive to changes in the labor market than completely school-based programs. Examples of cooperative programs include the Chrysler-Northwestern Program and Philadelphia's Business Experience and Education Program (BEEP).

After the 1967 riots in Detroit, the Chrysler Corporation renovated a wing of the city's predominantly black Northwestern High School and established a program to train auto mechanics and a placement office where industry personnel could test and interview the trainees. In addition, teaching grants were awarded to Northwestern instructors who wanted to develop new programs. In the Philadelphia program, public schools have cooperative work-study arrangements with about 20 employers. The participating students, almost 4,000 of them, receive on-the-job training and earn money for their labors. In 1969-70, their average earnings were $960.

In addition to participating in cooperative programs, many large companies are establishing their own schools. Ross Sackett, vice-president of the Columbia Broadcasting System, contends that his organization "has a major strategic commitment to operate well-run, quality schools because public education hasn't done the job." Industry schools can be extremely profitable. National Systems Corporation was reported to have grossed more than $15 million in 1970 operating courses for 50,000 students. Tuition per student at Honeywell Institute of Information Sciences is $1,900 a year; at five schools operated by Radio

2 Quoted in Roman C. Pucinski and Sharlene Hirsch (eds.), *The Courage to Change: New Directions for Career Education* (1971), p. 154.

Corporation of America it is $1,400; and for computer studies courses conducted by Bell & Howell Co. it is $1,300. Students appear willing to pay high tuition when there is a good chance they will get a job in the company when they complete the program. RCA, for example, places about 90 per cent of its graduates.

In addition to specific industry-run training schools, more than 7,000 private career schools operate in this country. These institutions enrolled about two million students in 1970 and collected about $2 billion in tuition. The Federal Trade Commission held hearings in 1970 arising from complaints that certain career schools had not delivered either the training or the jobs promised in their advertisements. The FTC can take only remedial action, that of issuing "cease and desist" orders, when it finds that a complaint is valid. Only if the orders are ignored is the offender subject to a fine (up to $5,000). Some 20 states and the District of Columbia have no laws regulating these schools. The U.S. Office of Education has delegated authority for accrediting career schools to the National Association of Trade and Technical Schools; its memberships is made up of the owners of trade schools.

The Washington Post published a series of stories between July 11 and 15, 1971, dealing with private career schools and the recruiting practices some of them used. Thomas Austin, a former director of a school operated in Washington by Career Enterprises, Inc., was quoted as saying: "You make real money by signing people up. The whole system is designed for everybody to put pressure on the man below him to go out and get students. In the process, everybody forgets about the students."

Theories of Education

Theories about the importance or wastefulness of vocational education have a long history. In *The Laws*, Plato wrote that training for manual skills is "mean and illiberal, and is not worthy to be called education at all." In contrast, Martin Luther advised the mayors and aldermen in Germany in 1524: "Boys should spend an hour or two a day in school, and the rest of the time work at home, learn some trade and do whatever is desired so that study and work may go together, while the children are young and can attend to both."

The 18th century philosopher Jean Jacques Rousseau, in his revolt against the intellectualism in the French education system, painted a rather idyllic picture of manual training in *Emile,* published in 1762. To learn the carpentry trade, Emile spent two days a week with a master carpenter. Rousseau's book had a direct influence on the Swiss educator Johann Heinrich Pestalozzi, who organized a school embodying many of Rousseau's ideas. Pestalozzi believed that a child learns by doing. Books were to be used "to supplement experience, and to supply those facts that are not readily accessible by direct investigation."

Pestalozzi's theories were brought to the United States by his pupil Francis Joseph Neff, who taught in a number of American schools before he was called to New Harmony, Ind., in 1825 to teach in a school founded by Robert Owen. Owen was in complete sympathy with the Pestalozzi method and called repeatedly for education "combining mechanical and agricultural with literary and scientific instruction...making every scholar a workman and every workman a scholar."

Higher Education Enrollments				
1971	8.4 million*		1966	5.9 million
1970	7.9 million		1965	5.5 million
1969	7.4 million		1964	4.9 million
1968	6.9 million		1963	4.5 million
1967	6.4 million		1962	4.2 million

*Estimate of U.S. Office of Education.

Gradually Owen's idea of combining general and vocational education grew and was embodied in the American landgrant colleges in the second half of the 19th century. The American educator, John Dewey argued that education was a tool to help the citizen combine culture and vocation. Dewey wrote: "Our culture must be consonant with realistic science and with machine industry instead of a refuge from them. And while there is no guaranty that an education which uses science and employs the controlled processes of industry as a regular part of its equipment will succeed, there is every assurance that an educational practice which sets science and industry in opposition to its ideal of culture will fail."[3]

However, with few exceptions, the idea that vocations should be taught in the schools was unacceptable to American educators. "American educational philosophy was merely a modification of English educational thought: it was essentially aristocratic and not democratic in its basic philosophy. The aristocratic concept of education held that education must be designed to meet the needs of the 'gentleman class.' If any of the 'laboring class' was willing or able to acquire such education, the educator did not object; in fact, he often urged the importance, in America, of taking 'culture' to the 'laboring classes' in order that they might be 'elevated.' "

The idea that a liberal arts education was the best preparation for any vocation was stressed by many American educators well into the 20th century. As late as 1944, Robert Maynard Hutchins, president of the University of Chicago, remarked: "The thing to do with vocational education is to forget it.... The task of the educational system is not to train hands for industry, but to prepare enlightened citizens for our democracy and to enrich the life of the individual by giving him a sense of purpose which will illuminate not merely the 40 hours he works but the 72 he does not."

John W. Gardner, former Secretary of Health, Education and Welfare, takes a different view. He has written: "We live in a society which honors poor philosophy because philosophy is an honorable calling, and ignores good plumbing because plumbing is a humble occupation. Under such practices, we will have neither good philosophy nor good plumbing. Neither our pipes nor our theories will hold water."[4]

Job Training in America

Vocational education in the United States developed in three stages: (1) through apprenticeship, (2) in private schools and colleges, and (3) in the public schools. The

3 John Dewey: "American Education and Culture," *The New Republic,* July 1, 1916, p. 216.
4 John W. Gardner, *Excellence: Can We Be Equal and Excellent Too?* (1969), p. 86.

Industrial Revolution which reached America in the early 19th century severely weakened the system of domestic apprenticeship. In that system, the trainee lived with his master who taught him the trade and provided him with food and clothing. The need for skilled workers and the decline of apprenticeship led to the establishment of a number of private vocational schools.

The Gardner Lyceum, the first school devoted entirely to practical studies like surveying, navigation, farming, carpentry and civil architecture, was opened in Maine in 1823. A year later, the Rensselaer Polytechnic Institute was founded in Troy, N.Y., to "apply science to the common purposes of life." These and a number of other private institutions were beset by lack of cooperation from the academic community. The majority of those established before the Civil War failed.

The Morrill Act in 1862 provided grants of land to endow, support and maintain state colleges devoted to agriculture and the practical arts "to promote the liberal and practical education of the industrial classes."

It was not until the 1880s that this concept of combining academic and vocational education was introduced into the secondary schools. A major reason for the delay was that the high schools had been used chiefly to prepare boys for college. In 1870, 80 per cent of all high school graduates went on to college. Beginning in 1880, with the adoption of compulsory school attendance laws in many states, high school enrollment doubled every 10 years while college enrollment grew at a much slower rate.

As the high school became the terminal point in the education of many young people, public demand for practical, career-minded education grew. The result was the merger of manual and academic training in the secondary school curriculum. Manual training was not conceived of as vocational training but as an attempt to "infuse new vitality into old curricula, to rouse student interest in school programs, to promote more sensible occupational choices, to raise the educational level of the laboring classes, and to elevate all occupations to a millennium of culture and refinement."[5]

Calvin M. Woodward, dean of the Washington University polytechnic faculty, opened the first manual training high school in St. Louis in 1880. Woodward's goal was a combination of mental and manual instruction, one which would "put the whole boy in school, his hands as well as his head." In less than four years, enrollment in Woodward's school increased from 50 to over 200. Similar schools were set up in many communities throughout the country. Other cities added manual training to their general high school programs.

However, near the turn of the century, some educators began to complain that the program of trying to train students for all vocations was actually training them for none. Many vocationalists believed that the only solution was the establishment of a separate public high school system devoted solely to vocational courses. This dual system of education was attacked by John Dewey and others as undemocratic. While the dual system in which administration and control of vocational and regular high schools are separate has not gained widespread acceptance in this country, a *de facto* dual system has emerged. State boards of vocational education, usually under the regular board of education, have become more influential.

Income and Education

Education of head of family	Family mean income	Number of cases
Grades 0-5	$ 4,000	143
Grades 6-8	6,300	410
Grades 9-11	8,820	402
Grade 12	9,480	415
Grade 12 plus non-college training	9,890	264
College, no degree	10,830	329
Bachelor's degree	13,030	239
Advanced or professional degree	16,460	109

SOURCE: Carnegie Commission on Higher Education.

The emergence of area vocational high schools has tended to reinforce this duality.

Soviet Career Education

In the United States, vocational education seldom begins before junior high school. In the Soviet Union, it starts much earlier. A Soviet educator has written: "Our general education school is also a trade and polytechnic school. From the very first elementary grades the children are taught how to handle simple tools and do simple repairs, the kind of thing every person needs to know, no matter what trade or profession he picks later. In the high schools, general education and polytechnic training go hand in hand. The teacher in each subject not only gives her students the theoretical knowledge, but also, to some degree, shows them how to apply it."[6] At least two hours a week of manual work is required of Russian students at every grade level. Occupational information and guidance is given even in the elementary grades. Older students work in school shops or farm plots and take courses at industrial or agricultural plants.

Before the Russian Revolution in 1917, most Russian workers were trained in apprenticeship programs. In the early 1920s, factory training schools were set up to provide both general and vocational education. These ran three to four years and required from four to seven years of previous general education. By 1937, factory training schools had prepared about two million skilled workers. But because every factory trained workers to meet its own needs, it was felt that a nationwide system geared to meet the needs of the whole country was essential.

To this end, a comprehensive system of vocational and industrial training schools was established in 1940. These schools at first required from four to six years of previous schooling; now at least eight, and preferably 10, years of general education are required for admission. The course of study is usually two years for those who have completed 10 years of general education and four years for those who left after eight years. Vocational school students divide their time between classroom and work experience. From four to six months a year are spent in apprenticeship training at factories, construction sites and state farms. Tuition, food, clothing, textbooks

---

5 Grant Vern, *Man, Education and Work* (1964), p. 49.

6 Tamila Zhurbitskaya, "The YCL in the High School," *Soviet Life*, May 1971, p. 52.

and accommodations are provided at no cost to the student.

Urban vocational schools train students for specific crafts in industry, construction, transportation, communications and public utilities, while rural schools prepare them to be farm machine operators, tractor drivers, electricians, mechanics and builders. The Committee for Vocational Training works closely with economic planning bodies to ensure that the Russian vocational schools train students to meet new technological and manpower requirements. Almost two million students were reported to be enrolled in the Soviet Union's 4,800 vocational-technical schools in 1971.

Early Legislation

During the 19th century, most financial aid for American vocational education was of state and local origin. Federal money was limited to the agricultural and mechanic arts. Under the first Morrill Act of 1862, the federal government donated "public lands to the several states and territories which may provide colleges for the benefit of agriculture and the mechanic arts." Twenty-five years later, the Hatch Act provided each state $15,-000 to "establish agricultural experiment stations to aid in acquiring and diffusing among the people of the United States useful and practical information respecting the principle and application of agricultural science." The second Morrill Act of 1890 provided another $15,000 annually for each of the land-grant colleges.

In the early years of the 20th century, a number of commissions were established to investigate vocational education needs and recommended programs for satisfying those needs. Invariably, these commissions advocated a great expansion of vocational education facilities at public expense. The Commission on National Aid to Vocational Education recommended to Congress in 1914 that national grants be made because the problem was too large to be worked out on a local basis. The commission's recommendations became the basis of the National Vocational Education (Smith-Hughes) Act of 1917. This act authorized $7-million a year for teaching vocational skills in agriculture, home economics, trade and industry. By 1920, enrollment in federally subsidized programs had doubled and federal, state and local expenditures had quadrupled.

Congress increased federal support of vocational education in subsequent legislation. The George-Reed Act of 1929 authorized the additional spending of $1-million a year to expand agriculture and home economics programs, the George-Ellzey Act of 1934 increased the supplementary funds authorization to $3-million, and the George-Deen Act of 1936 added $14-million to the basic $7-million Smith-Hughes grant. During World War II, Congress spent more than $100-million to finance a Vocational Education National Defense program for training seven million war-production workers. The George-Barden Act of 1946 authorized $29-million for training in agriculture, home economics, trades and industry. Sen. Walter F. George (D Ga., 1922-57) was co-author of the foregoing laws.

Federal Goals for Jobs

Soon after President Kennedy took office, he told Congress that "technological changes which have occurred in all occupations" call for a review of vocation-

al-aid laws, "with a view toward their modernization." To that end, the President established a Panel of Consultants on Vocational Education. Its report *Education for a Changing World of Work*, issued early in 1963, argued that vocational programs were not preparing enough students for work and that there was an urgent need for technical training after high school. The panel recommended that federal appropriations for these purposes be increased from $57-million to $400-million. The Vocational Education Act of 1963, signed into law by President Johnson on Dec. 18 authorized increased federal funding although it fell short of the amounts recommended by the panel.

Until the 1963 act was passed, federal funds for vocational education were limited to specific fields like agriculture and home economics. After 1963, these funds could be used for training in any occupation that did not require four years of college. This training could be offered in high school or afterward. Each state was required to match federal funds on a 50-50 basis. Most states contribute far more, often three times as much as they receive from the federal government.

Congress amended the act in 1968 "to provide vocational offerings so that persons of all ages in all communities of all states would have ready access to vocational training or retraining suitable to their needs and abilities." The 1968 legislation authorized $2.8-billion in federal spending over five years and required that at least 15 per cent of a state's basic allotment be spent for students who are disadvantaged mentally, physically or culturally.

The Higher Education Amendments of 1972 established a new program of federal aid for vocational education and authorized $100-million for fiscal 1972, $250-million for fiscal 1973, $500-million for fiscal 1974 and whatever sums necessary after that year. The legislation created a Bureau of Occupational Education within the Office of Education to administer vocational education aid programs.

Federal funds today account for about 20 percent of all public expenditures for vocational education. These combined expenditures in 1970 amounted to $1.8-billion *(see table, p. 21)* and represented a sevenfold increase since 1961. But they still were only a small slice of the total educational pie. Federal, state and local governments spent $85.1-billion on all types of education from kindergarten through graduate school in school year 1971-1972, according to the National Center for Educational Statistics in the U.S. Office of Education.

New Directions

Washington spends almost four dollars for retraining unemployed workers for every dollar it spends on "preventive programs"—those that prepare young people for employment at the beginning of their careers.[7] Hugh Calkins, chairman of the National Advisory Council on Vocational Education, has said that "this nation will never reduce its pool of unemployed until it gives as much attention to prevention as it gives to remediation."

He cited the Woodland Job Center in Cleveland where two programs have operated side by side. "One,

---

[7] The federal government spent at least $1.5-billion for retraining unemployed workers in 1970, compared with spending of $376-million on vocational education. For background on federal retraining programs, see Congressional Quarterly's *Congress and the Nation*, Vol. II (1969), pp. 734-743.

aimed at young adults who are already unemployed, is 100 per cent financed by federal dollars. The other, for youth not yet unemployed, but destined to be if they are not trained, is conducted with 100 per cent local dollars." Calkins estimated that the flow of untrained young into the unemployed pool amounts to about 750,000 young persons a year. "For the federal government to train half this number of young people, at an estimated cost of $1,500 each, and to provide a stipend of about the same amount to each, would cost...$1,125,000,000 each year. By contrast, if improved vocational education in the nation's high schools could lure the same number of students back into the schools, and if the federal government were to pay the additional cost of the vocational education program...the cost would only be 25 per cent as high."

Federal Testing of Proposals. More than seven of every 10 junior and senior high school students were enrolled in general and academic programs in the 1969-70 school year, although only two of the seven can be expected to complete four years of college. U.S. Commissioner of Education Marland spoke of this problem to the National Association of Secondary School Principals in Houston, Texas, Jan. 23, 1971: "Eight out of 10 high school students should be getting occupational training of some sort. But only two of these eight students are.... Consequently, half of our high school students, approximately 1,500,000 a year, are being offered what amounts to irrelevant, general education pap."

Marland suggested dropping the term "vocational education" in favor of "career education." "While it (career education) will necessarily and properly embrace many of vocational-technical education's skill-producing activities, if will also reach a large percentage of students now unexposed to the usual vocational education offerings. Instead of slightly less than 25 per cent of high school students now enrolled in some kind of vocational skills program, for example, the career education concept would affect, and affect in a fundamental fashion, as high as 80 per cent of these young people."

The National Center for Education Research and Development in the U.S. Office of Education has devised three plans for career education as substitutes for traditional general and vocational education. The first plan emphasizes career development from kindergarten through grade 12. As envisioned, a youngster would be introduced to a broad range of job ideas in elementary school. He could then choose a speciality in junior high school and pursue it in senior high in one of three ways—through preparation for work immediately after high school, preparation for two years of further education, or preparation for four years of college.

The second plan provides for students from 13 to 18 years old to work for various employers in the community in apprentice-type arrangements. Participating students could re-enter school and receive credit for their outside work or go forward in the work program and receive credentials at least equal to those offered by the school. The third plan is designed to make career education accessible to persons who have left school. This plan would make use of cable television, audio-visual cassettes, telephone and correspondence courses.

The Office of Education has awarded contracts amounting to $4.6-million to develop these plans. The Center for Research and Leadership Development in Vocational and Technical Education at Ohio State University has received $2-million on the first one. Another $2-million has been given to two educational laboratories, Research for Better Schools in Philadelphia and the Far West Laboratory in Berkeley, Calif., for feasibility studies on the second plan. In addition, the Center for Urban Education in New York City has been awarded $300,000 to study existing programs which could be used in developing this plan. The Education Development Center in Newton, Mass., has received a $300,000 grant for work on the third plan.

Innovative Work Programs. While the federal government is experimenting, many innovative programs are being carried out on the local level. The Seattle public school system has integrated career information and experience into the curriculum from kindergarten through grade 12 since 1965. Young children are introduced to different types of workers and the roles they play in the community. A second grader might learn to bake bread in mathematics and measurements classes. Junior high students choose from 30 courses dealing with career skills. Career courses in senior high are developed only at the request and with the cooperation of local labor, industry and business people, thus ensuring that the training fits local needs. Seattle public schools have also established a computerized data system to let students know what jobs are available and what fields are likely to need skilled workers in the next few years.

Many schools are using the cluster approach to career education. A student is taught the skills of related occupations which have similar knowledge requirements. This permits him to keep his career options open through high school and pursue advanced training in any one of several fields. Thus, changes in technology or manpower supply will not so readily render his skills obsolete. The Quincy, Mass., Vocational-Technical High School has developed 11 career programs providing instruction in more than 250 jobs. The programs are business education, data processing, electronics, food service, general piping, woodworking, commercial art, health care, home economics, metals and machines, and power mechanics.

The Work Opportunity Center (WOC) of Minneapolis is one of a growing number of experimental institutions established to provide school dropouts and potential dropouts of ages 16 to 21 with marketable skills. Students may enter the program whenever they wish, attend as many classes as they choose, and move through the program at their own pace. High school credit is given for completion of the program. Since it was begun in 1966, over 3,000 young people have graduated from WOC.

These programs and many others like them give some indication of how far vocational or career education has come in the past decade. The stereotype vocational program held in dingy high school basements, where the least talented and disciplined students endlessly hammer pieces of wood together until they are allowed to leave school, bears little resemblance to contemporary programs. There are still problems, to be sure. These include widespread public prejudice against vocational training, ignorance of its aims and innovations and inadequate financial assistance. But as America's trillion-dollar economy comes to demand more skilled para-professionals, the popularity and support of vocational education are bound to increase.

COALITION WORKS FOR HIGHER FEDERAL FUNDS IN 1971-72

Direct federal aid to education is more than a century old, but the question of how much federal money should be allocated is settled anew each year when Congress considers the money bill for the Office of Education in the Department of Health, Education and Welfare.

To work for increased federal money for aid to education, education interest groups in 1969 formed a powerful new coalition to mobilize support for federal spending for education. Most major education groups, more accustomed to competition than cooperation, joined this Emergency Committee for Full Funding of Education Programs, impelled in large part by the nationwide economic downturn which had serious repercussions in the education community.

This economic downturn, however, generated an equally strong determination by the Nixon Administration that federal spending—in education as in other areas—must be held down.

Three times during the first three years of the Nixon Administration these opposing forces collided:

• The White House won the first round; Congress in early 1970 upheld Mr. Nixon's veto of the appropriations bill to which the education coalition had won addition of $1-billion more than he had budgeted for fiscal 1970. Despite a concerted "Operation Override" mounted by the Emergency Committee, the House sustained the veto by a 226-191 vote.

• But the education coalition was victorious in the second confrontation, later in 1970. Congress added more than $500-million for education to the amount requested by Mr. Nixon for fiscal 1971; again he vetoed the bill. This time the coalition had the votes to override the veto and enact the bill anyway. The House voted 289-114 to override; the Senate followed suit, 77-16.

• The Emergency Committee lost its first battle in 1971—and came out only a partial victor in the final appropriations bill for fiscal 1972. The House rejected a committee-backed amendment to the appropriations bill, adding $729-million to the amount approved by the House Appropriations Committee.

A renewed effort won addition in the Senate of $816-million to the education funding bill, but the threat of another presidential veto convinced conferees to cut $470-million of that increase from the final version of the bill, reducing the total to $5.1-billion, $563-million more than in fiscal 1971.

By the first week in August 1972, it appeared that Nixon and proponents of increased education funding might once again be on a collision course. The House increased education funds in the Labor-HEW fiscal 1973 appropriations bill $655,288,000 over the budget request. Despite warnings of a presidential veto, the Senate added an additional $292,158,000. As the bill emerged from conference $791,365,000 over the request, presidential spokesmen continued to threaten a possible veto. *(p. 89)*

Federal Aid to Education

The idea that the federal government take some part in the support of education is an old one, dating from the post-Revolutionary years when certain land in every township in the Northwest Territory was set aside by Congress for support of public schools.

But not until 1862 did Congress act again to aid education, then establishing in each state land-grant colleges of agricultural and mechanical arts. In 1867, Congress approved a bill introduced by Rep. (later President) James A. Garfield, creating a non-Cabinet Department of Education. In 1917, Congress authorized federal aid to vocational education.

The federal government made its largest total financial contribution to education through the GI bill (Servicemen's Readjustment Act, 1944) and its successor laws.

In 1950, Congress authorized federal grants for schools in areas where federal activities were adding population while removing property from the tax rolls. But only after the Russians launched Sputnik did Congress pass the National Defense Education Act (NDEA) authorizing $1-billion in federal aid to education.

The decade of the 1960s, particularly the Administration of former schoolteacher Lyndon B. Johnson, brought the greatest extension of federal aid to education through the Higher Education Facilities Act of 1963, the Elementary and Secondary Education Act of 1965 and the Higher Education Act of 1965.

Interest Groups

As Congress enlarged the federal role in aiding education, many education groups set up Washington offices.

The American Federation of Teachers (AFT) moved from Chicago—where it had been chartered by Samuel Gompers in 1916—to Washington. The Association of American Universities (AAU) moved to Washington in 1962 at age 62. The National School Boards Association, founded in 1940, set up a Washington office in 1966.

By 1972, there were hundreds of such groups represented in Washington. Almost every type of institution and teacher was represented, as well as parents, libraries and educational administrators. School librarians and school secretaries each had their own group; as did college governing boards, college registrars and college business officers. In addition, dozens of the colleges and universities had their own Washington representatives. *(Partial listing of education interest groups, next page.)*

The education community covers a wide spectrum of groups and specific interests from the 1.1-million-member National Education Association and the 10-million-member National Congress of Parents and Teachers to the 56-member Council of Chief State School Officers

A List of Major Education Interest Groups, 1972

Teachers

American Federation of Teachers (AFT)—Union of classroom teachers; established 1916; affiliated with AFL-CIO; represents 250,000 teachers.

National Education Association (NEA)—Largest professional organization in world, representing 1.1 million teachers and educational administrators; established as National Teachers Association in 1857, became NEA 1870; a family of organizations including such affiliates as the American Industrial Arts Association and the Association for Education Communications and Technology, and associated organizations including the American Association of School Administrators, the Association for Educational Data Systems, the National Association of Secondary School Principals.

American Association of University Professors—Established 1915; represents more than 94,000 professors.

Education: General

American Education Lobby—Organized 1967 to oppose federal control (through aid) of education; 10,000 members.

Council of Chief State School Officers—Established 1928; 56 state or territorial commissioners of education.

National Association of School Boards—Established 1940; represents state and local school boards.

National Catholic Education Association—Established 1904; represents all types of Catholic schools.

National Congress of Parents and Teachers—Founded 1897; represents more than 10 million members.

Higher Education

American Council on Education—Established 1918; coordinating organization for higher education groups; represents 312 national and regional associations; 1,343 institutions of higher education, 83 affiliated groups.

American Association for Higher Education—Established 1870 as NEA department, independent in 1971; represents more than 7,000 persons working in higher education.

American Association of Colleges for Teacher Education—Established 1917 as American Association of Teacher Colleges; represents 853 institutions of higher education.

American Association of Junior Colleges—Founded 1920; represents 825 junior colleges.

American Association of State Colleges and Universities—Established 1961 from older organizations; represents 277 state colleges and universities.

Association of American Colleges—Founded 1914; represents about 850 liberal arts colleges; affiliated with National Council of Independent Colleges and Universities, founded in 1971 to speak for private higher education.

Association of American Universities—Established 1900; 46 major universities in the United States and two in Canada.

National Association for Equal Opportunity in Higher Education—Established in 1969 to give visibility to the needs of predominantly black colleges; represents 85 predominantly black colleges.

National Association of State Universities and Land Grant Colleges—Descendant of oldest higher education associations founded in 1885 and 1895; represents 118 major state universities and land grant institutions.

Graduate Education

Association of American Law Schools—Established 1900, represents 124 law schools.

Association of American Medical Colleges—Founded 1876; represents all medical schools, 47 academic societies and 400 training hospitals.

Council of Graduate Schools in the United States—Established 1960; represents 300 graduate schools.

Adult, Vocational Education

Adult Education Association of the U.S.A.—Founded 1951 to further the concept of continuing education.

American Vocational Association (AVA)—Established 1926; represents 50,000 vocational education teachers.

National University Extension Association—Founded 1915; represents 168 universities with extension divisions or divisions of continuing education.

Libraries/Broadcasters

American Library Association—Founded 1876; represents more than 37,000 librarians, libraries, publishing houses, business firms and individuals.

Association of Research Libraries—Founded 1931; represents 89 large research libraries.

National Association of Educational Broadcasters—Founded 1925; professional association of individuals and institutions interested in educational television and radio.

and the exclusive 48-member Association of American Universities.

The men and women who serve as congressional liaison for these different groups come from a variety of backgrounds. There are former government officials, such as Ralph K. Huitt, executive director of the National Association of State Universities and Land Grant Colleges, who served as assistant secretary of health, education and welfare for legislation during the Johnson administration, and Charles V. Kidd, executive secretary of the Association of American Universities, who served in the Office of Science and Technology in the Johnson administration.

There are former congressional staff members: John F. Morse, director of the American Council on Education (ACE) Commission on Federal Relations, who in 1962 directed a study of federal involvement in education for Rep. Edith Green (D Ore.), chairman of the House Education and Labor special subcommittee on education; Mary P. Allen, associate for governmental relations to the executive director of the American Vocational Association (AVA), for 12 years a staff aide to Rep. Carl Elliott (D Ala., 1949-1965), a member of the Education and Labor and Rules Committees.

There are former teachers—Carl J. Megel, former Chicago high school science teacher and coach, for 12 years president of the AFT, and, since 1964, AFT director of legislation. And there are former school officials— John M. Lumley, recently retired after 14 years as assistant executive secretary of the NEA for government relations and citizenship, who came to that position from the post of superintendent of schools in Wilkes-Barre, Pa. and Ira Silverman, assistant executive secretary of the Association of American Universities, formerly admissions officer at Princeton University. And there are parents— the six women volunteers who watch over the legislative concerns of the National Congress of Parents and Teachers.

Emergency Committee:
A New Umbrella

No umbrella is large enough to cover all education interest groups although for a brief period in 1970 it seemed that the Emergency Committee for Full Funding might be able to.

But then a policy reversal obligated the NEA to withdraw from active participation in the committee, of which NEA congressional liaison Stanley J. McFarland was serving as chairman. Late in 1971, the NEA rejoined the committee.

The National Congress of Parents and Teachers, which works independently for education funds, was advised by its legal counsel not to participate in the committee.

The committee itself, often described as the brain of the second most powerful lobby in Washington, was organized in April 1969 by Lumley, Steinhilber, Kenneth Young of the AFL-CIO and several other educational interest representatives concerned at the cutback in education funds proposed in the last Johnson budget and deepened by the Nixon budget amendments. As Young explained the rationale behind the committee's establishment, "If we can work together on authorizing legislation, why not get together and really work on appropriations?"

From Oregon—to which he had just retired after 13 years' service with Sen. Wayne Morse (D Ore. 1945-1969)—Charles W. Lee was summoned to serve as the committee's director. From 1962 to 1969, professional staff member of the Senate education subcommittee, Lee had a part in the drafting and passage of every education bill during those years. "No one knows more about the Senate and education legislation than Charlie Lee," said Mary Allen of AVA.

From week to week the composition of the committee's membership changes, said Lee. Supported by contributions from member educational institutions and groups, its work was directed by Lee from one crowded suite in the Congressional Hotel across the street from the House office buildings.

From its creation, Lee said, there was a core group of Senators and Representatives willing to work with the committee to win full funding of education programs. "We serve as a free-floating staff" for these persons, said Lee, putting together a package amendment which can be enacted and then providing the information which advocates can use to win votes for that package increase.

The committee's strategy was developed in breakfast meetings—usually held near the offices of member groups, frequently in the cafeteria at One DuPont Circle, the building owned by the ACE and housing many higher education groups.

In all three years, Lee was the center of a communications network, transmitting timely information to member groups so that each could act in the best interests of its constituents.

In 1971, Lee sent to member groups a package containing an analysis of the votes cast by about 250 individual representatives on the 1971 Hathaway amendment (for its House sponsor, Maine Democrat William D. Hathaway). An accompanying memo from Lee encouraged each group to forward this information to its members, asking them to contact their representative, thanking him for a "yes" vote on the amendment, asking the reason for a "no" vote, and asking absent members how they would have voted.

Lee is using a similar method in 1972. In addition, the committee—which dropped the "Emergency" from its name in 1972, is trying to collect information on education funding for specific projects in individual states and congressional districts. No matter how a representative votes, Lee said, he should have data on hand on the impact of funding levels on his district's schools.

The committee tries, said Lee, "to cut through the glass that surrounds Congress, to let them know that we are concerned out here, and that we know what is happening."

A Community of Interest

The emergency committee—its creation and operations—cast into relief the difficulty of fusing these diverse groups into an effective cooperating community and the sensitivity of many of them to any suggestion that they were lobbies in the traditional meaning of the word.

Despite a basic common interest, many conflicts arose between groups, related to the various sectors of education which each represented. Black colleges and community colleges often did not benefit from the same programs as do large universities, the all-teacher membership of the AFT might not see things the same way as the teacher-administrator groups within NEA.

Because of these divisions, categorical aid programs —library services and school lunch—were enacted by Congress long before any type of general aid to schools. A proposal for general aid brought out all the contradictions in the educational community—church-state, public-private—while categorical grant programs won support from certain groups without incurring the opposition of others.

In 1971, external threats contributed to an unusual unity within the educational community. The financial crunch produced the cooperative effort of the emergency committee where, Lee said, the groups could hash out their differences and then arrive at a common strategy.

Its "package approach," developing one amendment increasing funding for a variety of education programs, was designed to overcome the fragmentation which had often beset the education community.

The cooperation of the higher education associations working for institutional aid "just shows what the financial bind can do," said one of their representatives. The chief reason that Congress has not approved institutional aid for colleges and universities earlier, explained Ralph Huitt, was the inability of the higher education groups to agree on the type of program they wanted.

Early in 1971, most of the major higher education groups agreed upon one statement on institutional aid; later they agreed upon a formula whereby federal aid to institutions would be allocated on a per student basis. The groups reluctantly supported provisions of the Higher Education Amendments of 1972 (PL 92-318) providing institutional aid based instead on a combination formula related to the number of federally-aided students in each institution, the total annual amount of federal aid dollars provided to an institution's students and the number of graduate students at an institution.

A number of other prominent and often-disagreeing groups united to oppose a program of education vouchers, which was seen as a serious threat to the public school system. The Coalition on Education Vouchers was chaired jointly by AFT's Megel and NEA's Lumley.

Low-Key Lobby

The NEA and the AFT register their liaison men as lobbyists. But generally, education groups—all tax-exempt nonprofit organizations—shy away from that label.

"I virtually never go to the Hill except on request. I don't walk the halls," said John F. Morse of the American Council on Education. "We lobby by invitation," agreed Huitt of the land grant group. "Our members do the lobbying: it's more effective."

And one primary role for the Washington staff of these groups is to teach their members to do the lobbying. Mary Allen of the AVA has conducted workshops across the country for vocational education leaders. She explained the legislative process step-by-step, pointing out the way in which an individual may make his opinion heard at each step. "When a particular Congressman is the key to a bill or a provision," she said, "we see to it that the folks in his district let him know how they feel about it."

Through newsletters, education groups keep their members informed of legislation under consideration; when the crucial time arrives, a call for action is sent out asking constituents to contact their congressional representatives. These organizations also participate in the formulation of legislation by testifying before Congressional committees, usually represented by persons from their member institutions.

And Federal education officials often consult these interest groups. A hiatus between the Nixon administration and the education community during 1969 was ended in 1970 when HEW Secretary Elliot Richardson (formerly assistant HEW secretary for legislation 1957-59) restored communication.

The administration's own education lobbyist, Christopher Cross, deputy assistant HEW secretary for legislation in charge of education, keeps in contact with the education groups.

Some members of Congress criticized the public "high-pressure tactics" of the emergency committee—such as the whip system organized in 1969 to ensure that Representatives who had promised to vote for the committee-backed increase in education funds actually did get to the floor and vote—as out of keeping with the generally low-key behind-the-scenes approach of the education community to Congress. Some of the higher education groups reflected a similar feeling.

Rep. Green, staunch champion of education, questioned in a House speech the propriety of participation in the committee of groups which stand to profit from an increase in education funds, such as federally connected educational laboratories, consulting groups and equipment companies. Lee said that little if any of the group's funds come from such groups.

Rep. William H. Ayres (R Ohio), then ranking minority member of the House Education and Labor Committee, criticized the committee for bringing educators, parents and other citizens to Washington in January 1970 to lobby for overriding the education funds veto. Never in his 20 years in Congress, he said, had he seen "anything as brazen by any group coming here trying to influence legislation."

Commenting on the instructions which the committee issued to these arriving citizens to direct them in talking with their representative, Ayres noted that the committee instructed the person to tell his representative that he would be in the House gallery during the vote. Ayres' interpretation of this was "Big Brother will be watching."

And in regard to the committee's note that the constituent might tell the representative, if he promised to vote to override, that the constituent and his associates would do everything they could to assist him locally, Ayres commented, "in other words, in his next election. By inference, if you do not vote with them, you know what they are going to try to do. I think this is a disgrace to the good name of education." Ayres was defeated in his race for re-election in November 1970.

The NEA was criticized for its lobbying by persons who pointed out that tax-exempt organizations were not allowed to use a substantial part of their funds for legislative efforts.

Lee responded that the emergency committee merely focuses educational concerns and information into each member's office, adding its input to the decision-making process. "Decisions will be made, anyway," he said. "They might as well be made on our input. There's no law against lobbying in the public interest, and that's what we are doing."

Young of the AFL-CIO sees the work of the education community through the emergency committee in a larger context, as part of a long-needed effort to make the appropriations committees more responsive to public needs and concerns. "It was a good fight," he said, "and there ought to be more like it. It was something other groups should have done long ago. The education groups should be proud of themselves."

FIVE NEW PROPOSALS AND TWO FUNDING VETOES

President Nixon's program for "fulfilling the federal role in education and meeting the educational needs of the 1970s" consisted of five major elements:

● Student assistance "to assure that no qualified person would be barred from college by a lack of money."

● A national institute "to bring energy and direction to educational research."

● A national foundation "to encourage innovation in learning beyond high school."

● Education revenue sharing.

● Emergency federal aid "to help local school districts desegregate wisely and well."

By election year 1972, Congress had modified Nixon's student assistance plan, approved the institute, rejected the national foundation proposal, given perfunctory hearing to education revenue sharing, and authorized $500-million more than requested for desegregation aid.

Critics of the Nixon administration's attitude toward education pointed to the fact that, despite these education proposals, Nixon had twice vetoed education appropriations bills which he considered inflationary.

Education Funds Vetoes

One of the longest appropriations disputes in congressional history ended March 5, 1970—three months before the end of fiscal 1970—when President Nixon signed into law the fiscal 1970 appropriations bill (HR 15931—PL 91-204) for the Departments of Labor and Health, Education and Welfare (HEW). HR 15931 was the second bill for that purpose approved by Congress. The first, HR 13111, cleared Congress Jan. 26 but was vetoed by the President on nationwide television the same day.

The money contained in HR 13111—$19.7-billion—$1.1-billion more than the administration requested—Nixon said, was the "wrong amount for the wrong purposes for the wrong time." The veto, he said, "is in the vital interests of all Americans in stopping the rise in the cost of living."

"An example of the unfairness of the bill," the President said, was the program of school aid to federally impacted areas. He said the bill provided about $6-million in aid for the half-million residents of one of the richest counties in the nation (Montgomery County, Md.), while giving only about $3-million to the three million people who lived in the 100 poorest counties.

The bill contained $717-million for elementary and secondary education, $312.5-million more than the administration request of $404.5-million. The White House maintained that only $15-million of the increase was necessary.

The House failed to override the veto, and Congress began work on a new bill (HR 15931). As finally enacted, the measure contained $19.38-billion in appropriations—

still $579.7-million over the President's modified (compromise) request submitted Feb. 2 following the veto.

For the controversial impacted areas assistance, the final bill contained $80.4-million more than Nixon's compromise level, $318.4-million more than originally requested.

The Second Veto. In August 1970, President Nixon —proclaiming that his administration was determined "to hold the line against dangerous budget deficits"— vetoed HR 16916, a $4.4-billion appropriations bill for the Office of Education in fiscal 1971, because it appropriated $453-million over his request.

In his veto message, the President said the action meant "saying 'no' to bigger spending and 'no' to higher prices in the interest of all American people." The President argued that his budget request provided for a 28 percent increase in spending for education. Congress had appropriated $600-million more for education than in fiscal 1970, with major increases of $232-million for elementary and secondary education, $126-million for impact aid and $110-million for higher education.

Congress, however, overrode the President's veto by a 289-114 roll-call vote in the House, and a vote of 77-16 in the Senate.

Fiscal 1972. Although the bill (HR 7016—PL 92-48) appropriating $5.14-billion for the Office of Education and related agencies in fiscal 1972 contained $393-million more than requested by the administration, President Nixon signed the measure in July 1971.

ESEA Extension

A three-year, $24.6-billion extension of the 1965 Elementary and Secondary Education Act (ESEA) was signed by President Nixon in 1970, the largest authorization bill for education programs ever enacted. The administration had requested a two-year extension pending a full review of education programs.

Prior to final action, the Senate engaged in two major debates over equal enforcement of federal desegregation guidelines. The most heated Senate controversy centered around an amendment offered by John C. Stennis (D Miss.) and Abraham Ribicoff (D Conn.) which stated that federal guidelines on school desegregation must be applied equally to segregation in the North and South, whether *de jure* or *de facto*. Although the measure passed the Senate, House-Senate conferees required separate federal policies dealing with each type of discrimination.

The Nixon administration maintained a delicate position of neutrality on the amendment. In a formal statement, the President said (without endorsing the amendment) that "within the framework of the law, school desegregation problems should be dealt with uniformly throughout the land."

Major program revisions in the Elementary and Secondary Education Act extension (PL 91-230) included an increase to $4,000 from $3,000 in the maximum income level for determining eligibility of aid to school districts serving large numbers of poor children; and extension of impact aid to cover children living in federally financed public housing.

Budget requests and funding of these extended programs of aid to elementary and secondary education fell far below authorization levels for 1971 and 1972. *(Chart p. 43)*

Education Amendments of 1972

In mid-1972 Congress completed action on the most sweeping aid to education bill ever enacted. HEW Secretary Elliot L. Richardson praised the Education Amendments of 1972 (S 659—PL 92-318) as "truly a landmark in the history of education." The legislation differed significantly from President Nixon's original proposal for revising federal-aid-to-education programs.

The product of two and one-half years work, the bill authorized $19-billion for higher education programs through fiscal 1975, restructured existing higher education programs and established a new program of federal grants for qualified needy students. It also authorized a new program of federal aid to colleges and universities, and expanded federal aid for vocational education. The bill contained controversial provisions restricting school busing and provided $2-billion in aid for desegregating school districts. *(Details, Appendix)*

In 1970, Nixon sent Congress a special message proposing the refocusing of federal education aid to students from low-income families. He pointed out that a person whose family income exceeded $15,000 was five times more likely to attend college than one from a family with an annual income of less than $3,000.

Nixon also proposed that the financing of student loans be shifted to the private money market—phasing out the program of direct federal loans—and that Congress create a national foundation for higher education and a national institute of education to spark research and innovation in American education.

Critics of the administration's proposals said that they would substantially reduce aid to students from middle-income families, that the proposed shift to the private money market would reduce the amount of loan aid available and that aid should be provided to those already-strained colleges and universities which the additional government-aided students attended.

By late 1971, both the House and Senate had rejected the major thrusts of Nixon's student-aid proposals. The administration then supported the basic student grant program adopted by the Senate and a cost-of-education payment approach to general aid to colleges and universities. This payment would be based on the number of federally aided students attending an institution, to meet the cost of educating those students.

As cleared by Congress in June, the bill contained the Senate student-aid provisions which entitled any college student in good standing to a grant of $1,400 minus the amount his family could reasonably be expected to contribute toward his education expenses.

PL 92-318 also established a national institute of education within HEW, as requested by Nixon, to encourage educational research, and provided that direct federal aid be apportioned to higher education institutions on the basis of the amount of federal aid paid to students, the number of federal grant recipients attending each institution and the number of graduate students in attendance.

Desegregation Aid. President Nixon in 1970 requested $1.5-billion for improving schools in "racially impacted" areas and for aiding school districts to overcome problems caused by court-ordered desegregation.

Congress authorized $2-billion in desegregation aid as part of the 1972 education amendments.

Revenue Sharing

President Nixon April 6, 1971, sent Congress a special revenue sharing plan to consolidate into one program 33 existing categories of federal aid to elementary and secondary education. About $3-billion (roughly the same amount already provided in categorical grants) would be apportioned among the states on the basis of a formula taking into account the total school-age population in each state, the number of students from low-income families and the number of students whose families resided or worked on federal property.

Although the President stated in the expanded 1972 State of the Union address sent to Congress that he had "continuing confidence that special revenue sharing for education can do much to strengthen the backbone of our educational system...without compromising the principle of local control," Congress gave slight hearing to the proposal opposed by the education leaders.

Education interest groups were unenthusiastic about the proposal because it would erase existing categorical programs, which they considered effective, and provided only a small amount of additional funds.

Donald E. Morrison, president, National Education Association, told the Senate Labor and Public Welfare Subcommittee on Education Oct. 27, 1971:

"The problem with the federal aid programs is that they have never been fully funded, and the revenue-sharing proposal contains still-inadequate funds. It seems that the thrust of this bill is to provide administrative convenience and perhaps to bring political relief from the pressures for full funding of existing grant programs."

Education Property Taxes

In his 1972 State of the Union message, the President committed himself to a solution to the growing problem involved in the financing of local school systems through property taxes, which he described as "one of the most inequitable and regressive of all public levies."

Noting court decisions in California, Minnesota, Texas and New Jersey which held that the method of financing schools through property taxes was "discriminatory and unconstitutional," he promised legislative proposals on the subject in 1972.

The administration was known to be considering a value-added tax, a form of federal sales tax that is common in Europe, as a new source of revenue that could be earmarked for aid to education and as a relief to property owners, but Nixon did not specify the nature of his proposals. By mid-year the White House had made no more specific proposal. *(Financing p. 3)*

BUSING OF SCHOOLCHILDREN: OLD PRACTICE, NEW PROBLEM

When Massachusetts in 1852 became the first state to enact a compulsory education law, its legislators probably did not foresee all the complications that would ensue.

One of those complications resulted from the facts of a scattered population and a limited number of school buildings. Some way had to be provided for every pupil, particularly those in rural areas, to get to school. In 1869 Massachusetts became the first state to provide pupil transportation at public expense.

By 1919, all states were using tax revenues to transport pupils, and the most popular mode of transportation was the bus. The number of students bused to and from school grew steadily into the early 1970s. *(Table, next page)*

But since the mid-1960s, when federal courts began to order use of the school bus as one means of providing the quality education every state promised its pupils, busing has become such a controversial practice that its long history is often obscured.

The school bus has been bombed in Pontiac, Mich., overturned in Lamar, S.C., and damned around the country. Busing has become the symbol of federal interference in local affairs and the watering down of educational standards. It is one of the most emotional domestic political issue of 1972.

Busing was denounced as "massive" or "forced," despite estimates that busing for the purpose of desegregation accounted for only a very small percentage of total busing, according to official estimates.

The latest federal survey, for the 1969-70 school year, found a total of between 18 million and 19 million students, 43 percent of all public school students, being bused. No figures were available for the number being bused for desegregation purposes, but the office of civil rights in the Department of Health, Education and Welfare (HEW) and the U.S. Commission on Civil Rights agreed on an estimate of only 2 to 3 percent.

The Nixon administration articulated some of the complaints about busing, as reasons for its proposals, in a statement accompanying its anti-busing measures sent to Congress March 17, 1972. Busing, said the administration statement, was widespread, costly, harmful to the educational process and it created unnecessary administrative burdens.

Stephen Horn, vice chairman of the civil rights commission, refuted these charges in testimony before the House Judiciary Committee May 10, 1972. Horn said that population growth accounted for almost all busing and that the cost of busing had held steady at between 3 and 4 percent of total educational expenditures for 40 years. He reminded the committee that Secretary of Health, Education and Welfare Elliot L. Richardson had told Congress in 1970 that there had been more busing in past years to preserve segregated schools than there was in 1970 to desegregate schools.

"Desegregation," said Horn, "actually can cause many children to spend less time on the bus...because children are no longer bused past one segregated school to get to another, and hence the trip is much shorter." As an example, he cited Georgia, where the number of pupils bused rose to 566,000 in 1971 from 517,000 in 1967, but where the miles logged in a year by Georgia buses dropped to 51.3 million from 54 million.

The presidential campaigns of 1972 provided a clear contrast on the busing issue. President Nixon's opposition to busing was well known; George McGovern, the Democratic nominee, supported the use of busing, and the party platform contained an endorsement of the transportation of students as one means of achieving equal educational opportunity.

The Courts

The federal courts—and the judges who manned them—took the brunt of the criticism of busing, for almost all busing resulted from some court's directive. Technically, courts did not order busing, but it was their approval of plans that include busing, which have been drawn up by plaintiffs or school boards, that put those plans into effect.

Busing was approved as a means of desegregating schools by the Supreme Court's 1971 decision in *Swann v. Charlotte-Mecklenburg Board of Education.* Unanimously, the court held that "desegregation plans cannot be limited to the walk-in school." Busing was permissible so long as it did not risk the students' health or impinge on the educational process, it said.

The *Swann* decision was the latest in a series of Supreme Court rulings on school desegregation which began with its 1954 holding—in the case of *Brown v. Board of Education of Topeka*—that "separate educational facilities (for black and white students) are inherently unequal." This overturned an 1896 ruling *(Plessy v. Ferguson)* condoning separate-but-equal public facilities.

A year later, in a decision elaborating on the first *Brown* decision, the court called for desegregation "with all deliberate speed." But many southern school districts answered with delays and adopted plans which often did not achieve desegregation. In 1969 the court ruled that segregation must be eliminated "at once."

Black neighborhoods and white neighborhoods, found particularly in urban areas, result in black neighborhood schools and white neighborhood schools. In order to desegregate those schools some pupils must be assigned—and transported—away from their neighborhood schools.

National Pupil Busing Data: 1929-30 to 1969-70

School year	Total public school enrollment	Pupils transported at public expense		Expenditure of public funds for busing	
		Numbers	Percent of total enrollment	Total (excluding cost of new buses)	Average cost per pupil
1929-30	25,678,015	1,902,826	7.4	$ 54,823,000	$28.81
1931-32	26,275,441	2,419,173	9.2	53,078,000	24.01
1933-34	26,434,103	2,794,724	10.6	53,908,000	19.29
1935-36	26,367,098	3,250,658	12.3	62,653,000	19.27
1937-38	25,975,108	3,769,242	14.5	75,637,000	20.07
1939-40	25,433,542	4,144,161	16.3	83,283,000	20.10
1941-42	24,562,473	4,503,081	18.3	92,922,000	20.64
1943-44	23,266,616	4,512,412	19.4	107,754,000	23.83
1945-46	23,299,941	5,056,966	21.7	129,756,000	25.66
1947-48	23,944,532	5,854,041	24.4	176,265,000	30.11
1949-50	25,111,427	6,947,384	27.7	214,504,000	30.83
1951-52	26,562,664	7,697,130	29.0	263,827,000	34.93
1953-54	26,643,871	8,411,719	32.8	307,437,000	36.55
1955-56	27,740,149	9,695,819	35.0	353,972,000	36.51
1957-58	29,722,275	10,861,689	36.5	416,491,000	38.34
1959-60	32,477,440	12,225,142	37.6	486,338,000	39.78
1961-62	34,682,340	13,222,667	38.1	576,361,000	43.59
1963-64	37,405,058	14,475,778	38.7	673,845,000	46.55
1965-66	39,154,497	15,588,567	39.7	787,358,000	50.68
1967-68	40,827,965	17,100,873	42.1	981,006,000	57.27
1969-70	41,934,376*	18,200,000*	43.4*	$1,214,399,000*	$66.73*

*Preliminary figures   SOURCE: U.S. Office of Education, HEW

New boundaries for attendance zones and the use of "magnet" schools often did not achieve results fast enough or completely enough to satisfy the requirement of desegregation "now."

The South was the first region to feel the impact of the desegregation decisions and busing orders; its schools had been segregated by law (de jure). The effects were dramatic in the late 1960s: Black pupils attending all-black schools in 11 southern states dropped to 14 percent in 1970 from 68 percent in 1968, according to HEW statistics. There was virtually no change in the racial isolation in northern and western schools during that same period.

But what was once a regional issue became a national controversy when federal courts began in 1970 to order busing in cities outside the south. Members of Congress from the North and West began giving their support to long-ignored antibusing proposals in Congress.

Yet undetermined by the Supreme Court in 1972 was the question of whether segregated schools resulting from residential segregation (de facto) were also unconstitutional. Attorneys for black parents in non-southern cities argued that what appeared to be de facto segregation was really the result of official action because of the backing of agencies like the Federal Housing Administration, whose loan guarantees supported much housing construction, and who until the late 1940s had actively promoted racially restrictive covenants in property titles.

The Supreme Court had set arguments on the de facto issue for the fall of 1972. The decision which it would

reach in that case, which came from Denver, Colo., would have broad implications for the future of desegregation of schools outside the South.

In Denver Federal District Judge William Doyle had found in 1970 that its de facto segregation was in fact unconstitutional; he ordered implementation of a busing plan to overcome the segregation in that city's schools. He was overruled by the court of appeals, 10th circuit; that reversal was appealed to the Supreme Court.

Adding to the national uproar was the 1972 decision of a Richmond, Va., federal district court requiring busing across city and county lines to desegregate schools. Judge Robert R. Merhige Jr.'s ruling—which was overturned in June by the court of appeals, 4th circuit—merged the largely black Richmond city school system with the white suburban systems of Henrico and Chesterfield Counties. It required the busing of about 78,000 of the 104,000 pupils in the three systems, an increase of 10,000 over the number being bused in the three systems before the judge's order.

And in Detroit, Federal District Judge Stephen J. Roth, who had earlier found that city's schools deliberately segregated, ordered in June the preparation of a desegregation plan for Detroit and 53 suburban districts. On July 10 Roth directed the state of Michigan to purchase 295 buses. The orders were appealed by the state and the suburbs of Detroit; the court of appeals, 6th circuit, July 20 delayed the implementation of Roth's orders pending arguments Aug. 24 on the appeals.

The Administration

President Nixon responded with sympathy to busing opponents. In a major address March 16, he said the lower courts had gone beyond what the Supreme Court said was necessary in requiring pupil transportation.

"All too often," the President said, "the result has been a classic case of the remedy for one evil creating another evil. In this case, a remedy for the historic evil of racial discrimination has often created a new evil of disrupting communities and imposing hardships on children —both black and white—who are themselves wholly innocent of the wrongs that the plan seeks to right."

The President followed up his speech with a two-part legislative proposal to slow, if not stop, the use of busing for desegregation. It consisted of:

• The Equal Educational Opportunities Act which would allow busing only as a limited last-resort remedy for segregation and would concentrate $2.5-billion in federal funds for compensatory education programs in poor schools.

• The Student Transportation Moratorium Act which would bar implementation of all new busing orders until July 1, 1973, or until Congress passed the equal opportunity bill, whichever was sooner.

The Justice Department issued a list of more than 150 school districts in 25 states that would be affected by the moratorium proposal.

The constitutionality of the proposals was a point of much discussion. The administration said that Congress had the constitutional authority to limit the jurisdiction of the federal courts. Opponents of the proposals questioned whether or not Congress could withdraw from the courts the power to order the use of a remedy necessary to secure to individuals their constitutional right to an equal educational opportunity.

The administration could have avoided this controversy by endorsing a proposed constitutional amendment barring the use of busing, but President Nixon declined to do so, saying that the amendment process (requiring two-thirds approval by both houses and ratification by three-fourths of the states) was too slow.

Clarence Mitchell, chief lobbyist for the NAACP, called the President's plan "a stunning example of government sanctioning hysteria and chaos." Nixon was standing in the school house door much as Alabama Gov. George C. Wallace did in the early 1960s to prevent blacks from entering the state university, he said.

Southerners were cool toward the proposals, recognizing them as fulfillment of their predictions that busing would be halted when it hit the North. "What about the old busing?" asked Rep. Joe D. Waggonner Jr. (D La.), referring to the busing already in effect which the moratorium would not touch.

And Mrs. Irene McCabe, a Pontiac, Mich., housewife and leader of the anti-busing National Action Group (NAG), scolded the President for not endorsing the constitutional amendment route.

Northerners, on the other hand, saw the proposals as saving them from carrying out busing orders in their section. House Minority Leader Gerald R. Ford (Mich.) and Rep. Norman F. Lent (R N.Y.) endorsed the moratorium. But Lent, the sponsor of a constitutional amendment barring busing, said he would press for that measure if Congress failed to pass the moratorium bill.

Some criticism came from within the administration itself. In April, two-thirds of the lawyers in the Justice Department's civil rights division signed a letter to Congress calling on it to reject any measures that would limit the remedies available in the federal courts. And 40 black federal officials, calling themselves the Council of Black Appointees, criticized the proposals and called for major revisions.

The administration pressed ahead with its proposals, and by mid-year the Justice Department had intervened on the side of anti-busing forces in important busing cases in Detroit, Richmond, Nashville, Dallas, Oklahoma City and Fort Worth.

The President, signing the higher education bill which contained anti-busing amendments on June 23, scolded the legislative branch for refusing to act on his proposals. John D. Ehrlichman, the senior White House adviser on domestic affairs, said that if Congress failed to act on the administration's measures before it adjourned for the elections, the President would "go to the country" to rally support for a constitutional amendment.

Immediately after reconvening from the Democratic convention, a House Education and Labor subcommittee approved, for full committee consideration, a modified version of the President's equal educational opportunity bill. The subcommittee dropped from the bill the provisions concentrating funds, retaining the guidelines for use of busing only as a last resort measure.

Forces Pro and Con

Arrayed behind—and often ahead of—the politicians on the busing issue was a variety of pressure groups. Anti-busing forces were chiefly grass roots organizations. They were not highly organized, but were effective.

Among them were the National Action Group (NAG) whose head, Mrs. McCabe, walked 600 miles from her home in Michigan to Washington, D.C, to dramatize her campaign for the Lent amendment. A group of parents from Richmond took part in a motor caravan to Washington to promote anti-busing legislation.

Also opposing busing was the Congress on Racial Equality (CORE), a leading black civil rights group. CORE's position was that only black-controlled schools could provide quality education for blacks, whereas busing would perpetuate white dominance of schools and school boards.

Other opponents included citizen action groups, school boards and local PTAs. A 1971 Gallup Poll found 77 percent national opposition to busing. Blacks split almost evenly on busing, it found.

Busing proponents counted on the support of labor, minority and civil rights groups. George Meany, president of the AFL-CIO, denounced the President's proposals as "political chicanery." The moratorium, he said, was "a cynical attempt to reward those who said 'never,' and to undermine the moral leadership of those citizens who endeavored to comply with the Constitution and the Supreme Court's 1954 decision."

The national PTA went on record supporting busing at its national convention in May—but by the slimmest of margins—302-296. The vote came on a resolution recommending that the group strive for "solutions that could, by rational means, reduce isolation through transportation."

The National Association for the Advancement of Colored People adopted a resolution at its 63rd annual convention in July condemning the President for his anti-busing views and asserting he had aroused "passions of hate and bitterness" among Americans.

Civil rights groups—127 of them—gathered under the umbrella of the Leadership Conference on Civil Rights to oppose the President and the trend in Congress.

Howard A. Glickstein, former staff director of the civil rights commission, directed the conference's battle to keep busing alive as a means of desegregating schools. People were "hysterical and irrational" over busing and the President "was anxious to make an issue of it," Glickstein said.

He predicted that the President would "keep the pot boiling" with attempts to stir Congress into action on the issue, and that Nixon would win points regardless of what Congress did. If Congress acted, Nixon could take the credit, and if it did not, he could blame them, Glickstein explained.

The anti-busing amendments to the 1972 Higher Education Act, which the conference opposed, could have more than their desired effects on busing, he went on. Noting that one amendment delayed transfers in addition to busing, he said the effect might be to stop all integration. In any case, Glickstein said, "It's an invitation to litigation...to delay."

Other pressures on Congress and the President came from state legislatures. Voters in Florida on March 14 and in Tennessee May 4 voted overwhelmingly, in non-binding referendums, to support constitutional amendments barring busing. The vote was 74 percent in Florida and 80 percent in Tennessee for such an amendment. These states were also easily carried by George Wallace in presidential primaries.

The Virginia Senate had voted 36-3 February 15 in favor of a resolution asking Congress to amend the Constitution to bar busing to integrate schools.

Confusing the issue, Florida voters, at the same time they voted against busing, gave 78 percent approval to another question on the ballot: "Do you favor providing an equal opportunity for quality education for all children, regardless of race, creed, color and place of residence, and oppose a return to a dual system of public education?"

Congress

The 92nd Congress responded to the busing pressures by approving its strongest anti-busing language in the Higher Education Act (S 659—PL 92-318). The amendments were a compromise between stronger House language and less rigid Senate provisions. They:

• Postponed until all appeals had been exhausted, or the time for them expired, the implementation of all federal district court orders requiring the transfer or transportation of pupils to achieve racial balance. The provision was to expire Jan. 1, 1974.

• Limited use of federal funds for busing intended to desegregate a school system to cases where the local officials requested the funds.

• Barred busing where it would risk the pupil's health or require him to attend a school inferior to his former school.

• Barred federal pressure on local school boards to induce them to use busing "unless constitutionally required."

But busing opponents were unsatisfied with these limitations and by mid-August were pressing for even stricter controls, specifically the President's proposals.

The President's moratorium was stronger than S 659 because it would put a complete ban on all new busing orders, whereas the anti-busing amendments to S 659 would bar implementation of busing orders until appeals—or the time for them—had been exhausted.

In order to get House action on stiffer busing control bills, proponents pulled off a rarely used power play through the Rules Committee that pried one bill out of the pro-busing Judiciary Committee and forced another out of the liberal Education and Labor Committee.

Under House rules, the Rules Committee was authorized to discharge a bill from a legislative committee by majority vote. This was seldom done—only four times since 1953—because the wishes and prerogatives of committee chairmen usually were honored by other committee chairmen.

But William M. Colmer (D Miss.), retiring chairman of the Rules Committee, was an ardent busing opponent who felt the Judiciary Committee was stalling action on the Lent amendment and the President's moratorium bill. The amendment had been in the committee for more than a year. Hearings were held on it and the moratorium, but no other action was taken.

Colmer issued an ultimatum to Chairman Emanuel Celler (D N.Y.) of the Judiciary Committee June 29 that one of the bills would have to be reported out of his committee by Aug. 1 or the Rules Committee would attempt to discharge them.

"This Congress should not adjourn without taking favorable action on this matter," he told the House. "It should be settled and not left as a political football to be kicked around in this election year."

Celler and the Judiciary Committee refused to act on the ultimatum and on Aug. 1 the Rules Committee voted 9-6 to discharge the Lent amendment and send it to floor. The amendment read, "No public school student shall, because of his race, creed or color, be assigned to or required to attend a particular school."

The language, seemingly equalitarian, had been denounced by constitutional experts at hearings as likely to bar desegregation as well as busing.

At the same time, the Rules Committee voted 11-4 to delay a discharge attempt on the President's moratorium proposal. The two votes made clear, however, that there was enough strength on the committee to force anti-busing legislation out of the Education and Labor Committee, too.

Feeling the pressure, the Education and Labor Committee voted 21-16 Aug. 8 to report an amended version of the President's equal educational opportunities bill putting strict limits on busing.

As ordered reported, the bill required that any pupil in the elementary grades (1-6) be allowed to attend the public school "closest or next closest" to his home. It also reserved $500-million annually for compensatory education from the sums appropriated for aid to desegregating school districts. The committee rejected an amendment which would have made the $500-million a newly authorized sum, instead of simply earmarking part of already-authorized funds.

The committee also rejected a provision in the bill as proposed by Nixon that would have allowed reopening of school desegregation orders to determine whether they conformed with the provisions of the new legislation.

The Senate Judiciary Committee had not begun hearings on the moratorium proposal. Education Subcommittee Chairman Claiborne Pell (D R.I.) said after holding several days of hearings on the equal opportunity bill that he was having trouble finding witnesses who would testify in its favor. "It's hard for us to report out a bill that nobody comes out for," he said. An aide to Peter H. Dominick (R Colo.), the bill's sponsor, said it was questionable whether the bill would come to the Senate floor.

In the 92nd Congress an anti-busing majority consolidated itself in the House. As court orders were issued requiring busing in the North and West, representatives from those parts of the country began to join their southern colleagues in opposition to busing.

A leading example of this new majority was the Michigan Democratic delegation, five of whose members served districts in Detroit or its suburbs and had pro-civil rights voting records.

Four of the five—James G. O'Hara, Lucien N. Nedzi, William D. Ford and John D. Dingell—voted for the amendment to the higher education bill, approved by the House in 1971, that delayed the implementation of court busing orders until appeals had been exhausted.

The amendment was authored by William S. Broomfield (R Mich.) specifically to delay any cross-district busing in the Detroit area. O'Hara and Ford previously had been opponents of anti-busing amendments.

The four Michigan Democrats, joined by Martha W. Griffiths (D Mich.), later signed the petition aimed at discharging the Judiciary Committee from consideration of the constitutional amendment barring busing.

Although the Broomfield amendment was approved 235-125, it failed to gain the support of some southerners who knew it would have little effect on southern school districts already engaged in busing. Jack Edwards (R Ala.) stated their position:

"We are busing all over the 1st District of Alabama.... A lot of people say to me, 'How in the world are we ever going to stop this madness?' I say, 'It will stop the day it starts taking place across the country, in the North, in the East, in the West.'

"And so busing is ordered in Michigan and the first thing the members from Michigan do is come in with this amendment and ask us to delay it for them. But, my friends, we are not going to stop the busing as long as we let them off the hook the minute it hits them. Let it hurt them, and we will get their votes as we try to stop busing once and for all."

The underlying divisions on busing were further exemplified by William Jennings Bryan Dorn (D S.C.), who distinguished himself from the majority of his southern colleagues by voting consistently for federal aid for districts undertaking busing.

During debate in March on a motion instructing House conferees on the higher education bill not to compromise away the strong anti-busing language approved by the body, including that limiting federal funds for busing, Dorn said:

"There is no way my schools can continue to operate and function properly without busing. In the school yard of my home town high school at this moment there are 88 buses. To deny federal aid to continue this busing operation is to hamper and hamstring quality education.

"The result will be increased property taxes on the citizens of my district, taxpayers who are already saddled with excessively high taxes, local communities which are desperately seeking means to raise revenue. It would be incredible to tax them further to bus school children and deny them urgently needed federal funds."

(College Financing continued from p. 19)

education over a lifetime, reducing the amount of time spent on it early in life and spending additional time on formal education later in life as desired and needed.

John G. Kemeny, president of Dartmouth College, has suggested "professional sabbaticals" to bring business executives and professional men and women back to campuses every fifth summer at their employers' expense. He proposes that colleges and universities enter into lifetime agreements with alumni to provide courses they need as they move through or change careers.

The most unorthodox of the new lifetime learning attempts has begun in Britain. It is called simply the Open University, and its aim is to provide college instruction on television and radio for all adults who want a second chance, or perhaps a first chance, to get a degree. The only prerequisites for enrollment are a minimum age of 21 and payment of a tuition fee of $60 a year. The program, which started Jan. 10, 1971, offers 36 weekly lessons on both television and radio. In addition, the student receives monthly homework assignments by mail in each of the four courses—science, math, art and social science—currently being offered. The plan also features 250 study centers, staffed by tutors and counselors, which the students are urged to visit. There are also mandatory one-week residential summer school sessions.

Costs of the entire program are expected to run at about $10 million per year. Costs per student will be only 10 per cent of what they would be at a convention university. A similar non-residential college will be established by the State University of New York, aided by grants from the Carnegie Corporation and Ford Foundation.

This radical departure from traditional methods has aroused hostility both in Britain and the United States on the part of those who are afraid that such a venture will bring on inferior academic standards. Anastasios Christodoulou, the secretary of Open University, insists that "We won't pass people just so the university can survive politically." A drop-out and failure rate of about 30 per cent is anticipated by the university's administrators.

"We're going to beat our critics all hollow," Christodoulou added. "The idea of an elite class coming out of elite universities simply doesn't hold water any more." The open university is, however, just entering its period of testing. And many other suggested reforms are merely hopes for the future. Meanwhile, the search for solvency is becoming desperate. The unresolved question is whether change will mean only budget cutting or will lead to the effective reform of higher education.

RESTORE PRAYER IN SCHOOLS: THE MOVE THAT FAILED

Despite the support of a majority of the House of Representatives, a proposed school prayer amendment failed Nov. 8, 1971, to win the approval of the necessary two-thirds when it came to its first House vote. The vote was 240-162; the supporters of the proposal lacked 28 votes of two-thirds of the 402 members voting.

(Constitutional amendments require approval of two-thirds majorities in the House and Senate and ratification by three-fourths of the states.)

The vote capped intense lobbying efforts for and against the proposed constitutional amendment, designed to override the Supreme Court's decisions in 1962 and 1963 outlawing officially prescribed or officially backed religious observances in the public schools.

As modified on the floor, the proposed amendment (H J Res 191) would have added to the Constitution a statement that voluntary prayer or meditation in public buildings, by persons lawfully assembled, was constitutionally permissible. *(Text of amendment, box next page)*

It was introduced in 1971 by Rep. Chalmers P. Wylie (R Ohio) and was similar to one proposed in 1967 by then-Senate Minority Leader Everett McKinley Dirksen (R Ill. 1951-1969).

Wylie and supporters of the amendment—mobilized in a two-year grassroots lobbying effort by Ohio housewife, Mrs. Ben Ruhlin—said that H J Res 191 would modify the Supreme Court decisions to restore the freedom of religious expression—through voluntary prayer in the schools—which the 1st Amendment was written to guarantee.

Opponents of the amendment, led by the National Council of Churches, House Judiciary Chairman Emanuel Celler (D N.Y.), James C. Corman (D Calif.) and Fred Schwengel (R Iowa), said that the amendment was unnecessary, that it merely ensured that which the 1st Amendment already protected. Tampering with the Bill of Rights, they said, would "whittle down" the present freedom of religion enjoyed by Americans and would open a breach in the wall separating church and state.

The politically explosive proposal came to the House floor through the extraordinary procedure of a discharge petition. Mrs. Ruhlin asked Wylie to file such a petition to pry the resolution from Celler's committee, to which it had been referred and from which it had received no attention. After a majority (218) of the members of the House sign such a petition, the committee is discharged from consideration of the measure which then can, on approval of a motion by a majority, be brought directly to the House floor.

This rarely effective tactic succeeded in bringing the school prayer resolution to the floor chiefly through the efforts of Mrs. Ruhlin, her Prayer Campaign Committee and related groups. They mobilized citizen pressure across the country to persuade members to sign the discharge petition.

This intense pressure on members to support the petition may have backfired. On the crucial vote the amendment was defeated by the defection and abstention of members who had signed the discharge petition.

On the vote of approval, 28 who had signed the petition either did not vote or opposed the amendment, exactly the number needed to reach the necessary two-thirds majority. Twelve of the 28 did not vote; 16 opposed the amendment.

Background: Church and State

Separation of church and state was a unique premise of the national structure of the United States, the direct result of the experience of the founding fathers whose families had fled to the New World from persecution at the prompting of a state church.

After considerable debate, Congress approved as the 1st Amendment the simple statement that: "Congress shall make no law respecting an establishment of religion or prohibiting the free exercise thereof."

Supreme Court decisions during the 1940s held this guarantee binding on the states as well as on Congress.

"The First Experiment." "Almighty God, we acknowledge our dependence upon Thee, and we beg Thy blessings upon us, our parents, our teachers and our Country."

This prayer, recommended by the New York State Board of Regents for daily use in that state's public schools, was challenged by the parents of certain students as contrary to the 1st Amendment ban on establishment of religion. One hundred and seventy years had passed since the adoption of the 1st Amendment. During this time no challenge to school prayer had come before the Supreme Court.

The Supreme Court held for the plaintiffs in June 1962, ruling that the New York practice violated the 1st Amendment—despite the fact that the prayer was non-denominational and that students who did not wish to recite the prayer were excused from the room. Justice Potter Stewart dissented. *(Engel v. Vitale)*

For the majority, Justice Hugo Black wrote that the 1st Amendment "must at least mean...that it is no part of the business of government to compose official prayers for any group of the American people to recite as part of a religious program carried on by government."

"The 1st Amendment," he continued, "was added to the Constitution to stand as a guarantee that neither the power nor the prestige of the federal government would be used to control, support or influence the kinds of prayer the American people can say."

"When the power, prestige and financial support of government is placed behind a particular religious belief, the indirect coercive pressure upon religious minorities to conform to the prevailing officially approved religion is plain," wrote Black. But the reason for the Establishment Clause was also the belief that a union between government and religion tended to destroy one and degrade the other, he said, adding:

"The Establishment Clause thus stands as an expression of principle on the part of the founders of our Constitution that religion is too personal, too sacred, too holy, to permit its 'unhallowed perversion' by a civil magistrate."

The 1st Amendment was adopted, the Court said, "to quiet well-justified fears which nearly all of them felt arising out of an awareness that governments of the past had shackled men's tongues to make them speak only the religious thoughts that government wanted them to speak and to pray only to the God that government wanted them to pray to. It is neither sacrilegious nor antireligious to say that each separate government in this country should stay out of the business of writing or sanctioning official prayers and leave that purely religious function to the people themselves."

To those who argued that the prayer concerned was too general and brief to pose any danger of establishing religion, Black repeated the warning of James Madison, one of the authors of the 1st Amendment: "It is proper to take alarm at the first experiment on our liberties.... Who does not see that the same authority which can establish Christianity, in exclusion of all other religions, may establish with the same ease any particular sect of Christianity, in exclusion of all other sects?"

In dissent, Justice Stewart said he could not "see how an 'official religion' is established by letting those who want to say a prayer say it. On the contrary, I think that to deny the wish of these schoolchildren to join in reciting this prayer is to deny them the opportunity of sharing in the spiritual heritage of our nation."

Reaction was immediate and generally adverse. The Court, headlines reported, had outlawed prayer in the public schools. Constitutional amendments to override the decision were promptly introduced in Congress, but after two days of hearings by the Senate Judiciary Committee, Congress took no further action in 1962.

A Position of Neutrality. Public outcry had no apparent effect on the Court. In June 1963, with Justice Stewart again dissenting, the Court held that Maryland and Pennsylvania were violating the 1st Amendment by requiring public schools to begin the school day with classroom Bible reading or recitation of the Lord's Prayer. *(Murray v. Curlett, Abington School District v. Schempp)*

The states cannot require such religious exercises as part of the curricular activities of students who are required by law to attend school, Justice Tom C. Clark wrote for the majority. It is irrelevant that such practices may seem "relatively minor encroachments on the 1st Amendment. The breach of neutrality that is today a trickling stream may all too soon become a raging torrent."

The Court's ruling did not, wrote Clark, set up a "religion of secularism" in the schools. The study of religion had its place in the curriculum and the Court made clear that "nothing we have said here indicates that such study of the Bible or of religion, when presented objectively as part of a secular program of education may not be effected consistently with the 1st Amendment."

School Prayer Amendment

H J Res 191 would have added the following amendment to the Constitution:

"Nothing contained in this Constitution shall abridge the right of persons lawfully assembled, in any public building which is supported in whole or in part through the expenditure of public funds, to participate in voluntary prayer or meditation."

Before the House amended the resolution on the floor, the language had provided for participation in non-denominational, rather than in voluntary, prayer.

The 1st Amendment commands the government to maintain a strict neutrality, neither aiding nor opposing religion, Clark said. Even with the consent of the majority, a state could not require a religious exercise.

"The place of religion in our society is an exalted one," Clark said, "achieved through a long tradition of reliance on the home, the church and the inviolable citadel of the individual heart and mind. We have come to recognize through bitter experience that it is not within the power of government to invade that citadel, whether its purpose or effect be to aid or oppose, to advance or retard. In the relationship between man and religion, the state is firmly committed to a position of neutrality."

Justice Stewart dissented, arguing that the facts before the Court were insufficient to support any decision. "What our Constitution indispensably protects is the freedom of each of us, be he Jew or agnostic, Christian or atheist, Buddhist or Freethinker, to believe or disbelieve, to worship or not worship, to pray or keep silent, according to his own conscience, uncoerced and unrestrained by government. It is conceivable that these school boards... might eventually find it impossible to administer a system of religious exercises during school hours in such a way as to meet this constitutional standard."

Reaction to the Court's second school prayer decision came quickly. Evangelist Billy Graham said he was shocked: "Why should the majority be so severely penalized by the protests of a handful?"

And despite the opposition of most major religious organizations to any constitutional amendment overriding the Court's rulings, mail advocating such an amendment flooded into congressional offices.

A SCHOOL PRAYER AMENDMENT?

Rep. Frank J. Becker (R N.Y. 1953-1965) had introduced a proposed amendment before the second Supreme Court decision. His amendment provided that nothing in the Constitution should be interpreted to bar "the offering, reading from, or listening to prayer or biblical scriptures, if participation therein is on a voluntary basis, in any governmental or public school institution or place." After the 1963 decisions, Becker filed a petition discharging the House Judiciary Committee from consideration of his proposal. Committee Chairman Celler had made plain his opposition to any such constitutional amendment.

By early 1964 the petition had gathered 164 of the 218 signatures needed. Celler agreed to hold hearings. For six weeks, the Judiciary Committee received testimony. The printed record filled three volumes totaling almost 2,800 pages. The committee took no further action; Celler said it had found no way to approve any of the proposed amendments without infringing upon existing guarantees of freedom of religion.

The Dirksen Amendment. Despite the lack of congressional action, the school prayer issue did not disappear. In mid-1965 a court of appeals upheld the action of a New York principal who had refused a request by a group of children that time be set aside for them during school hours to recite two prayers. The Supreme Court refused to review this decision. *(Stein v. Oshinsky)*

Supporters of a school prayer amendment point to this decision and later ones as evidence of the need for an amendment to "clarify" the Supreme Court's 1962 and 1963 holdings. But major church groups remain opposed to any amendment.

Senate Minority Leader Dirksen in 1966 proposed an amendment stating that the Constitution should not be interpreted to bar any public school authority from providing for or permitting the voluntary participation of students in prayer. His amendment specifically stated that it did not authorize any authority to prescribe the form or content of a prayer.

The Dirksen amendment was not directed to the required religious exercises outlawed by the Supreme Court but instead at situations such as that in the *Stein* case, where a principal forbade student-requested prayer periods during school hours.

There was strong grassroots support for the amendment, Dirksen said, especially after the Court by refusing to reverse the *Stein* decision had closed the door on voluntary prayer in the schools. Birch Bayh (D Ind.), chairman of the Judiciary Subcommittee on Constitutional Amendments, maintained that voluntary school prayer was still permissible. Sam J. Ervin Jr. (D N.C.) opposed the Dirksen amendment as an "annihilation of the principle of the 1st Amendment."

Bayh held hearings in 1966 but took no further action on the Dirksen resolution. In September the Senate agreed to substitute the text of the school prayer amendment for that of a pending bill. But the Senate then failed, by nine votes, to give the Dirksen amendment the necessary two-thirds vote.

Dirksen introduced a new school prayer amendment in 1967. It was identical to H J Res 191.

Wylie's involvement began soon after his 1967 arrival in Washington as a freshman Representative. After receiving a petition from constituents asking him to support the Dirksen amendment, Wylie visited Dirksen and offered his assistance. Dirksen suggested that Wylie introduce an identical resolution in the House. Wylie did, but no action was taken on either measure by the 90th Congress. Both resolutions were reintroduced in the 91st Congress; no action was taken on them before Dirksen's death in September 1969. Observers felt then that the school prayer issue would probably fade away.

A year later, in October 1970, Howard H. Baker Jr. (R Tenn.), Dirksen's son-in-law, proposed the school prayer resolution as an amendment to the proposed constitutional amendment guaranteeing women equal rights. The Senate agreed, 50-20, to add on the school prayer resolution but did not complete action on the whole package during the 91st Congress.

1970 PRAYER CAMPAIGN

But even while the school prayer amendment appeared to be losing strength in Washington, a vigorous prayer amendment campaign was under way in other parts of the country.

In Cuyahoga Falls, Ohio, Mrs. Ruhlin was disturbed by remarks of her teenage son concerning the impact which the absence of prayer in the schools might be having on religious beliefs of the young. Pursuing this concern, she was told by the local school board to look to Congress or the courts for clarification of the school prayer situation.

Working with her Representative, William H. Ayres (R Ohio 1951-1971), Mrs. Ruhlin researched the issue and began her campaign. In the summer of 1970 she paid visits to Sen. James O. Eastland (D Miss.), chairman of the Senate Judiciary Committee and to Celler, asking them to report out the prayer amendments.

About the same time, Mrs. Ruhlin placed $6,000 worth of coupons in major newspapers across the country. Persons supporting the movement to put prayer back in the schools were to fill out the coupons and send them to the House Judiciary Committee.

Through this self-financed effort, Mrs. Ruhlin contacted women across the country who became her Prayer Campaign Committee. In September 1970 the committee conducted a poll of House members to ascertain how many of them would support a discharge petition to force the school prayer amendment from the Judiciary Committee to the floor. The results indicated that such an effort would work.

Mrs. Ruhlin told Congressional Quarterly that Celler said his committee would report out an amendment in 1971, but that when she talked with him early in 1971, he changed his position and said that he would not.

"She's standing on her head when she says such a thing," Celler told Congressional Quarterly Oct. 27, 1971, referring to Mrs. Ruhlin's statement that he had said he would report out the amendment. "I never said such a thing," he said.

Mrs. Ruhlin then visited Wylie, bringing petitions bearing more than 100,000 names and urging approval of a school prayer amendment. Ayres had been defeated in the 1970 election by John F. Seiberling (D Ohio) who was not sympathetic to Mrs. Ruhlin's campaign. Ayres suggested that Wylie would be the best Representative to lead the school prayer effort in the House.

In her conversation with Wylie, Mrs. Ruhlin asked him to talk to Celler to ask him to hold hearings and, if that failed, to file a discharge petition to bring his resolution (H J Res 191) to the floor.

Wylie was unsuccessful in persuading Celler to hold hearings. Wylie filed a discharge petition April 1, 1971.

Mrs. Ruhlin and her committee contacted Representatives who had indicated their willingness to support a discharge effort and asked them to sign the petition and send the committee confirmation that they had done so. Members who failed to sign received phone calls and visits from constituents on the prayer committee.

By mid-1970 Mrs. Ruhlin and the Prayer Campaign Committee, with its members from all parts of the country, were working with several other groups with similar aims: the Back to God movement, Citizens for Public Prayer, Project Prayer, Parents for Prayer and Citizens for Public Reverence. The major organized religious group working for the amendment was the National Association of Evangelicals, composed of 37 evangelical denominations and some 38,000 individual persons and churches belonging to almost every Protestant group.

Members of these groups spent most of the summer of 1971 in the House office buildings, visiting Representatives who had not signed the discharge petition and bringing pressure on them—directly and through mail and constituent contacts—to do so.

The major talking point of Mrs. Ruhlin and her coworkers' drive was that the majority of the American people wanted a school prayer amendment to restore religion to its rightful place. The Rev. Robert Howes, national coordinator of Citizens for Public Prayer, cited an Opinion Research poll early in 1971 which indicated that 80 percent of the American people favored putting prayer back in the public schools.

Among the other persons and groups listed by Wylie and Mrs. Ruhlin as backing H J Res 191 were: Billy Graham, Patrick Cardinal O'Boyle, the North Carolina Baptist Convention, Bishop Fulton J. Sheen, the National Council of Catholic Youth, the Rev. Theodore Hesburgh—chairman of the U.S. Commission on Civil Rights—Orthodox Greek Diocese of North America, the national Junior Chamber of Commerce, the Veterans of Foreign Wars, the American Legion, the legislatures of Massachusetts, Maryland, North Carolina and Louisiana, the National Federation of Republican Women, the National Kiwanis Club, the National Conference of Mayors, the National Conference of Governors and the National Grange.

OPPOSITION: LATE START

The major opponents of a school prayer amendment were undisturbed by the now-perennial rumblings of support for such an amendment, confident that Celler's adamant opposition and Dirksen's death made action by either chamber unlikely.

Celler was one of the first to realize that a major battle was brewing. In mid-July he wrote a letter to every Representative, accompanied by the weighty record of the 1964 Judiciary Committee hearings. Celler's letter asked each Representative not to sign the discharge petition, pointing out that after full consideration and discussion in 1964, his committee had been unable to reach a consensus on any amendment which would not infringe upon freedom of religion as already guaranteed by the Bill of Rights. He asked that each Representative consider the evidence presented to the committee.

The National Council of Churches and the Baptist Joint Committee on Public Affairs became aware of the situation about the same time. (The National Council is a federation of 33 national Protestant communions and denominations; the Joint Committee consists of persons representing each of the eight Baptist conventions in the United States.)

The first effort of these groups was directed toward holding the number of signatures on the discharge petition below the requisite 218, persuading members not to sign—or if they had already signed, persuading them to remove their signatures.

Recognizing that this effort was unlikely to succeed in the face of the intensive efforts of the prayer campaign members, the religious groups working together in opposition issued a statement Sept. 15, 1971. Hand-delivered to every representative's office, the letter was signed by leaders of all eight Baptist conventions, of the Board of Social Ministry of the Lutheran Church in America, of the Presbyterian Church in the United States and of the United Presbyterian Church.

In addition to the Joint Committee and the National Council, the letter was also signed by the Friends Committee on National Legislation, the Church of the Brethren, the executive council of the Episcopal Church, the council for Christian social action of the United Church of Christ, the joint advisory committee of the Synagogue Council of America and the National Jewish Community Relations Advisory Council, the Unitarian Universalist Assn. and the board of Christian concerns of the United Methodist Church. Many of these groups maintain active lobbying operations in Washington.

The letter expressed the view that the First Amendment adequately protected the right of school children and others to pray voluntarily without government authorization or supervision. By approving the proposed amendment—the first change in the Bill of Rights—Congress would be opening the door for government intrusion into religious matters, the letter said.

Less than a week later on Sept. 21, 1971, the last of the 218 signatures was added to the discharge petition; 111 Republicans and 107 Democrats had signed.

The rules for the discharge procedure provide that a petition, once fully signed, must wait seven days before being brought before the House. It can be considered only on the second or fourth Mondays of the month. These requirements plus the House's holiday schedule in October meant that Nov. 8 was the earliest day on which the discharge motion could be considered. This seven-week interval was the opposition's best break.

On Sept. 27, 1971, a meeting was convened in the office of Rep. James C. Corman (D Calif.), an outspoken opponent of the proposed amendments since 1964. At the meeting besides Corman were Jim Hamilton of the National Council of Churches, and Reps. Fred Schwengel (R Iowa), Don Edwards (D Calif.), Mike McCormack (D Wash.) and Robert F. Drinan (D Mass.), a Roman Catholic priest.

This group became the organizing force for the opposition. Through colleague-to-colleague persuasion and through pressure from constituents mobilized by the opposing churches, the anti-amendment forces began to work, concentrating chiefly on those members who had not signed the discharge petition or introduced a school prayer resolution.

The opposition's objectives were two-fold: to convince each Representative to take a careful look at the amendment and its implications and to assure him that he would not be committing political suicide by voting against a prayer amendment.

By Oct. 4, 1971, the opposition was gaining strength. A group of clergymen and Representatives held a press conference announcing their united opposition to the Wylie resolution as "a very real threat to religious freedom." In addition to the group which had met Sept. 27, the participants included Representatives Celler, Bob Eckhardt (D Texas) and Don Fraser (D Minn.), Carl

Bates, president of the Southern Baptist Convention and six other religious leaders.

Also Oct. 4, 67 Representatives formed the Congressional Committee to Preserve Religious Freedom and sent to all other Representatives a "Dear Colleague" letter urging opposition to the amendment: "We believe that the House should not now undertake to tamper with the First Amendment after a scanty one-hour floor debate, particularly where the meaning and possibly far-reaching consequences of the pending resolution are far from clear." Among the 59 Democrats and 8 Republicans signing the letter were Seiberling and some, including Shirley Chisholm (D N.Y.), who had signed the discharge petition.

"Almost everybody on careful reflection opposes the amendment," said Corman, who feared what he felt was the opportunity it might provide for religious indoctrination in the schools, "but it is an issue that lends itself to pressure."

The strongest pressure on members of the House of Representatives is that exerted by the votes of their constituents. And as a member of the staff of one southern Representative explained: "It's just very difficult to explain a vote against prayer. If you are voting strictly on political considerations, you vote for it."

PRO: THE WILL OF THE PEOPLE

"The American people want a prayer amendment," declared Mrs. Ruhlin, who emphasized that in a democracy, a government by the people, the will of the majority should rule.

Wylie followed suit. Critics of his amendment manifested "total ignorance of the will of a majority of the people," he said Oct. 21, 1971. Supporters of the amendment dismissed the opposition of religious leaders and national church organizations as that of generals without armies. Mrs. Ruhlin said that she and her colleagues had polled many churches and found that almost all of their members supported a school prayer amendment.

Adoption of the proposed constitutional amendment is necessary to clarify the Supreme Court's decisions, said Wylie. Clarification would prevent "hairsplitting" lower court decisions such as that which in 1968 upheld a court order barring the compulsory recitation, by public school kindergarten children, of a thank-you verse. (*DeSpain v. DeKalb County Community School District 428*) The Supreme Court refused to review that decision, as in 1970 it refused to review the decision of New Jersey courts barring the school board-approved practice in one school district of providing a pre-school period during which prayers were read from the *Congressional Record* to anyone who wished to attend. (*State Board of Education v. Board of Education of Netcong, N.J.*)

Adoption of the prayer amendment would benefit society generally, Wylie said. The ban on prayer in schools had called into question the validity of prayer and religion, he contended, particularly in the minds of students. Since 1962, he noted, church membership had declined, while crime, juvenile delinquency and drug abuse had increased sharply.

Advocates of the Wylie amendment said it would restore the 1st Amendment guarantees to their original meaning. They were intended to prevent state preference of one denomination over another, not to prevent state preference for religion over atheism. The Supreme Court should not have added atheists and agnostics to the groups protected by the 1st Amendment, Wylie said, "and the American people want Congress to undo the damage of this Warren Court decision."

To those who questioned the concept of a non-denominational prayer, Wylie pointed to the New York Regents prayer in *Engel v. Vitale*. In answer to those who fear his amendment could lead to state use of the schools for religious indoctrination, Wylie replied that "some inculcation in the schools might spark interest."

Evangelist Billy Graham urged passage of the amendment Nov. 4 in a telegram to Wylie. He warned that atheism and secularism might become America's unofficial religion. He said: "I see no damage to this amendment....I believe that the overwhelming majority of the American people want prayer in the schools. It is interesting...that when we took prayer out of the schools, sex permissiveness, rebellion, drugs and even crime came in."

BOOMERANG OR BOOBY TRAP

"Don't booby-trap religious freedom by an innocent-sounding prayer amendment that is in fact a time-bomb against religion," warned a pamphlet published by the Baptist Joint Committee, stating the position of a variety of religious groups, including Southern Baptists and Unitarians, Masons and Mennonites.

The opposition argued first, that the proposed amendment was unnecessary and, second, that it was undesirable.

Schwengel, who believes firmly in prayer and carries 17 prayers in his coat pocket, said the amendment was unnecessary because the Court did not throw God out of the schools or restrict the individual's right to pray. Voluntary prayer, he says, is permissible anywhere.

This point was repeated in an October 1971 editorial in the Jesuit magazine *America*. H J Res 191 was "sheer tokenism," it said. asserting "what very few would deny, that there is no constitutional interdict on truly 'private' prayer in public buildings."

Critics say that the proposed amendment was undesirable because it would restrict religious freedom, provide the opportunity for a government role in religious matters, divide religious groups in its implementation, dilute religion into non-denominationalism and set a dangerous precedent for tampering with the Bill of Rights.

Religious leaders and church groups expressed concern for the potential for government interference. In the Sept. 15 letter, these groups stated: "We deny that an elected body or governmental authority has the right to determine either the place or the content of prayer as is implied in the proposed constitutional amendment." An Oct. 22 statement by Americans United for Separation of Church and State took a similar view.

The grand commander of the Scottish Rite of Freemasonry in the United States issued a call Sept. 26 to all Masons to oppose the "boomerang" school prayer amendment. He warned that its adoption would be "the foot in the door, the camel's nose in the tent, sure to result in further and eventual fatal intrusions" into fundamental constitutional rights.

The U.S. Catholic Conference, in a statement released Nov. 3, announced its opposition to the school prayer amendment.

A number of constitutional experts voiced opposition to the amendment in letters to Celler, and more than 300 attorneys, law professors and deans released a statement Nov. 2 opposing it, saying: "If the first clause of the Bill of Rights...should prove so easily susceptible to impairment by amendment, none of the succeeding clauses will be secure."

Floor Debate

Wylie urged the House to approve the motion discharging the Judiciary Committee from consideration of H J Res 191. Approval of the motion, which required a simple majority vote, would open the way for House consideration of the amendment. Wylie called for adoption of the resolution in order to clarify the Supreme Court decisions which, he said, had, "for all practical purposes, voided school prayer."

Celler, holding the three heavy volumes of testimony on the prayer amendment issue before his committee in 1964, asked the House not to try to write a constitutional amendment on the floor in the one hour allotted for debate on H J Res 191. He reminded them that the full Judiciary Committee, after the lengthy 1964 hearings, was not able to draft appropriate language for an amendment which, he said, would not do violence to the 1st Amendment.

Robert L. F. Sikes (D Fla.) urged approval of the motion, saying "there is such a thing as too much freedom of speech. The same Court which stopped prayer in the schools has said the news media can lie about you with absolute immunity. It has said a Communist-oriented newspaper can publish any secrets it can buy or steal without regard to national security....This is the freedom of speech you are being asked to protect....If you are one of those who plan to vote against the prayer amendment today, I want to be around to hear you explain to your constituents your vote against prayer to God and for the Court."

House Majority Leader Hale Boggs (D La.) said a vote against the amendment meant not that a Representative was against prayer but that he was concerned about an amendment which would for the first time qualify the freedom of the 1st Amendment.

The House agreed to the motion to discharge the committee by a roll-call vote of 242-156. The large vote against the motion indicated that opponents of the amendment might well have the strength to block approval of the amendment.

The House then moved to debate the merits of the amendment. G. V. (Sonny) Montgomery (D Miss.) discussed the practical politics of the issue: "A vote for the proposed constitutional amendment is going to be a lot easier to explain back home than a vote against it. I know that if I vote against the resolution today, my opponent next year will make me do a lot of explaining....I still believe that the people we represent want this measure adopted....It is up to us to give them what they want."

William J. Keating (R Ohio) asked how members of the House could participate in the prayer which began each day's session of the House and say that it was unconstitutional for their children to do the same thing in school each day.

William M. McCulloch (R Ohio), ranking minority member of the Judiciary Committee, spoke against the amendment as "not good law...not good theology."

In a brief emotional statement, Speaker of the House Carl Albert (D Okla.) opposed the amendment, saying he was unprepared "to let the meddling hand of government at any level in any degree be placed on any man's altar."

Schwengel pointed out that Wylie said local school boards would make the determination on what was a non-denominational prayer, subject to review by the courts. This, said Schwengel, made it the business of government to determine the content of prayer.

Drinan, opposing the amendment, noted that there was no satisfactory definition of non-denominational He pointed out that for the first time American Roman Catholic bishops had spoken out to oppose the amendment. He said that if the House and Senate passed the proposed amendment, state legislatures would be "threatened, not by a majority, not by a well-informed and rational lobby, but by a tiny minority of shrill persons who have sought to intimidate me as they have sought to intimidate every member of this House." The amendment's adoption, he said, would be a disaster.

K. Gunn McKay (D Utah) opposed the amendment: "You cannot legislate morality or religion. You build it in the home and the church and when the home and church breaks down...propping it up in any school will never change that."

Samuel L. Devine (R Ohio) called the church leaders who opposed the amendment "generals without armies" and said the same clergymen who argued for separation of church and state were "first in line with hat in hand seeking government money."

John Buchanan (R Ala.), a Baptist minister, proposed to amend H J Res 191 by substituting the word "voluntary" for "non-denominational" to describe the type of prayer allowed—and by adding meditation to the activity allowed. These changes, he said, would answer the primary arguments against the amendment and would remove the danger that the state would prescribe any religious activity.

Abner J. Mikva (D Ill.) asked if prayer was voluntary when one considered that children must be in school and must stand in silent prayer—or not in prayer as he or she, perhaps at age 6 or 7, chose. He said that if "non-denominational," was deleted, the prayer would be denominational, "and we are back in the same box... whose denomination is going to choose the prayer?"

The Buchanan amendment was agreed to by voice vote. H J Res 191 then was voted on and failed to win the necessary two-thirds majority, receiving 240 votes to the opposition's 162.

Reaction. In early 1972, Mrs. Ruhlin was actively working to defeat representatives in the 1972 elections who had voted against the amendment. By early May, almost 50 billboards bearing the message that the local congressman "voted against the voluntary school-prayer amendment" were scattered from New England to Texas. Mrs. Ruhlin predicted that more than 200 billboards would be displayed "before we're through."

FUNDING GAP: DIFFERING VIEWS OF KEY COMMITTEES

Federal aid to education—which means dollars with which college students pay their tuition and with which elementary and secondary schools buy more books for their libraries and new equipment for their labs—is the product of a long legislative process.

Chief protagonists in this process—which recurs in some dimension each' year—are four congressional subcommittees: the House and Senate appropriations subcommittees which review the budget requests of the Department of Health, Education and Welfare (HEW) and the House special education subcommittee (of the Education and Labor Committee) and the Senate education subcommittee (of the Labor and Public Welfare Committee) which have jurisdiction over almost all legislation authorizing or revising programs of federal aid to education. (The major exception to this jurisdiction is GI Bill educational benefits which are considered by the veterans' affairs committees in each chamber.)

Authority and Appropriations

Each year a large gap yawns between the amount which Congress has said *could be provided* in federal aid to education and the amount which Congress *actually provides* through the appropriations process.

In fiscal 1972, a total of almost $5-billion was authorized for federal aid to elementary and secondary education. Congress appropriated just under $2-billion for these programs—about $4 provided for every $10 promised. *(Chart p. 44)*

This gap reflects the differing roles and views held by the members of the appropriations and authorization subcommittees on education. The members of the latter in many cases regard themselves as the congressional champions of and advocates for education. Many of them are more junior in congressional service to their counterparts on the appropriations subcommittees and are often more liberal in their attitudes toward an increased federal role and increased federal spending for social purposes, such as education.

A significant factor in the attitudes of these members toward spending federal dollars for education may be the records of their states in spending for education Forty percent of the members of the House appropriations subcommittee and 55 percent of the Senate appropriations subcommittee represent states whose per-pupil spending for education falls below the median level of spending per pupil for the 50 states. But only 15 percent of the House special education subcommittee and 30 percent of the Senate education subcommittee represent states with this lower level of education expenditure. *(Box p. 6)*

Indicative of the tension between those who authorize federal spending for education and those who actually recommend appropriations for those programs

were exchanges on the floors of the two chambers during debate on certain education bills in 1971.

During debate on the omnibus higher education bill (S 659—PL 92-318) in August of 1971, Sen. Warren G. Magnuson (D Wash.), chairman of the Senate appropriations subcommittee dealing with the education budget, warned: "The people who are running these great universities and the people in higher education should not start planning right now on $18-billion (at that time authorized by S 659) to spend because under present conditions they will not get that much."

Earlier, in an exchange with education subcommittee chairman Claiborne Pell (D R.I.), Magnuson had placed on the record the total authorized by the bill, warning that after the bill was passed, "the full funding people (will) show up (before the Appropriations Committee).... The members of the Committee on Labor and Public Welfare are great authorizers. Then...*we* take all the problems." (Italics added)

Reflection of a similar concern with the realities of providing these authorized dollars marked another speech—during House consideration of the same education bill in October. George Mahon (D Texas), chairman of the House Appropriations Committee, warned that he would probably oppose the bill although he favored the concept of federal aid to higher education: "I find myself reluctant to vote for expanding old programs and initiating far-reaching new programs at a time when we are threatened with economic instability and the collapse of the dollar."

But members of the authorizing committees protested that the appropriations committees, by refusing to recommend funds for programs, "could say 'no' as a matter of substance to a program that Congress has authorized."

The appropriations-authorization gap sparked creation—in 1969—of a new education coalition, the Committee for Full Funding of Education Programs. Representatives of education interest groups, who had worked together during the 1960s to win authorization of federal aid-to-education programs, united to obtain appropriations equal to the authorized level for those programs. *(Education lobby story p. 26)*

And in a related development, the provisions of PL 92-318 revealed a certain adjustment of authorization figures to the reality of the appropriations process. Several existing aid-to-education programs were extended by that law at authorization levels substantially below those for fiscal 1971, and perhaps more in the range of possible appropriations. *(Box p. 44)*

The Office of Education

Once federal aid-to-education programs have been authorized and funded, they are implemented—and

ESEA Appropriations-Authorization Gap

(figures in millions of dollars)

ESEA Titles	1969 Authorized	1969 Appropriated	1970 Authorized	1970 Appropriated	1971 Authorized	1971 Appropriated	1972 Authorized	1972 Appropriated
I-Educationally deprived children	$2,776	$1,123	$2,523.3	$1,339	$3,457.4	$1,500	$3,642.8	$1,597.5
II-Library resources, textbooks	165	50	206	42.5	206	80	216.3	90
III-Supplementary education centers	528	165	566.5	116.4	556.3	143.4	592.3	146.4
V-Strengthening state education departments	80	30	80	29.8	110	29.8	130	33
VI-Handicapped children	179	31	206	29.2	206	34	216.3	37.5
VII-Bilingual education	30	7	40	21.3	80	25	100	35
VIII-Dropout prevention	30	5	30	5	30	10	31.5	10
Total	$3,788	$1,411	$3,651.8	$1,583.1	$4,645.7	$1,822.2	$4,929.2	$1,949.4

SOURCE: HEW Office of Education, Budget Division

the funds allocated—through the executive branch, chiefly through the Office of Education within the Department of HEW.

Created in 1867, the Office of Education that year received $18,592 in appropriations. Two years later it became part of the Interior Department—a move reflecting its primary responsibility, administration of the land grant college program. It remained in the Department of Interior for 70 years, until becoming part of the Federal Security Agency in 1939—by which time its appropriations had risen to almost $17-million. In 1953, it came to its present position in the new Department of HEW.

The 1972 education law (PL 92-318) created a new division of education within the HEW Department, composed of the existing Office of Education (which is headed by a commissioner of education) and the newly created research body, the National Institute of Education. The new division was to be headed by an assistant HEW secretary, who was not to serve concurrently as the commissioner of education. In mid-1972, the then-commissioner, Dr. Sidney P. Marland, was named to the new assistant secretary post.

Under Marland the Office of Education had been reorganized into major areas of management (budget, manpower), external relations (public affairs, legislation), development (experimental schools, research, statistics, program planning and evaluation, personnel development), school systems (elementary and secondary education, compensatory education, impact aid, adult, vocational and technical education) and higher education (including international studies and libraries and educational technology). Each of these major areas was headed by a deputy commissioner of education.

The rapid growth of a federal role in education was mirrored in the growth of the Office of Education

during the 1960s. A 1967 study noted that in fiscal 1967 the Office of Education budget was larger than that of eight of the Cabinet-level departments, that it employed as many consultants and readers as fulltime personnel, and that since 1960 its staff had doubled, its programs quadrupled and its funds multiplied by eight.

The relationship between the authorizing subcommittees in Congress and the Office of Education has been less than cordial during the Nixon administration. The subcommittees have often expressed their feeling that the office was failing to carry out the intentions which Congress had expressed in legislation establishing certain aid programs. The office, on the other hand, feels that Congress is exceeding its mandate when it attempts to direct the way in which the office should be organized to carry on its business.

This tension was reflected in the Senate committee report on the higher education bill (S 659) in mid-1971. *(Story p. 90)*

In the report the committee noted that in creating the Teacher Corps program in 1965, it had expressly required that the corps be as independent as possible within the office. Twice since 1965 the committee had, in its reports, insisted on this independent status. "However," continued the report, "the Office of Education...has not seen fit to provide the requested independence," making the corps a unit within another bureau, cutting its staff and its budget despite the quadrupling of appropriations for the program. "In the face of the refusal of the office... to heed repeated statements of congressional intent, the committee finds itself compelled to legislate independent status for the Teacher Corps within the Office of Education." Similar complaints led the committee to include language creating a new community college unit, and bureaus of occupational, adult and Indian education within the Office of Education.

FEDERAL GOVERNMENT AIDS ALL LEVELS OF EDUCATION

Support of elmentary and secondary education is primarily a local responsibility; college education traditionally has been furnished by the states and private citizens. Yet in the 1971-72 school year, the federal government provided 7.9 percent of all funds spent on elementary and secondary education and 16.7 percent of higher education funds. *(See box p. 5)*

Direct federal contributions to education date back to the Morrill Act of 1862, establishing land-grant colleges in the states. But federal involvement grew slowly over the next 100 years. A dramatic change occurred in the middle 1960s—a landmark period in American education.

By 1966, the Federal Government was aiding education at all levels, from pre-school through graduate school to adult education for those bypassed along the way. From nursery schools to university campuses, it would be hard by the late 1960s to find a single pupil, teacher or classroom not in some way affected by the federal government's interest and assistance.

From the Morrill Act which helped establish colleges to the Smith-Hughes Act of 1917 which supported vocational training at the high school level, the government moved piecemeal into the education field. In the 1940s and 1950s Congress authorized the government to buy school lunches, to supply funds to improve the teaching of science, mathematics and foreign languages, to lend colleges money to build dormitories, to educate veterans and to grant funds for school construction, operation and teachers' salaries in areas "impacted" by tax-free federal property and the school-age children of federal employees.

Until 1965, however, no aid program was enacted which could be considered a general subsidy for education or for college students. The Elementary and Secondary Education Act of 1965 launched a federal program so broad in application as to constitute the first general aid-to-education program ever adopted by Congress. In the same year the government for the first time assumed responsibility, in the Higher Education Act, to pay for a college education for talented but needy students.

Elementary and Secondary Education

Until the 1940s it was a truism that responsibility for the lower levels of education rested entirely in the states and local communities. But growing financial strains on local and state governments and the greater taxing power of the federal government led to slowly rising support in Congress for some general kind of federal contribution to education. A key portent was the conversion of the pre-eminent leader of conservative Republicanism, Sen. Robert A. Taft (R Ohio 1939-53). Taft declared in 1946 that the nation's schools no longer could provide an adequate education for all without federal assistance.

Two years later, the Senate for the first time passed a general school aid bill, but the House remained opposed to the concept. It did not give in until 1960, only to see final action on the legislation stymied by the Rules Committee, which refused to let the House-passed bill be sent to conference with the Senate. Five years later, the first broad general-aid bill was enacted.

Over the years, opposition to general aid was based primarily on the contention that federal aid meant federal control of the schools, particularly if teachers' salaries and textbooks were part of the aid package. Two other basic issues added to the controversy: the Government's position with regard to racially segregated schools and church-related schools.

The segregation issue reached its peak after the Supreme Court's 1954 decision outlawing the doctrine of "separate but equal" schools. It was largely resolved by the Civil Rights Act of 1964, which authorized federal court suits for desegregation of schools and the withholding of federal funds from institutions that practiced segregation.

The church-state issue, based on the First Amendment's ban on federal laws concerning religion, was not resolved until 1965. Legislation in the late 1940s had proposed to let the states spend federal education funds as they did their own tax revenues, supporting public schools and, in some states, parochial schools as well. Opposition to this proposal was too strong to overcome, and in the next decade Congress considered legislation that would specifically prohibit aid to private schools. Opposition then came from the Roman Catholic church and its spokesmen in Congress. The impasse continued until, in the

Federal Financial Aid

Federal aid to education comes in a variety of garbs—from the fellowship check to a graduate student to the non-profit, tax-exempt status enjoyed by most institutions of higher education.

Most existing federal aid to education consists of aid directly to the students—like fellowships and GI educational benefits—and of *categorical grants*, which provide aid for clearly defined categories of school needs.

Another form of aid, often advocated by Republican members of Congress, is the *block grant*. This type of grant is simply a chunk of money given to a state or institution which then decides how it should be divided up among various needs. *Education revenue-sharing*, as proposed by the Nixon administration, is an expansion of the block grant concept: under this proposal, each state would receive a certain amount of money—to be spent as the state decided within general areas of emphasis delineated by the federal government.

1965 Act, federal aid was focused on disadvantaged children no matter what kind of school they attended.

ELEMENTARY AND SECONDARY
EDUCATION ACT (ESEA)

This Act, the first general aid to education law (PL 89-10), was signed by President Johnson April 11, 1965, outside the former one-room schoolhouse at Stonewall, Texas, where he first attended classes. The President, a former school teacher himself, said no measure he had "signed, or will ever sign, means more to the future of America."

Enactment of the law took only three months—largely because old controversies were stilled by the new emphasis on aid to children, not schools, and because the Democratic party had achieved huge majorities in Congress in the November 1964 elections. To make sure there was no hang-up in conference, the Senate accepted the bill exactly as the House had passed it, which was almost as submitted by the Johnson administration.

The heart of the Act was Title I, which directed its funds to school districts on the basis of the number of children from low-income families in the area. Thus, although 95 percent of the nation's counties were eligible for aid, the bulk of the money was to be concentrated on the inner city and impoverished rural areas where the neediest children lived.

The appeal to all geographical segments was underlined by Title I's formula for providing federal funds, which was based on each state's average spending per student and its number of children from low-income families. Thus it appealed to the poorer states by taking into account their many poor children and to the richer states by recognizing their higher expenditures per child. The formula was made more generous to the poorer states in 1966 by permitting them to use the national average expenditure per child instead of their own, smaller figure.

The church-state controversy which had blocked so many school bills in the past was overcome by ESEA's focus on aid to needy children rather than schools. The school districts were directed to include private school children in compensatory programs and to lend (but not give) federally funded school books to needy private school children. Such aid was not comprehensive enough to offend powerful opponents of private school aid and was satisfactory to lobbyists for aid to parochial schools.

SUMMARY OF ESEA PROVISIONS. Following are the main provisions of the Elementary and Secondary Education Act (ESEA) as passed in 1965 and amended in 1966, 1967 and 1970. Technically, the entire Act was an amendment to the "impacted area" school law of 1950 (PL 81-874), but it is generally treated as an entirely separate law.

Title I. This title allocated funds to local school districts (through state agencies) under a formula that multiplied the number of school children from low-income families (under $2,000 a year or on public assistance) by one-half of the state's average expenditure per school child. In 1966 Congress raised the low-income figure to $3,000, to take effect in fiscal 1968, but the next year this provision was made conditional upon the availability of sufficient appropriations to fulfill the goal. With appro-

priations for fiscal 1968 and 1969 falling far short of amounts authorized in the revised formula, the new income level was not put into effect.

The 1966 amendments to ESEA made another change in the formula, one that greatly benefited the poorer states. It allowed any state to use the national average expenditure per school child, instead of its own expenditure figure, in determining its Title I allotments. As a result, most Southern states received a substantial increase; the poorest state, Mississippi, went from $23.5 million in fiscal 1967 to $44.8 million in fiscal 1968.

"Incentive" grants were authorized but not funded. They were to go to states that spent a larger share of their resources on education than the national average.

The purposes for which Title I funds could be used were largely left up to the local school districts. The Act said only that the money was for programs "designed to meet the special educational needs of educationally deprived children." The schools could reduce their class sizes, hire remedial reading teachers, buy special equipment, serve breakfasts at school—the possibilities were endless.

Private school children, however, had to be included in some of the programs. The act said the local school agency must make provision for special services (such as dual enrollment, educational TV programs or mobile educational facilities) in which private school children could participate.

Reviewing the first three years of the program, HEW Secretary Wilbur J. Cohen said in January 1969 that the trend among participating schools was to put "increasing stress on activities most directly serving the student's needs: improving the quality of instruction and offering such services as medical care, guidance and counseling, and food." The percentage of money spent on construction and equipment had dropped sharply from the first year, while the proportion spent on instruction and, to a much smaller extent, services had increased, Cohen said.

Over 9 million children participated each year in Title I programs, about 500,000 of whom were private school students. In addition, children of migrant farmworkers, residents in state institutions for neglected, handicapped or delinquent children, and those attending Indian schools received separate Title I allotments.

The failure to appropriate up to the level authorized, however, meant a reduction in per capita spending over the first three years. The number of poor children covered in the formula went up from 5,600,000 to 6,670,000 between 1966 and 1968 and to 7.9 million by 1973 while the amount spent per child declined from $210 to $173. (The other children included in the 9 million Title I total were attending the same schools as the "formula" children but were from families with incomes above the Act's poverty definition.)

Authorizations under the formula rose from $1-billion for fiscal 1966 to $3.6 billion for fiscal 1972, but appropriations were much lower and reached only $1.6 billion in fiscal 1972.

The most important change made by the 1970 act in Title I was an expansion of the program to include children from families earning up to $4,000 rather than $3,000 yearly.

Title II. Unchanged since its enactment in 1965, Title II authorized federal grants to the states for school library resources, textbooks and other printed material for the use of children and teachers in public and private schools. To avoid conflict with the First Amendment's clause on religion, the ESEA specified that title and control of all materials furnished under Title II must remain with a public agency and that all materials, including books, must have been approved for use in public schools.

Because many states and school boards provide free textbooks for their schools, the emphasis under Title II has been on library resources. Almost $300 million was appropriated for the program in ESEA's first three years. In subsequent years the level of funding decreased.

Title III. This title was designed to introduce innovative programs into the schools. Federal grants were provided for supplementary educational centers and services that could serve as models for regular school programs or as centralized supplements to the curricula of individual schools.

The act specified a number of different services that might be offered, including: specialized equipment and instruction for students in advanced scientific subjects and foreign languages; art and music courses; production of educational radio and TV programs; special services for people in rural areas, including mobile units; and counseling and social services to encourage dropouts and adults to resume their education.

Originally, grants were made directly from the U.S. Commissioner of Education to the agencies applying for funds, although there was a general allotment of funds by state, based on their population.

In 1967 Congress rewrote the program to give most of the control to state education agencies. State plans for use of the funds were to be drawn up, and after fiscal 1969 the state agencies would distribute all of the money. However, 15 percent of the funds were to be spent on special programs for handicapped children. (Title VI of ESEA, which was added in 1966, was directed entirely at handicapped children.) In 1970 Congress consolidated Title III of ESEA and Title V (a) of the National Defense Education Act (guidance, counseling and testing) and authorized programs under Titles III and V for gifted and talented children.

Authorizations for Title III programs, like those for Title I, increased sharply over the years but appropriations remained relatively stable. The program began with a $100 million authorization increasing to $556-million for fiscal 1971 and $592-million for fiscal 1972. Appropriations for 1971 and 1972, however, were only $143-million and $146-million, respectively.

Title IV. The Cooperative Research Act of 1954, providing federal construction aid for educational research facilities, had funded research centers on a pilot basis at four universities. In 1965 the program was written into ESEA as Title IV and was expanded to permit contracts or grants to various kinds of research groups. A five-year authorization of $100 million for cooperative research construction was provided.

The 1970 act extended the $100-million authorization through fiscal 1974, and the Education Amendments of 1972 authorized additional funds; but total appropriations were far below these levels.

Title V. To strengthen state departments of education, Title V of ESEA authorized direct federal grants for such purposes as statewide planning, reporting of educational data and programs to improve the competence of employees of educational agencies and of teacher training efforts.

Originally, 85 percent of each appropriation was to be alloted directly to the states and 15 percent reserved for allotment by the U.S. Commissioner for experimental projects or services that might help state agencies on a regional or nationwide basis. In 1967 the Commissioner's share was reduced to 5 percent. About $30 million a year was appropriated under the title although the authorization permitted $110-million in fiscal 1971 and $130-million in 1972.

The 1970 act authorized new programs of grants for strengthening local education agencies, grants to aid planning and evaluation on local and state levels and of advisory councils on quality education.

Title VI. Enacted in 1966, this title authorized federal funds to assist the states in the education of mentally and physically handicapped children. It was expanded in 1967 to include funds to improve the recruitment of personnel for the field, to establish regional resource centers and model centers for deaf-blind children.

Under the state grant program a number of services were provided for the first time: mobile units for rural areas, work-study programs, and special transportation arrangements, for example. Nearly 225,000 children were helped under the program in its first years.

Title VII. At the initiative of Congress, particularly the delegations from California and Texas, a program to improve the education of children from non-English-speaking families was authorized in 1967. About 3 million children of school age were expected to benefit from special programs funded under this Bilingual Education title.

However, although $100-million was authorized for aid to school districts and teacher training in fiscal 1972, the appropriation was only $35-million.

Title VIII. Two other Congressionally initiated programs were added to this title in 1967. One authorized grants for local programs to prevent school dropouts. The demonstration programs were to focus on schools which have a high concentration of children from low-income families and a high dropout rate. The authorization was for $30 million a year, but the first appropriation, granted in fiscal 1969, was for only $5 million, which was expected to finance five projects; by 1972 the appropriation had risen to $10-million.

The second new program in Title VIII authorized a small technical assistance project for rural schools to help them apply for federal aid. In 1968 this was replaced by a more general provision for collection and dissemination of information which was written into the Vocational Education Amendments of 1968.

Federal Control. The 1965 Act stated that there was to be no federal control over the curriculum, selection of books or personnel of any school aided by the ESEA, nor was there to be any payment of funds for religious worship or instruction.

Desegregation. After a bitter battle in 1966, Congress wrote into the law language prohibiting the Federal Government from requiring the assignment or transportation of students or teachers to overcome racial imbalance—in other words, to alter de facto segregation. The provision left intact the Government's au-

(Continued on p. 50)

Major Trends in Education: Projections of . . .

Population is increasing less rapidly or declining.

	1958	1968	1978
		(change in millions)	
Elementary school age	30.9	37.2 (+20%)	35.5 (— 5%)
Secondary school age	10.9	15.1 (+39%)	16.8 (+11%)
Higher education undergraduate age	9.0	14.3 (+59%)	16.9 (+18%)

The high school graduation rate is increasing.

Graduates as percent of 18-year-olds

1958-59	64%
1968-69	77%
1978-79	88%

The proportion of high school diplomas awarded to boys is increasing and is expected to exceed 50 percent before 1979.

Boys as percent of all graduates

1958-59	48.2 % (790,000 of 1,639,000)
1968-69	49.8 % (1,408,000 of 2,839,000)
1978-79	50.6 % (1,908,000 of 3,773,000)

Proportionately more people are earning college degrees.

Bachelor's degrees as percent of graduation age population

1958-59	17.5 %
1968-69	22.0 %
1978-79	25.4 %

A larger proportion of degrees earned are advanced degrees.

	Master's as percent of total	Doctor's (except first-professional) as percent of total
1958-59	15.6% (72,500 of 462,000)	2.0% (9,400 of 462,000)
1968-69	19.4% (188,600 of 969,700)	2.7% (26,100 of 969,700)
1978-79	24.9% (368,400 of 1,481,400)	3.8% (57,000 of 1,481,000)

The proportion of bachelor's and first-professional degrees awarded to women is increasing.

Women as percent of bachelor's and first-professional-degree recipients (numbers)

1958-59	33.5% (127,000 of 380,000)
1968-69	42.5% (321,000 of 755,000)
1978-79	46.8% (494,000 of 1,056,000)

*SOURCE: *Projections of Educational Statistics to 1978-79*, Office of Education.

. . . Enrollment and Expenditures from 1958 to 1979*

Degree-credit enrollment in 2-year institutions is growing faster than in 4-year institutions.

	Degree-credit students in 2-year institutions as percent of all degree-credit students (members)
1958	11.9% (386,000 of 3,236,000)
1968	18.6% (1,289,000 of 6,928,000)
1978	21.1% (2,176,000 of 10,318,000)

The ratio of public elementary and secondary students to classroom teachers is declining.

	Ratio of students to classroom teachers		
	Total	Elementary	Secondary
1958	26.1	28.7	21.7
1968	23.1	25.4	20.3
1978	22.4	24.5	20.2

The cost of educating elementary and secondary students is increasing.

	Current expenditure per pupil in average daily attendance (1968-69 dollars)	Total expenditures by school systems (in billions)
1958-59	$440	$20.7
1968-69	696	39.8
1978-79	885	52.0

The cost of educating college students is increasing.

		Current expenditures per full-time-equivalent student for student education (1968-69 dollars)	
	Total	Publicly controlled institutions	Privately controlled institutions
1958-59	$1,355	$1,350	$1,361
1968-69	1,772	1,638	2,100
1978-79	2,089	1,865	2,833

Expenditures by higher education institutions is increasing.

		(billions of 1968-69 dollars)	
	Total	Publicly controlled institutions	Privately controlled institutions
1958-59	$7.8	$ 4.4	$ 3.4
1968-69	21.3	13.6	7.7
1978-79	35.4	22.8	12.6

thority to require desegregation of schools that were run on a discriminatory basis; it also permitted school districts, if they wanted, to use federal funds for busing students in order to improve the racial balance of their schools.

A time limit was set for determination by the U.S. Commissioner of Education of a district's compliance with the nondiscrimination requirements of the 1964 Civil Rights Act. Title VI of that Act authorized the Commissioner, after holding hearings, to withhold federal funds from any school district found in noncompliance with the Act.

Adult Education. The community action program authorized in the 1964 Economic Opportunity Act, the basic antipoverty law, included as one of its many undertakings projects to upgrade the education of adults. In 1966 Congress transferred this activity to the U.S. Commissioner of Education. Specific authorization of funds for the program was made, and the Federal Government's share of the cost of each local undertaking was set at 90 percent. Most of the money was to go to state agencies for distribution, but 20 percent was reserved for experimental projects funded directly by the Commissioner.

TEACHER CORPS

The National Teacher Corps was first proposed in 1965 by Sens. Edward M. Kennedy (D Mass.) and Gaylord Nelson (D Wis.). Kennedy had noted the success of trained volunteers who taught Negro students in Prince Edward County, Va., when the public schools were closed to avoid integration. Nelson was impressed with the impact of former Peace Corps volunteers who participated as teacher interns in ghetto schools in Washington, D.C.

The two Senators offered their Teacher Corps proposal as an amendment to the Higher Education Act. The idea was quickly endorsed by President Johnson and became labeled a Great Society program.

The National Teacher Corps was created by Title V, Part B of the Higher Education Act of 1965 (PL 89-329). The Corps had no difficulty in the Senate, but it survived in conference with the House only after a motion by Albert H. Quie (R Minn.) to delete it was rejected on a 152-226 roll-call vote of the House.

The Corps was designed to improve elementary and secondary education in city slums and impoverished rural areas by sending in teams of an experienced teacher and several young college graduates to strengthen local school programs. The Act authorized the Commissioner of Education to recruit teachers and interns to serve in the Corps for up to two years.

There were two stages in the program—a three-month summer training period at a designated college, followed by an in-service period during which a team was assigned to a local school. The interns had their tuition paid for part-time graduate work at a nearby university.

The primary goal of the program was to improve public education in poverty areas. But the program was also intended to encourage idealistic college graduates to enter training in the country.

PL 89-329 authorized $36,100,000 for fiscal 1966 and $64,715,000 for fiscal 1967. In 1967, in PL 90-35, the Teacher Corps was extended for three years, through fiscal 1970, and the word "National" was removed from its name. Authorizations for the Corps were set at $33

million in fiscal 1968, $46 million in 1969 and $56 million in 1970. In 1970 the authorization for fiscal 1970 was increased to $80 million and to $100 million for fiscal 1971. The Education Amendments of 1972 reduced the authorization level through fiscal 1975 to $37.5-million (the amount appropriated for fiscal 1972) or one-quarter of the total appropriation under Title V of the 1965 Higher Education Act, whichever figure was greater. The reduced level of authorization in the 1972 amendments reflected low levels of appropriation—rising from only $9.5 million for fiscal 1966 to $37.5 million for fiscal 1972.

Opposition to the Teacher Corps was always something of a mystery. It was extremely popular with school authorities; it provided direct assistance to the neediest schools while at the same time training young school teachers to cope with the most difficult of educational problems. To overcome opposition, Congress specified that not only the local schools but also the state agencies must request the assignment of Teacher Corpsmen and that 10 percent of their salaries must be furnished by the schools they were serving. The opposition came from the "conservative coalition" of Republicans and Southern Democrats and was generally based on the need to economize in federal spending.

IMPACTED AREA SCHOOLS

Although no general school aid program was approved by Congress until 1965, from 1950 on there were two highly popular programs of federal grants to build and operate schools and pay teachers in federally "impacted" areas. The programs were begun as the outgrowths of federal commitments in the Lanham Act of 1940 to provide school aid in areas where federal activities brought in more families and reduced taxable property. Amendments raising the amount of federal support and liberalizing the qualifications for aid over the following 10 years led to a broad program which some Congressmen, mainly those from recipient areas, said merely honored a federal commitment to supplant lost taxes, and which others, mainly those from non-recipient areas and those who supported general school aid, said had developed into a massive, "pork barrel."

Repeatedly, Presidents Eisenhower, Kennedy and Johnson were rebuffed in attempts to cut back the impacted areas program to what they said would represent more accurately the need of each "impacted" district.

The two 1950 laws (PL 81-815 and 81-874) authorized federal grants to areas "impacted" by tax-free federal property and installations, Indian reservations or Government contractors. PL 815 authorized federal payments for school construction; PL 874 authorized federal payments for building maintenance and teachers' salaries. The two laws did not authorize specific money appropriations but set criteria for determining whether a school district was entitled to assistance and, if so, how much it could receive.

Under PL 874 the Government paid 100 percent of the local share of the cost of educating each child whose parents both lived and worked on federal property (Section A). It paid 50 percent of the local share of the cost of educating children whose parents lived or worked on taxable property (Section B). It also authorized payments of 100 percent the first year and 50 percent the second where there were sudden increases in federal contract activity (Section C).

Under PL 815, the Government paid 95 percent of the cost per pupil of construction for Section A children, 50 percent for Section B children and 45 percent for Section C children.

Section A of both laws was permanent; the others carried expiration dates.

In 1970 the program was amended to include children living in federally financed public housing, but through fiscal 1972 this part of the program had not been funded.

College and Graduate Education

Unlike the elementary and secondary field, federal aid to institutions of higher education was well established before 1965. But the late 1960s and early 1970s produced a dramatic new emphasis on aid to college students, especially those from families who could not afford a college education for their children.

Federal scholarships were authorized in the Higher Education Act of 1965, though they were disguised as "educational opportunity grants," not scholarships. The same Act also authorized interest subsidies on private loans to middle-income students and transferred the anti-poverty agency's work-study program for college students to the Office of Education.

Federal financing of direct loans to students dated back to the 1958 National Defense Education Act (NDEA); the subsidized-interest program was intended to replace NDEA loans, but Congress insisted on retaining both programs. As interest rates zoomed up in 1966 and again in 1968, the private, subsidized program fell far below expectations in the number of students it helped. A plan, popular with some Congressmen and endorsed by the Republican party, to offer tax credits for college education costs never was authorized.

The principal laws aiding colleges and universities were the 1950 Housing Act, the 1963 Higher Education Facilities Act, the 1958 National Defense Education Act, the Economic Opportunity Act of 1964 and the Higher Education Act of 1965.

COLLEGE HOUSING AND CLASSROOMS

The 1950 Housing Act authorized 40-year, low-interest Government loans to public and private colleges and universities for construction of dormitories and infirmaries. The program was operated through a revolving fund administered by the Housing and Home Finance Agency, which became the Department of Housing and Urban Development. The agency was authorized to borrow $300 million from the Treasury to set up the fund, and this authorization was regularly reviewed. In 1965 a flat 3 percent interest rate was set on the loans. In 1968 Congress enacted a program of debt service grants (i.e., subsidized interest on private loans). Since 1968 this program has financed construction of college housing. The direct loan revolving fund also continues and is used for those colleges which cannot get market loan financing.

A more controversial program of federal aid for college classroom construction was included in the Higher Education Facilities Act of 1963. The Act authorized $1.2 billion over three years in federal grants and loans for facilities at public and private colleges and universities. The funds for grants were earmarked for libraries and classrooms where science, engineering, mathematics or modern language courses were taught.

When the program was extended in 1965, these categorical restrictions, similar to those in the original NDEA law, were removed.

By fiscal 1971 annual authorizations for the program had reached $936 million for grants for undergraduate facilities, $120 million for graduate facilities and $400 million in loans. But authorization levels were sharply cut for fiscal 1972 and 1973.

NATIONAL DEFENSE EDUCATION ACT (NDEA)

Enacted in 1958 in reaction to Russian achievements in space technology, symbolized by the 1957 orbiting of the first earth satellite (Sputnik), and in awareness of the country's need for more scientists, the NDEA focused on encouraging the study of science, mathematics and foreign languages. All school levels were covered by the Act. Its major titles provided equipment for elementary and secondary schools; financed loans for college students; and authorized three-year graduate fellowships, with preference for prospective college teachers.

By the end of 1968, after several extensions, NDEA's focus on limited, mainly scientific, categories was ended and aid for study of almost all subjects was authorized under the Act. For the principal programs the 1968 extension authorized: $130 million in fiscal 1970 for purchase of equipment for lower schools, plus an additional $160 million for schools receiving ESEA Title I funds (those in disadvantaged areas); $275 million for student loans; and 7,500 new graduate fellowships a year, with matching payments to the graduate schools of $3,500 per fellow.

The NDEA student loans grew out of a proposal by President Eisenhower in 1958 for 10,000 federal scholarships a year. The House Education and Labor Committee reported a bill providing 23,000 scholarships and, in addition, $220 million for a federal student loan fund. The scholarship provision was stripped from the bill on the floor, and the $120 million authorized for the scholarships was added to the loan fund. The Senate version was accepted in conference and became law. Under its provisions, the Federal Government provided 90 percent and the individual schools 10 percent of the money in loan funds set up and administered by each participating college.

Under the original NDEA, undergraduates were eligible for loans of up to $1,000 a year, not to exceed $5,000 during a student's undergraduate years. The 3-percent interest rate did not go into effect until the repayment period began, nine months after the student left college. The repayment could be deferred up to a total of three years while the recipient was attending graduate school or serving in the armed forces, the Peace Corps or Volunteers in Service to America (VISTA). Repayment could extend over a 10-year period.

If the borrower became a full-time school teacher or college professor, half of the loan was cancelled at 10 percent for each year of teaching. If he taught at designated "hardship" schools in low-income areas or was a teacher of handicapped children, he could have the additional 50 percent cancelled at 15 percent a year.

To receive a loan, students had to sign an oath of loyalty to the United States.

Since the loans were made directly by the institutions, students applied directly to their colleges.

Office of Education figures showed that through the end of the 1966-67 college year, one million students had borrowed more than $1 billion since the program began.

The Education Amendments of 1972 increased authorizations for direct student loans to a level of $375-million for fiscal 1972 and $400-million annually for 1973-1975 and set a $2,500 aggregate limit on direct loans to an undergraduate student in his first two years of study (replacing a $1,000 per year ceiling).

The 1972 act also restricted the kinds of jobs or service in the armed forces for which part of these loans could be cancelled.

WORK-STUDY PROGRAM

The Economic Opportunity Act of 1964 (PL 88-452), the basic anti-poverty law, authorized grants to colleges to pay 90 percent of the wages of students with part-time jobs in the college or other nonprofit institutions. The grants were to support students from low-income families.

The Higher Education Act of 1965 transferred the work-study program to the Office of Education, removed the requirement that students be from low-income families and permitted colleges to provide their matching share through services and equipment, including tuition and books. The Act authorized $129 million in fiscal 1966, $165 million in fiscal 1967 and $200 million in fiscal 1968. A further extension was made in 1968, raising the authorization to $285 million by fiscal 1971 and setting the federal matching share at 80 percent of the grants. The Education Amendments of 1972 authorized $330-million for fiscal 1972 and $366-million for 1973.

The work-study program was administered by the colleges, which passed upon the applications of their students and received the matching funds from the Government.

Work under the program was limited to an average of 15 hours a week while classes were in session and 40 hours a week during summers and vacation periods. The on-campus work could be anything from running the soda fountain in the student union to acting as faculty aides or laboratory assistants.

HIGHER EDUCATION ACT OF 1965

Enacted with wide bipartisan support in Congress, the Higher Education Act (PL 89-329) was revolutionary in several aspects, particularly in its student aid provisions. For the first time in U.S. history Congress approved federal scholarships for undergraduate students. The $70 million authorized annually for first-year scholarships was estimated to provide 140,000 students of "exceptional financial need" with scholarships each year. Scholarships had been approved by the Senate in past years only to die in the House. When HR 9567 was first debated by the House, an amendment to remove scholarships from the bill was defeated on a 58-88

standing vote. No further efforts were made to delete the provision.

Another new aid program for college students was insurance on loans, with federal subsidies on interest payments. Federally insured loans had been proposed by President Johnson when he was in Congress, and were subsequently requested by President Kennedy in 1963. Insured loans and scholarships, combined with the expanded work-study program also authorized by the Act, were expected to help students from middle-income as well as low-income backgrounds. They were designed to supplement NDEA loans.

Five titles of the 1965 Act provided aid for colleges and universities. For the first time, funds were voted ($50 million a year) to buy library materials, including books. Other programs in the Act provided grants to develop university extension courses related to community problems and funds to raise the academic quality of impoverished small colleges. The latter program was authorized for only one year because the Senate insisted on making junior colleges eligible, and the House was opposed.

Another key program established by the Act was the Teacher Corps *(see above)*.

Title I of the Education Amendments of 1972 incorporated in the 1965 Act, as amended, certain programs established by the National Defense Education Act of 1958, and the provisions of the Higher Education Facilities Act of 1963. The 1965 Act thereby became the basic federal-aid-to-higher-education law covering almost all programs with the exception of veterans' benefits.

HIGHER EDUCATION ACT PROVISIONS. The principal programs in the Act, as amended by Congress in 1966, 1968 and 1972 were:

Title I. Matching grants to the states were authorized for community service programs conducted by public or private nonprofit colleges and universities. They were to give particular emphasis to urban and suburban problems, including housing, poverty, employment, transportation, health and other local issues.

Beginning at a $25 million level, the grants rose to an authorized $60 million for fiscal 1971, but the failure of appropriations to reach this level resulted in reduction of authorizations to $10-million for fiscal 1972 and $30-million for 1973.

Title II. The library title of the Act, this section authorized basic grants for college library books and materials, special purpose grants for colleges with special needs, training grants to increase the supply of college librarians and to develop new techniques, and a small amount for the cataloging service of the Library of Congress. The 1968 extension of the Act authorized $75 million for this title in fiscal 1970 and $90 million in fiscal 1971. Authorizations for fiscal 1972 and 1973 were $39-million and $87-million.

Title III. Colleges which "are struggling for survival and are isolated from the main currents of academic life," defined as "developing institutions," received special help under this title. The colleges, many of them small, largely Negro institutions in the South, could apply for federal grants to raise the academic quality of their programs. Faculty and student exchange programs with more established colleges were part of the offering, along with national teaching fellowships for graduate students and junior faculty members who wished to strengthen the developing colleges' faculties. Two-year colleges and technical institutes were eligible for aid as well as institutions that grant B.A. degrees. For fiscal 1970 and 1971, $70 million and $91 million, respectively, were authorized for this title of the Higher Education Act. The 1972 Act authorized $91-million for fiscal 1972 and $120-million for 1973.

Title IV. The Student Assistance title of the Act authorized federal scholarships ("educational opportunity grants"), federally insured loans and subsidies on interest for full-time college students and transferred the work-study program authorized in the 1964 Economic Opportunity Act to the Office of Education.

The scholarships section authorized (in Part A) $70 million annually in fiscal 1966-68 for grants to institutions of higher education for first-year scholarships to full-time students "of exceptional financial need," plus whatever sums were necessary to continue scholarships beyond the first year.

It limited the amount of each scholarship to the lesser of $800 or half the amount of financial aid provided the student by the college or a state or private scholarship program, including loans and scholarships under the Act but excluding aid under work-study programs. (To be eligible for a federal scholarship, a student had to receive an equal amount of other financial aid.) A $200 bonus could be awarded scholarship students who in their preceding college year placed in the upper half of their class. In 1968 the bonus was dropped and the maximum scholarship was raised to $1,000.

Scholarship funds were allotted to the states according to the ratio of the number of each state's college students to the number nationally. The colleges receiving funds were forbidden to cut back their other student aid below the average amount furnished in the preceding three years.

Funds provided for these scholarships allowed 296,-800 new grants to students for the 1971-72 academic year and 266,700 for 1972-73.

The 1972 Act redesignated the educational opportunity grant program the "supplemental educational opportunity grant program," and established a new basic educational opportunity grant program under which any college student in good standing was entitled to a grant of $1,400 minus the amount his family would reasonably be expected to contribute to his educational expenses.

Upward Bound—A provision in the 1965 act authorized the U.S. commissioner of education to contract with public or private groups for the singling out of talented students who needed encouragement to attend college. This program, known as Talent Search, was directed in the 1968 law to take over, beginning in fiscal 1970, the better known Upward Bound program of the Office of Economic Opportunity, which had similar goals. Funds for the merged programs, including special services to help disadvantaged students stay in college, were set at $56.7 million for fiscal 1970 and $96 million for fiscal 1971. Under the 1972 act authorizations were $96-million for fiscal 1972 and $100-million annually for fiscal 1973-75.

Guaranteed Loans—Part B of Title IV established a guaranteed, interest-subsidized loan program designed for middle-income families. The program was proposed by the Johnson administration in the hope that private

loans could replace the direct federal cost of NDEA student loans, but Congress clung to the popular NDEA program as well as approving the new program.

The new program sought to encourage state and private nonprofit insurance for student loans and authorized the Federal Government to pay the interest costs while a student was in college and 3 percent during the repayment period on loans made by private sources at a maximum rate of percent. The subsidy was available to families with net income, before taxes, of less than $15,000. The 1972 Act allowed students from families earning more than $15,000 to obtain loans in some cases.

In its first three years, the program fell far below its predicted scope as banks and other lenders found the interest rate too low and the administrative details too cumbersome to be profitable. By the end of 1968 the number of students receiving loans under the program was about 750,000 whereas the goal for the first year alone had been 950,000.

In 1968 Congress set the maximum interest rate at 7 percent and removed the interest subsidy during the after-college repayment period.

In 1969 Congress approved the Emergency Insured Student Loan Act, which authorized special payments to lenders in times of high interest rates. The 1972 act extended this act through 1974.

The 1972 Act also set up a student loan marketing association backed by the federal government through fiscal 1981 to provide a secondary market and warehouse for student loans.

Work-Study—The work-study program, originally part of the antipoverty law, became Part C of the Higher Education Act of 1965. *(Details, p. 52)*

Cooperative Education—In 1968 Part D was added to Title IV. Entitled Cooperative Education, the program was to encourage alternate periods of full-time study and full-time employment. Beginning in fiscal 1970, grants of $8 million the first year and $10 million the second year could be made to colleges and universities to plan and carry out these programs.

Direct Loans. The 1972 Act added language authorizing the direct loan program established by Title II of the National Defense Education Act to Title IV of the Higher Education Act. *(Details in NDEA p. 51)*

Title V. This title established the Teacher Corps (described in the preceding section on Elementary Education) and a number of programs to improve teacher education, mainly by fellowships for graduate study.

The title was expanded in 1967 and given the name of the Education Professions Development Act. It added special grants for the educational upgrading of persons teaching or preparing to teach in elementary and high schools, and for the recruitment of qualified personnel in areas of critical teacher shortages.

Title VI. This title, the equipment section of the Higher Education Act, authorized 50-50 matching grants to the states for laboratory and audiovisual equipment and closed-circuit television equipment. The program was generally funded at $10 to $15 million a year.

Title VII. This title completely revised in 1972 to contain the provisions of the Higher Education Facilities Act, authorized grants for construction of classrooms and other academic facilities by undergraduate and graduate institutions and authorized loans for this construction.

Title VIII. Added to the Act in 1968, this title was given the name Networks for Knowledge. It was intended to encourage colleges to share educational facilities and resources such as closed-circuit TV, computers and special library collections. The Commissioner of Education was authorized to make contracts to facilitate such sharing. Planning funds were authorized for fiscal 1969, plus grants of $4 million in fiscal 1970 and $15 million the next year.

Title IX. The 1972 Act consolidated into a new Title IX a number of categorical programs of aid to graduate students. They included: aid to improve graduate programs (previously Title X) aid for graduate programs in public service, graduate fellowships for students intending to be college teachers (previously Title IV, NDEA), graduate fellowships for students intending to follow careers in state, local or federal governmental service and fellowships for students interested in mineral resource conservation.

Title X. The 1972 Act created a new Title X which contained a new program of aid to states for the planning of the expansion of their community college systems and of aid to the community colleges to assist their development and expansion. In addition the newly-written title also contained a new and expanded program of federal grants to improve post-secondary occupational education and to increase the preparation for such training in elementary and secondary schools.

Title XI. This title authorized contracts with law schools to pay 90 percent of the cost of programs providing clinical experience for law students. The hope was to train more trial lawyers. The authorization was $7.5 million annually in fiscal 1970 and 1971, but lack of funding resulted in a drop of authorization to $5-million for fiscal 1973.

Title XII. As in other education acts, this title specified that nothing in the Act authorized any federal control over curriculum or personnel or any aid to religious instruction or departments of divinity. In addition, it specified that there was to be no federal control over college organizations, such as fraternities, which were financed entirely by private funds and whose facilities were not owned by the college.

NATIONAL SCIENCE FOUNDATION

The National Science Foundation was established by Congress in 1950 (PL 81-507) to promote basic scientific research and education of future scientists and to establish and coordinate national scientific policies.

The 1950 Act directed the NSF to "develop and encourage the pursuit of a national policy for the promotion of basic research and education in the sciences." The NSF was authorized to (1) make grants and loans for basic research in the mathematical, physical, medical, biological, engineering and other sciences; (2) undertake military research for national defense; (3) award scholarships and graduate fellowships to U.S. citizens; (4) aid the interchange of information among scientists in the United States and other countries; (5) correlate its programs with private and other public research projects; and (6) maintain a roster of scientific and technical personnel and in other ways provide a central clearinghouse for information on such personnel.

The Act authorized appropriation of $500,000 to establish the Foundation and get its program under way,

and eventual appropriations of $15 million. In the first year of operation, fiscal 1951, the NSF received an appropriation of $225,000. In 1953, the $15-million ceiling was removed, but total appropriations did not exceed that level until 1956. In the next 11 years, appropriations increased rapidly until, in fiscal 1968, they reached a total of $495 million, reflecting a vast enlargement of the Foundation's activities. In fiscal 1969, however, over objections in the Senate, NSF appropriations dropped to $400 million.

Authorizations for NSF increased from $477.6 million in fiscal 1970 to $703.9-million for fiscal 1973. Appropriations for fiscal 1972 were $622-million.

Only minor amendments to the 1950 Act were made between 1952 and 1959. Major changes came in 1962, by Presidential initiative, and in 1968, by Congressional order. President Kennedy's 1962 Reorganization Plan No. 2 established a new Office of Science and Technology in the Executive Office of the President and transferred to the new Office the NSF's responsibility for shaping, evaluating and coordinating Government scientific policy Under the Plan, the NSF could continue to originate policy proposals and make recommendations, but the policy was actually set by the Office.

Because the NSF authority had been granted on a permanent basis, the principal Congressional review of the Foundation's operations had come during the annual appropriations process and was conducted by the Appropriations Committees of both chambers. In view of the increasing importance of science, the House in 1959 established a Science and Astronautics Committee and gave it legislative jurisdiction over the NSF, as well as over other scientific matters. Senate jurisdiction was in the Labor and Public Welfare Committee, which handles education bills.

The House Subcommittee on Science, Research and Development, headed by Rep. Emilio Q. Daddario (D Conn.), began the first comprehensive legislative review of the NSF late in 1964. The review resulted in proposed legislation to expand NSF's scope. The House passed the bill in 1966 and again in 1967, only to have the Senate fail to act.

1968 Action. The Senate in 1968 passed a bill that closely followed the language of the 1967 House bill in updating operations of the NSF. It gave the Director greater authority over NSF management, although the National Science Board, to whom he would continue to report, remained responsible for overseeing NSF policies. The bill also enlarged the Foundation's scope so that it could support applied science as well as basic science, and research in the social sciences as well.

A Senate provision required that henceforth the NSF must seek an annual authorization from Congress for its activities. This was the traditional way for Congressional legislative committees to influence an agency's policies and also to inform Appropriations Committee members (sometimes in vain) of emphases the legislative committee members felt should be given to programs.

The House accepted the Senate amendments to its 1967 bill and it became law (PL 90-407) July 18, 1968.

FOUNDATION ON ARTS AND HUMANITIES

After several years of growing Congressional and private support for federal aid for the study, development and presentation of the arts and humanities, Congress in 1965 established a National Foundation on the Arts and Humanities. The final bill was based on an Administration proposal, which was submitted after Congressional hearings had begun on a number of bills introduced in the Senate and House. Earlier attempts to win Congressional approval for federal support of the arts had met with failure, most often because action was blocked in the House.

The National Foundation established in PL 89-209 consisted of two autonomous subdivisions, a National Endowment for the Arts and a National Endowment for the Humanities. Each endowment had a chairman and a 26-member advisory council—one on the arts and one on the humanities. Each endowment was authorized to make grants—most of them to be matched—for a wide range of activities. The operations of the National Foundation were to be coordinated with other federal activities through a nine-member Federal Council on the Arts and the Humanities, made up of representatives of various agencies.

In addition to establishing the Foundation, Pl 89-209 (S 1483) authorized two small programs of financial assistance to be carried out by the Office of Education. These were to help schools buy equipment for teaching the humanities and the arts and to finance training institutes for teachers of these subjects.

The bill authorized appropriations for each endowment of $5 million for each of three fiscal years, 1966, 1967, and 1968. An additional annual maximum of $5 million for the Humanities Endowment and $2.25 million for the Arts Endowment were authorized to match gifts or bequests. Another $2.75 million was authorized for the Arts Endowment for matching grants to state arts agencies of $50,000 annually to each state. States without such an agency could receive a one-time grant of $25,000—without matching requirements— to establish arts councils.

As enacted, S 1483 authorized total appropriations of $63 million from fiscal 1966 through 1968.

In 1968 Congress extended the Foundation for two years. PL 90-348 (HR 11308) authorized appropriations of $34 million over two years, plus sums to match up to $13.5 million in private gifts to the Foundation.

In contrast to the funds finally enacted, the figures initially recommended by the House Education and Labor Committee totaled $135 million over two years. In the first of many signs of "economy fever" in Congress, the House initially rebuffed the Committee by reducing the first-year authorization to $11.2 million and entirely deleting the second-year authorization. The Senate put back the two-year authorization and the House went along with it.

Appropriations for the Foundation in its first four years remained around the $10-million level annually. These were the figures (carried in the annual appropriations bill for the Interior Department and Related Agencies, one of which had for years been the Commission on Fine Arts): Fiscal 1966, $10.7 million; 1967, $9 million; 1968; $12.2 million; 1969, $11.5 million.

In 1970 Congress authorized a three-year extension of the Foundation with authorizations set at $40-million for fiscal 1971, $60-million for fiscal 1972 and $80 million for fiscal 1973. Appropriations for fiscal 1972 were $61.2 million.

Support for the Foundation. Pressure for federal support of the arts and humanities was, in part, a reaction to the Government's concentration on advancing scientific activities. Efforts in behalf of artistic fields got under way some years before promotion of the humanities was undertaken.

Congress in 1910 established the Commission of Fine Arts, which reviews and comments on architectural and urban design affecting federal areas within the District of Columbia. In 1958 federal land was donated for a National Cultural Center in Washington, D.C., to be built by private donations. After President Kennedy's assassination, Congress in 1963 authorized federal matching contributions for the center and renamed it for Kennedy.

This was a recognition of the late President's sponsorship of federal support for the arts. In 1961 he backed legislation to establish a Federal Advisory Council of the Arts, as President Eisenhower had done in 1955. The Kennedy bill was defeated in the House Sept. 21, 1961, on a 166-173 roll-call vote. In 1962 President Kennedy appointed August Heckscher as his Special Consultant on the Arts. At their urging, the Senate in 1963 passed a bill to establish a National Arts Foundation to make grants to the states and to professional groups to encourage and support the arts. The bill was not passed by the House, but in 1964 Congress did establish an advisory body, the National Council on the Arts, in the Executive Office of the President.

To promote the humanities, a private group, the National Commission on the Humanities, was established in 1963 by the American Council of Learned Societies, the United Chapters of Phi Beta Kappa and the Council of Graduate Schools in the United States.

In a 1964 report, the Commission called for the establishment of a National Humanities Foundation to support study, teaching and research in the arts and humanities through federal grants and fellowships and through assistance in construction and expansion of libraries, classrooms, etc. The report said that the United States faced "a crisis of national leadership" because the development of the humanities lagged far behind science and technology.

Although President Johnson had expressed support for a foundation on the humanities in 1964, he asked in his January 1965 State of the Union message only for a foundation on the arts. However, numerous bills introduced in Congress called for both foundations and in March the President submitted a bill to establish the dual National Foundation on the Arts and the Humanities. Over considerable opposition in the House (an effort to kill the bill lost in the House on a 128-251 roll-call vote), the legislation was enacted in September 1965. It was supported by a great many educators, artists, musicians and actors as well as their private patrons.

The top officials appointed to the Foundation in 1965 were: S. Dillon Ripley, Secretary of the Smithsonian Institution, as chairman of the Federal Council on the Arts and the Humanities; Barnaby C. Keeney, retired president of Brown University and chairman of the private commission on the humanities, as chairman of the National Endowment for the Humanities; and Roger L. Stevens, chairman of the National Council on the Arts established in 1964, as chairman of the National Endowment for the Arts.

APPENDIX

Chronology of Education
Legislation 1945-1972

Education Amendments of 1972

CQ

CHRONOLOGY OF EDUCATION LEGISLATION: 1945-1964

In the postwar period from 1945-64 the federal government undertook several programs to aid public and private education at various levels, but the central question of the federal government's proper role in education remained controversial and unresolved.

National policy had always assumed—through enactment of early ordinances, establishment of land-grant colleges, and New Deal recovery programs—a federal interest in the national educational level. Before and after 1945, Congress moved into the educational field, undertaking a broad range of often expensive programs to meet special needs. But despite this acknowledgement of a limited federal role, it refused to make a total commitment to responsibility for the general level of the nation's education.

In the post-World War II period, Congress authorized the government to buy school lunches, to supply funds to improve the teaching of science, mathematics and foreign languages, to lend colleges money to build dormitories, to educate veterans, and to grant funds for school construction, operation and teachers' salaries in districts "impacted" by tax-free federal property. But it rejected all proposals to subsidize generally the building or operation of the nation's elementary and secondary schools.

The debate on Capitol Hill often provided a major election issue. It was partly philosophical: Those in favor of a broad program of federal aid to public elementary and secondary schools argued that the level of education given American students was a national concern, and its determination could no longer be left to the states. This concern began as early as World War I, when the draft revealed a high level of illiteracy, particularly in the poorer states. World War II showed that those conditions persisted. Following the war, proponents of federal aid argued the proven illiteracy, plus crowded classroom conditions caused by the lack of building during World War II and the population growth engendered after it, necessitated federal help. They also argued that teachers, underpaid relative to what they could earn in other jobs, were leavint the profession or not joinint it in enough numbers, and were not of adequate professional caliber. Local taxes were inadequate to meet these needs.

Opponents argued that education was traditionally and rightfully a state and local concern and responsibility. They warned that federal control and regulations would inexorably follow federal aid.

1945

General School Aid. Several bills were introduced, but there was no committee action in the Senate. The House Education Committee (which in 1947 was merged with the Labor Committee to become the House Education and Labor Committee, as specified in the 1946 Congressional Reorganization Act) in December voted 10-9 not to report an education bill similar to the earlier Thomas-Hill bill. An informal bipartisan Committee for the Support of Federal Aid for Public Schools had been formed in the House earlier in the session. Co-chairmen of the group were Reps. Jennings Randolph (D W.Va.) and Everett McKinley Dirksen (R Ill.).

Defense Area School Aid. Part of the Lanham Act of 1940, Defense Area School Aid was slightly increased by $30 million to a total authorization of $530 million (PL 79-125). The Act authorized the money to provide for the operation in congested defense plant areas of hospitals, schools, child-care centers and other facilities. *(Lanham Act box, p. 59)*

1946

General School Aid. A bill (S 181) was reported to the Senate floor, but not acted on; the idea of general school aid did, however, win an important new advocate —Sen. Robert A. Taft (R Ohio).

In his State of the Union message President Truman urged passage of federal aid to education. The Senate Education and Labor Committee held hearings on S 181, and on a broader, more expensive measure (S 717), which authorized aid to private schools. The committee reported a substitute for S 181, which authorized a permanent program of federal grants to all but the wealthiest states beginning at $150 million and going to $250 million in the third year and thereafter, in order to provide a minimum of $40 for each school-age child in the country. Funds could be spent for private schools, and—according to the prevailing "separate but equal" racial doctrine—states maintaining separate schools for racial minorities had to spend for them according to the minority's proportion of the population in the state.

Taft said that testimony given to the Senate committee had convinced him that in many states children were not receiving a basic education, even though some poor states were spending as high a proportion of their tax sources as the larger, wealthier ones. "Education," Taft said, "is primarily a state function—but in the field of education the federal government, as in the fields of health, relief, and medical care, has a secondary interest or obligation to see that there is a basic floor under those essential services for all adults and children in the United States."

The bill did not come up on the Senate floor before adjournment.

Defense Area School Aid. Congress approved a bill (PL 79-452) extending federal aid to schools in war-affected communities.

1947

Educators and lawmakers warned that a school crisis was at hand—teachers were leaving the profession in unprecedented numbers because of low salaries, and school enrollments were steadily rising. A Senate committee school aid bill was reported, but never came to a floor vote, and in the House a similar bill received subcommittee approval.

The National Education Association, generally known as the "teachers' lobby," estimated that the average teacher's salary in 1957-58 would be about $2,250, and that there would be about 450,000 more students but only about 7,000 more teachers.

General School Aid. A Senate bill allotted about $300 million a year permanently in order to provide that each state spend at least $45 and later $50 on each school-age child. It required the states to spend at least one

Federal Aid to Education Developments Before 1945

Several types of legislation, dating back to the Survey Ordinance of 1785, established a federal role in education before the post-World War II period. Following are the significant developments in federal aid to education before 1945:

1785. The **Survey Ordinance,** adopted by the Congress of the Confederation for the disposal of public lands in the Western Territory, reserved one section of every township for the endowment of schools within that township.

1787. In the **Northwest Ordinance,** which provided for the government of the Northwest Territory, Congress made the policy declaration: "...religion, morality, and knowledge being necessary to good government and the happiness of mankind, schools and the means of education shall forever be encouraged."

1862. The **Morrill Act** provided for grants of federal land to each state for establishment of colleges specializing in agriculture and mechanical arts. These became known as "land-grant colleges." The original Act authorized grants to the states of 30,000 acres of land, or the equivalent in scrip, for each U.S. Representative and each U.S. Senator to which the state was entitled in 1860. The proceeds from the grants were to be used for support of the colleges. After several land-grant colleges had been in operation for a number of years, and the states were having difficulty supporting them, Congress in the second Morrill Act of 1890 authorized annual federal grants to the states for the operation of the colleges. The purpose of the Morrill Acts was to provide both liberal and practical education for the working classes.

Changes in the Morrill Act made by the 1907 Nelson Amendment, the 1935 Bankhead-Jones Act and other legislation raised the annual grants to the colleges to $5,051,500 a year between fiscal 1954-61. Legislation passed in 1960 (S 3450—PL 86-658) increased the annual authorization to $14,500,000 starting in fiscal 1962. Of the total, $2,550,000 was for distribution under the so-called Morrill-Nelson Act, $7,650,000 was for flat grants of $150,000 each to the states and $4,300,000 for allocation according to population. The funds could be used by the colleges for any educational expense,

but not for construction of facilities. At the end of 1964, there were 67 land-grant colleges in the 50 states and Puerto Rico.

1867. Congress established an independent federal **"Department of Education."** Its name was changed to U.S. Office of Education after 1929. It was part of the Interior Department from 1869-1939, then transferred to the Federal Security Agency, which in turn became the Department of Health, Education and Welfare in 1953.

1917. The **Smith-Hughes Act** set up the first program of federal grants-in-aid to promote vocational education in the public schools below college grade. Funds were provided for courses and teacher training in the fields of agriculture, home economics, trades and industries. This was extended and expanded over the years.

1930s. Various federal emergency agencies set up during the depression years engaged in educational activities as part of the relief program. For example, the Public Works Administration made loans and grants for school construction, and the Federal Emergency Relief Administration developed adult education and nursery school programs.

1940. The **Lanham Act** authorized federal aid to local governments for construction, maintenance, and operation of facilities, including schools. Aid was given to communities with populations swollen by increased military personnel and defense workers. This was the forerunner of temporary legislation between 1946 and 1950 for "emergency" school aid and, beginning in 1950, "impacted" areas aid.

1944. The Servicemen's Readjustment Act **(GI Bill of Rights)** set up a program of educational benefits for World War II veterans which was unprecedented in scope. A more limited program was provided for veterans of the Korean war, and congressional controversy developed over whether "Cold War" veterans should receive similar benefits. *(Later legislation providing veterans' benefits p. 73, 89)*

percent of their income on education and, where this was sufficient to pay the desired amount-per-child, a flat grant of $5 per school child was offered. Thus even the wealthiest states were to benefit. The bill allowed the states to spend the money as their own education funds—for any school purpose, including private school aid. This last provision aroused the most controversy.

1948

General School Aid. A bill (S 472) authorizing $300 million permanently reported in 1947 was passed April 1 by the Senate, with the provision allowing the states to spend the money for private schools, the crux of the debate. An amendment to limit all aid to public schools was defeated by a 5-80 roll call, with four of the five "yea" votes by Southerners.

The bill stipulated that states maintaining racially segregated schools must provide equally for them, and the Senate accepted an amendment by Tom Connally (D Texas) prohibiting any limitations in future appropriation bills on the use of federal aid to education funds. Connally said this would prevent appropriations committees from attaching provisos which would forbid use of funds in states which maintained segregated schools.

1949

Both party platforms of 1948 endorsed federal aid to education. President Truman's "Fair Deal" program presented to the Democratic 81st Congress made education aid a key point. "We are not yet assuring all children of our nation the opportunity of receiving the basic education which is necessary to a strong democracy," the President said in his State of the Union message. But though a school bill passed the Senate with relative ease, a controversy over aid to private schools that was to plague the issue for years broke out among key House members and public figures.

General School Aid. The Senate bill (S 246), like the one passed in 1948, authorized $300 million a year in grants to the states, with most of the money "equalized" between rich and poor states, for any elementary and secondary educational purpose on which state funds were spent (thus the funds could go to private schools). It also required equal expenditures for Negro and white schools.

In the House, Education and Labor Committee Chairman John Lesinski (D Mich.) appointed Graham A. Barden (D N.C.) to head a subcommittee to consider the school bill. Barden introduced a bill (HR 4643) authorizing grants of $300 million annually, but restricted the aid to public schools only, made no mention of aid to schools for racial minorities, and authorized any taxpayer in the state to apply for an injunction to halt violations of the provision that federal funds go only for "current expenditures for public elementary and secondary schools within the state."

Lesinski, a Catholic, sponsored a bill authorizing up to $1 billion a year after 1955 primarily for public schools, but with funds earmarked for health and welfare activities in both public and private schools.

A letter came to the subcommittee from Columbia University President Dwight D. Eisenhower, who said that he supported federal aid under formulas which aided areas where the tax-paying potential could not provide adequate education, but added: "I would flatly oppose any grant by the federal government to all states in the Union for educational purposes." He warned "...unless we are careful even the great and necessary educational processes in our country will become yet another vehicle by which the believers in paternalism, if not outright socialism, will gain still additional power for the central Government."

The subcommittee June 9 approved the Barden bill. While the full committee remained deadlocked over aid to private schools, the issue long restricted to the committee room broke into the open with a blast by Lesinski accusing Barden of writing an "anti-Negro" and "anti-Catholic" bill which "dripped with bigotry and racial prejudice." He said the Barden bill would never be permitted out of the full Committee and accused Barden of writing the bill with just that aim. Barden said he was "utterly astounded" by Lesinski's charges, and denied them.

Impacted Areas School Aid. The beginnings of the more long-range impacted areas school aid program were embodied in a bill (S 2317) authorizing $5 million in grants to the states, to pay for half the cost of surveys to determine the need for more school buildings, and authorizing aid to local school agencies for school construction when a state certified an acute shortage of facilities caused by war, defense or other specific federal activities. S 2317 passed the Senate by voice vote Oct. 17.

1950

The religious controversy continued to rage around the general school aid bill, and ultimately killed it for

the 81st Congress. But the impacted areas school aid program was begun, the National Science Foundation was authorized, and the college housing program was enacted as part of the 1950 Housing Act.

General School Aid. The House Education and Labor Committee took up the bill passed by the Senate in 1949 (S 246), which allowed expenditure of funds for private schools, and ultimately rejected it by a 12-13 vote, apparently in the belief the issue had become too heated to put to a House test. Among committee members voting to kill the bill were Reps. John F. Kennedy (D Mass.), Richard M. Nixon (R Calif.), Lesinski and Barden.

Impacted Areas School Aid. Programs were enacted with time limitations set so that their success could be studied from time to time.

The school construction bill passed by the Senate in 1949 (S 2317) was passed by the House Aug. 22 by voice vote and became PL 81-815; a bill originating in the House (HR 7940) was passed July 13 and became PL 81-874, authorizing aid to help maintain and operate schools in federally impacted areas. PL 815 was authorized for two years, through June 30, 1952, and PL 874 for four years, through June 30, 1954. In passing HR 7940 (PL 874), Congress indicated that this would be a permanent program.

In the fall of 1954, 1,183 school districts in 47 states (all but Louisiana), Alaska and Hawaii, were found eligible for almost $30 million of aid under PL 874 for the first year.

During House committee hearings on S 2317 (PL 815), U.S. Commissioner of Education Earl J. McGrath said 300,000 new classrooms were needed in the next few years. He said the new law would be no substitute for general school aid, since he considered more funds for teachers of greater importance than the building program.

National Science Foundation. A bill passed by the Senate in 1949 (S 247) was passed with amendments by the House and enacted into law in 1950 (PL 81-507). The new law established the National Science Foundation and commissioned it to promote scientific research, correlate and evaluate research supported by other government agencies, improve the teaching of science, mathematics and engineering (this was a minor role at first, but developed in later years), cooperate in international scientific interchange, and disseminate scientific information.

1951

General School Aid. Old approaches to general school aid were abandoned, and moves to find resources for general school aid from the disputed offshore "tidelands" oil deposits began in 1951. Most of these proposals ran headlong into the opposition of the powerful groups interested in guaranteeing coastal state control of offshore oil deposits. It was only when, in 1953, the proposed education revenues were to be taken from offshore lands clearly in the federal government's domain, that the proposals came near to succeeding.

Impacted Areas School Aid. A bill (HR 5411) to extend PL 815, which was to expire June 30, 1952, was pocket vetoed by President Truman Nov. 2 on the grounds it would promote segregation of schools. The source of

Truman's concern was an amendment added in the Senate by Lister Hill (D Ala.) which required schools receiving federal aid to conform to state laws. This would have forced segregation in some non-segregated schools operating on federal property in the South.

1952

General School Aid. "Oil for education" amendments were again unsuccessfully offered to proposals to give the coastal states claim to certain offshore oil deposits and reserving others for the federal government. (A bill was passed, but vetoed by President Truman. The veto was not overridden.)

1953

In 1953, the Department of Health, Education and Welfare, requested by President Eisenhower, was established, general school aid was again considered in Congress only as part of a solution to the offshore oil dispute and rejected, and impacted areas aid was put on a new footing.

General School Aid. Two submerged oil lands bills became law, but neither had a provision setting aside revenues for general school aid.

Impacted Areas School Aid. PL 81-815 and PL 81-874 were extended and revised. PL 815's authorization had actually lapsed for a year because of President Truman's 1951 veto and no 1952 action on it. However, there had been sufficient funds remaining from earlier appropriations to carry out the school construction program through June 30, 1953. The 1953 law extended it again through June 30, 1954. PL 874, school maintenance aid, was extended through June 30, 1956.

1954

In the year that the Supreme Court overturned its own earlier "separate but equal" racial doctrine and ruled *(Brown v. Board of Education of Topeka, Kansas)* that segregated schools were no longer legal—which was to add a new dimension to the complex question of segregated schools in the school aid issue—the philosophical and fiscal dispute between President Eisenhower and congressional Democrats over school aid broke open. Even some Republicans (who controlled the 83rd Congress) were dismayed by the President's program, which eschewed general school aid grants and proposed (1) a national conference to study education problems; (2) authorization for the U.S. Office of Education to help the states conduct education surveys; (3) an advisory committee on education in the office of the Secretary of HEW; and (4) extension of PL 815 (impacted areas construction grants), which was to expire June 30, 1954. In his Jan. 21 budget message making these proposals, the President said: "I do not underestimate the difficulties facing the states and communities in attempting to solve the problems created by the great increase in the number of children of school age, the shortage of qualified teachers, and the overcrowding of classrooms.... At the same time, I do not accept the simple remedy of federal intervention."

Education groups generally backed the President's proposals, but termed them "grossly inadequate." All four were enacted.

White House Conference. PL 83-530 authorized the President to hold a White House Conference on Education in 1955.

Joint Studies. PL 83-531 authorized the Office of Education to make contracts and cooperative arrangements with colleges and universities for joint studies of educational problems.

National Advisory Committee. PL 83-532 authorized establishment of a nine-man National Advisory Committee on Education to advise the Secretary of HEW on pressing problems in education. It never was set up.

Impacted Areas School Aid. PL 83-731 extended impacted areas school aid under PL 815 through June 30, 1956. In a related development, Secretary of Defense Charles E. Wilson Jan. 12, 1954 issued an order that no new schools on military installations be opened on a segregated basis and that schools already segregated, desegregate no later than Sept. 1, 1955.

General School Aid. The President notwithstanding, general school aid grants were pushed in Congress, but unsuccessfully. The Senate Labor and Public Welfare Committee July 19 reported a bill (S 2601) authorizing "emergency" school construction aid in grants of $500 million for two years to the states, based on need, to pay up to 40 percent of construction costs. The bill was opposed by HEW Secretary Mrs. Oveta Culp Hobby who sent a letter to the committee saying school aid legislation should await the outcome of the 1955 White House Conference, and that the pending bill was not in accord with the administration's efforts to balance the budget or with the maintenance of state and local control of public education. There was no Senate floor action on the bill before the end of the 83rd Congress.

1955

General School Aid. President Eisenhower sent Congress a school aid proposal to authorize a three-year, $1.1 billion program of federal aid for school construction, with all but about $200 million to be repaid. The new Democratic Congress was not pleased and began work on its own bills. The funds in the administration bill would have been used for federal purchase of school bonds issued by communities unable to sell the bonds "at a reasonable interest rate" (later estimated as 3-1/8 percent); federal support of a program under which states would build schools and rent them to school districts until the principal and interest were repaid and the districts took title to the buildings; grants of $200 million to districts financially unable to issue bonds or participate in a lease-purchase program, limiting this aid to an amount sufficient to enable them to undertake bond issues or a rental program; and federal payment of half the administrative cost of state programs designed to work out long-term solutions of school financial problems.

The President's State of the Union message said there were "grave educational problems" and an "unprecedented classroom shortage" (about 300,000 class-rooms needed). Spelling out again his education aid philosophy, Mr. Eisenhower said: "Without impairing in any way the responsibilities of our states, localities, communities, or families, the federal government can and should serve as an effective catalyst in dealing with this problem." His program, however, was greeted by Congressional Democrats as "government by gimmick," a plan "conceived by investment bankers and dedicated to the money lenders," and an "empty hoax." Education lobbies urged programs of direct grants of substantially higher sums.

The Senate Labor and Public Welfare Committee held hearings on a number of bills, but took no further action before the first session adjourned.

The House Education and Labor Committee July 28 reported a bill (HR 7535) authorizing: grants of $1.6 billion over four years, to be matched equally by the states, for school construction; $750 million for federal purchase of local school construction bonds; $150 million to help pay off the principal and interest ("debt service") of school construction bonds worth $6 billion.

The bill remained in the House Rules Committee for the rest of the session.

Impacted Areas School Aid. Aid for school construction in impacted areas (PL 81-815), was extended until June 30, 1957 (PL 84-382).

White House Conference on Education. Began Nov. 28 amidst charges that it was "stacked" by those against federal aid to education. It ended, however, Dec. 1, with an endorsement of federal financial aid to education, with only a very small minority dissenting.

1956

General School Aid. The school aid bill (HR 7535) reported to the House in 1955 was killed on the House floor. Chief contributor to the death was an accepted amendment offered by Adam C. Powell (D N.Y.) which would have barred federal aid to states which failed to comply with (desegregation) decisions of the Supreme Court. A contributing factor was opposition by Republicans.

President Eisenhower revised his 1955 school aid proposal by raising federal grants to $250 million annually for five years. But Democrats stayed behind HR 7535, which authorized, among other things, grants of $400 million a year for four years.

Substantial debate over the principle of the Powell amendment took place before the bill came to a vote. The amendment, backed by the NAACP, was opposed by the NEA, the AFL-CIO, and the President. All those opposed said that the issues of segregation and school aid should be kept separate, and several indicated the ultimate effect of a Powell amendment—arousal of sufficient opposition by Southern Democrats which, joining Republican opposition to federal aid in general, could kill the bill.

The exact weight of the Powell amendment against the bill's passage was unclear. A substantial number of Southerners opposed the bill anyway, and had expressed fears earlier that an anti-segregation proviso would be put in a later school aid appropriation bill. Sixteen more

votes would have been needed for passage of the final bill which was defeated 194-224 (D 119-105; R 75-119). The strength of the Republican opposition came as a surprise to the bill's backers.

Earlier in the year, 101 Southern members from 11 states—19 Senators and 82 Representatives—March 12 presented a "Declaration of Constitutional Principles" criticizing the Supreme Court for its 1954 desegregation decision. The so-called "Southern Manifesto" had no legal standing in Congress and required no congressional action.

Impacted Areas School Aid. Aid to federally impacted areas for both school construction (PL 815) and school maintenance (PL 874) was extended through June 30, 1958 (PL 84-949).

1957

General School Aid. General opposition, segregation problems, and budget-cutting zeal again combined to kill a school bill on the House floor. The defeat came at a moment when Democrats offered to back the administration's bill. Both Republicans and Democrats charged that President Eisenhower, less than ardent in backing his bill, ignored an opportunity to gain enough bipartisan backing to get his bill through the House. The Senate took no action on general school aid in 1957.

The President's proposal was similar to the 1956 bill, but condensed into four years, thus honoring a 1956 election campaign pledge. It would have authorized a four-year, $1.3 billion program of federal grants to the states for school construction, $750 million for school bond purchases and authority to back the credit of school bonds. The grants were based on school-age population, weighted by relative state income per school child. The President said his bill should be considered an "emergency" measure, designed only to "stimulate" state and local efforts and asked that it "be enacted on its own merits, uncomplicated by provisions dealing with the complex problems of integration." The bill was attacked by school aid backers as inadequate and categorically opposed by others, notably the Chamber of Commerce of the U.S., which argued that there was "no critical national shortage in classrooms."

The House Education and Labor Committee May 28 reported a bill (HR 1) combining Administration and Democratic proposals. It authorized $1.5 billion in grants over five years for school construction, $750 million for bond purchases and $150 million to back bond credit. Half of the grants were based on school-age population and half on school-age population weighted by income.

In July 25 House floor action, an anti-segregation amendment offered by Stuyvesant Wainwright (R N.Y.), an avowed foe of the bill, was accepted. With the House sitting for final consideration of the bill and amendments to bring the bill to the President's original requests pending, Democrats Stewart L. Udall (Ariz.) and Lee Metcalf (Mont.) said they could compromise "all the way" and accept the Administration program in order to get a bill passed. At this point, Howard W. Smith (D Va.) moved to strike the enacting clause (kill the bill) and his motion was agreed to by a roll-call vote of 208-203 (D 97-126; R 111-77). A switch of three votes would have saved the bill.

In answer to charges that he could have saved the bill himself, President Eisenhower said he "never heard" that House Democrats were willing to support his proposals, that he "spoke up plenty of times for the (school aid) principles in which I believe.... I have compromised twice in the proposals that I have placed before the Congress...but am getting to the point where I can't be too enthusiastic about something that I think is likely to fasten a sort of albatross...around the neck of the federal government.... I don't get up and make statements every 20 minutes. I don't think that is good business."

Impacted Areas School Aid. PL 815 was extended for one year, to June 30, 1959 (PL 85-267).

1958

The National Defense Education Act cleared Congress in 1958. Passage of the $1 billion program geared basically to the sciences, mathematics and foreign languages followed in the wake of warnings that the U.S. was falling behind in the scientific field, coupled with evidence of Russian advances—their first earth satellite (sputnik) had been fired Oct. 4, 1957.

The Joint Atomic Energy Committee March 28, 1956 released a report stating the atomic energy program was "in serious danger of lagging unless something drastic is done immediately" to expand the education of engineers and scientists.

The Presidential Committee on Education Beyond the High School Aug. 10, 1957 recommended that the government institute a "work-study" program under which the United States would subsidize work projects for college students. The Committee asked for more borrowing for college students.

The President's Committee on Scientists and Engineers Nov. 26, 1957 urged a step-up in U.S. scientific training to place the nation's scientists on a par with Russian scientists and technologists.

National Defense Education Act. The NDEA bill moved through Congress with relative ease. It was based largely on requests made by President Eisenhower in a Jan. 27 special education message to Congress requesting a $1.6 billion federal-state education program emphasizing science, engineering, mathematics and foreign languages.

The chief controversy was over the President's request for 10,000 federal college scholarships a year for four years. The House Education and Labor Committee approved a bill with 23,000 scholarships a year and $220 million for a federal loan fund to aid college students. The bill was stripped of the scholarship provision, which was considered its key provision. The $120 million to finance them was then placed in the loan fund.

The NDEA bill (HR 13247) was approved by the House by voice vote Aug. 8.

Tht Senate Labor and Public Welfare Committee reported the bill with a provision for 23,000 scholarships annually for four years and the Senate approved, passing the bill Aug. 13. The House loan provision was accepted in conference and by both chambers.

President Eisenhower signed the bill Sept. 2 (PL 85-864), saying it would "do much to strengthen our American system of education so that it can meet the broad and increasing demands imposed upon it by considerations of basic national security."

Impacted Areas School Aid. Aid for school construction (PL 81-815) and operation (PL 81-874) was extended through June 30, 1961. Aid on behalf of children whose parents both live and work on federal property (Section A) was made permanent. President Eisenhower had requested cutbacks in both programs. In Jan. 20 testimony before the House Education and Labor General Education Subcommittee, Elliott L. Richardson, Assistant Secretary of Health, Education and Welfare, said grants should be limited to "situations where there is a clear and direct federal responsibility." He said a large program was, in effect, "favored treatment for many hundreds of communities as compared with others of equal or greater need." He said the need for federal savings was one reason for the recommended legislation.

1959

Proposals for federal aid to education centered again on general aid for school construction and teachers' salaries, and once more the Eisenhower administration and the Democratic Congress were at odds. The dispute was heightened in 1959 (and through 1960) because the Administration turned away from any kinds of outright grants, and Democrats, flushed with sweeping victories in the 1958 Congressional elections, and preparing already for the 1960 Presidential election, were less in a mood to compromise. Another factor was the heightened intransigence of the House Rules Committee. Although the Committee was nominally in the hands of Democrats, 8-4, Chairman Howard W. Smith (D Va.) and William M. Colmer (D Miss.) could frequently be counted on to vote with the four conservative Republicans on welfare issues, thus tying up legislation.

General School Aid. The administration in 1959 submitted a plan (S 1016, HR 4268) calling for federal payments stretched out over a period of 30-35 years to help local public school districts pay off the debt service (interest and principal) costs of $3 billion in long-term school construction bonds, which were to be issued within five years of enactment of the bill. There were no provisions for teachers' salaries or for direct grants to needy areas. Cost of the bill was estimated at $85 million a year, stretched out over the life of the bonds, with an eventual cost of about $2 billion.

The plan was attacked by northern Democrats as a "bankers bill" designed to cost the Eisenhower administration's budget little, but burdening future administrations with debt.

Northern Democrats supported proposals for immediate large-scale grants to the states for both public school construction and teachers' salaries. Their initial bill (S 2, HR 22) called for $4.4 billion annually in nonmatching grants for these purposes, to continue indefinitely.

The House version of the bill, sharply cut so that it provided $1.1 billion a year for only four years for school construction and teachers' salaries, was reported July 8 by the House Education and Labor Committee, but was never sent to the House floor by the Rules Committee. With this bill locked in the Rules Committee, Senate

Democrats on the Labor and Public Welfare Education Subcommittee wrote a new bill (S 8) that was reported by the full Committee Sept. 12.

S 8 called for an emergency two-year program of federal matching grants to the states for school construction only. The bill authorized $500 million in federal payments each year, and provided a variable 3-1 equalization between the wealthiest and poorest states—the poorest states would receive three times as much in allocations per school-age child as the wealthiest states. There was no Senate floor action on S 8 in 1959.

Impacted Areas School Aid. The President again sought cutbacks in aid to impacted areas, but his proposals were rejected by a House Education and Labor Committee subcommittee. Congress dealt Mr. Eisenhower another blow by appropriating more money than he had asked for impacted areas aid in fiscal 1960.

Loyalty Oath. A bill to remove the loyalty oath and non-Communist affidavit required of recipients of aid under the National Defense Education Act of 1958 was recommitted and thus killed by the Senate July 23 by a 49-42 roll-call vote. The affidavit and loyalty oath requirements had been inserted into the NDEA in the Senate Labor and Public Welfare Committee by Sen. H. Alexander Smith (R N.J.) in 1958 and received little notice during floor consideration. Under the requirements, a recipient of NDEA aid had to submit with his application an affidavit attesting that he did not believe in violent overthrow of the government, and did not support or belong to organizations believing in or teaching violent overthrow. The applicant was also required to swear an oath of allegiance to the United States. Senators Joseph S. Clark (D Pa.) and John F. Kennedy (D Mass.) led the attempt to remove the requirements. The Senate debated the bill heatedly for two days before rejecting it. Repeal of the requirements was favored by several colleges and academic groups and by the Department of Health, Education and Welfare, which protested that it singled out students and implied extra security precautions had to be taken regarding them. Several colleges refused to participate in the NDEA student loan fund because of this. Backers of the requirement said that no one should be reluctant to declare his loyalty to the United States.

1960

General School Aid. A general aid to education bill came close to passage, but was stymied when the House Rules Committee, by a 5-7 vote (D 5-3; R 0-4), refused to authorize a House-Senate conference that might have compromised differences between the House and Senate version of the legislation.

The Senate passed the bill which had been reported in 1959, S 8, with amendments Feb. 4 by a 51-34 roll-call vote. It authorized $1.8 billion in federal grants for school construction and teachers' salaries, with payments to be spread so that poorer states would receive more money per school-age child than richer ones. Before passage, Sen. Joseph S. Clark (D Pa.), with 22 co-sponsors, offered an amendment to authorize $1.1 billion a year for an indefinite period for construction and salaries. This narrowly missed acceptance on a 44-44 (D 39-17; R 5-27) roll call. A motion to table a move to reconsider the vote

carried, 45-44 (D 16-40; R 29-4), Vice President Richard M. Nixon casting the deciding vote. An amendment by Clark and A.S. Mike Monroney (D Okla.) authorizing $20 per school-age child for two years for construction and salaries was then accepted by a roll-call vote of 54-35 (D 46-11; R 8-24), thus shaping the final bill. The Eisenhower bill, authorizing funds to help pay the debt service on long-term school bonds, was rejected 25-61.

The House May 26 passed a bill (HR 10128) providing $1.3 billion in grants for school construction only, with no equalization formula. It also included a Powell anti-segregation amendment, which was adopted by a 218-181 roll call.

Even had the legislation not been finally blocked in the House Rules Committee, its provision of direct federal grants was expected to lead to a presidential veto.

In addition to financing policy, the Administration and Northern Democrats were at loggerheads over teachers' salaries. Democrats backed provisions allowing school funds to pay for salaries, saying that in many areas the need for higher salaries was greater than for more classrooms, and that states should have the option on how to spend the money. When asked about teachers' salary aid at a news conference, President Eisenhower said: "I do not believe the federal government ought to be in the business of paying a local official. If we're going into that, we'll have to find out every councilman and every teacher and every other person that's a public official of any kind...and try to figure out what his right salary is.... I can't imagine anything worse for the federal government to get into."

This developed into a major issue in the subsequent presidential campaign. Vice President Nixon sided with President Eisenhower and said aid for teachers' salaries would invite dangerous federal control over what is taught. Democratic candidate Kennedy backed the Senate-passed bill containing salary aid, pointing out that the government had been aiding salaries under the impacted areas school operations program (PL 874) since 1950, that about 60 percent of the nearly $2 billion that had been appropriated under the program went for teachers' salaries, and that there had been no complaints of federal control.

Loyalty Oath. Another fight over the student affidavit and loyalty oath in the NDEA took place. The Senate June 15 passed a bill (S 2929) eliminating the non-Communist affidavit requirement and instead making it a crime for a Communist or other "subversive" to apply for or accept federal aid under the NDEA. The loyalty oath was left intact. The only House action was a one-day Committee hearing.

Repeal of the affidavit had been requested by Mr. Eisenhower in his 1960 budget message and was backed by a number of education organizations. As of November 1960, 29 colleges refused to participate in the NDEA because of the affidavit (20 had participated and then withdrew) and a large number of institutions were on record against the affidavit. Other groups, such as the American Legion and Veterans of Foreign Wars, opposed the repeal move.

College Classroom Construction. Proposals received hearings in the Senate and the House, but were not reported. The Eisenhower Administration backed a proposal

(S 1017—HR 4267) to offer federal grants to help pay off the principal and interest costs of long-term construction bonds sold to the public. Democrats backed a revolving fund (S 3007), like the one for already existing college housing, to make long-term loans for college classroom construction. (President Eisenhower in January 1960 had requested that the college housing program be terminated, but it was extended in a stop-gap housing measure (H J Res 784—PL 86-788).

1961

Despite a new Democratic administration pledged to passage of a general school aid bill, and expansion of the House Rules Committee to give administration supporters a one-vote margin, a school aid bill was again defeated and the Rules Committee had a large hand in the defeat.

President Kennedy was thus handed a sharp defeat on what he had described as "probably the most important piece of domestic legislation" of the year. The bill was a victim of a combination of factors: strong and well organized opposition of Republicans and Southern Democrats, the racial and religious issues which had traditionally plagued school bills, and the lack of consistent, coordinated leadership. The bill's failure carried with it administration proposals for loans for college classroom construction and for college scholarships, for substantive changes in the NDEA, and for cutbacks in the impacted areas programs.

That the religious issue was such a large factor was a supreme irony for the first Catholic President, who was at pains in the campaign to convince skeptics that he would not favor the Church and who in 1961 suffered his greatest legislative defeat because of opposition by the Catholic bishops.

All that survived was a $900 million bill extending the NDEA without change for two years (estimated cost: $500,200,000) and the impacted areas programs (estimated cost: $402,992,000).

General School Aid. In his education requests, the President asked for: grants of $2.3 billion over three years to be used by the states primarily for construction of elementary and high school classrooms and for boosting teachers' salaries; loans to colleges of almost $2.8 billion over five years for the construction of dormitories, classrooms, laboratories, libraries and other academic facilities (dormitory loans were increased in the 1961 Housing Act); grants of $892 million for four-year federal college scholarships, averaging $2,800 each, for 212,000 prospective college students, and $350 a year to the college for cost of educating each student holding a federal scholarship. The administration's general school aid bill (S 1021, HR 4970) contained provisions to extend the expiring portions of the impacted areas laws (PL 815, PL 874) at about half the existing rates. It was hoped that inclusion of the popular impacted areas aid would swing votes for the new school bill.

The President's message said that no general school aid funds were allocated for private schools, "in accordance with the clear prohibition of the Constitution." The Catholic Church hierarchy issued a statement saying the public school bill should include private school loans or it should be defeated. At a press conference, the President said he believed "across-the-board" loans as well as grants to private schools were unconstitutional. This formed the outlines of the religious school aid controversy that raged for the entire session of Congress and ultimately led to defeat of the bill.

To the school aid bill's natural enemies in the House—conservative Republicans and Southern Democrats—who already posed a formidable threat to passage, was added the prospect of a sizeable number of the House's 88 Catholic members, many of whom had supported school bills in the past.

It was clear to the bill's backers that it had to be insulated from the controversies that were swelling around it, including the desegregation issue.

With an eye to southern and border-state votes in the House, Abraham A. Ribicoff, Secretary of HEW, repeatedly stated that he would not withhold school aid funds from segregated school systems unless Congress so directed. Powell himself, now chairman of the House Education and Labor Committee, pledged to withhold his anti-segregation amendment.

To disentangle the parochial school aid issue from the public school bill was more difficult. Various, sometimes conflicting strategies were devised by the House, Senate, White House and HEW leaders backing the bill. The idea finally carried through was for the administration to send to Congress proposals for extending and expanding the NDEA. The Act, scheduled to expire June 30, 1962, already authorized (in Title III) loans to private schools (and grants to public schools) for equipment for teaching science, mathematics and foreign languages. The administration would ask that a number of amendments be made to the Act, basically expanding it to include more fellowships and add English and physical fitness as subjects to be aided. From Congress would come a proposal that Title III also provide loans to private schools for construction of classrooms in which science, mathematics, foreign languages, English and physical fitness were taught. The private school loans would thus be for special "defense" purposes, not "across-the-board"; and the administration would not appear to be backing private school aid.

The Senate May 25 passed S 1021, authorizing $2.5 billion in grants to the states for operation, maintenance and construction of public schools and for teachers' salaries. The passage vote was 49-34 (D 41-21; R 8-22) and followed eight days of debate, during which supporters of the bill beat off 15 amendments designed to raise or resolve latent civil rights and religious issues, to limit the bill, or to substitute other forms of aid to education. The principal amendment accepted, sponsored by Winston L. Prouty (R Vt.), broadened the bill to pay for bus service, textbooks and school health services, as well as construction and salaries.

The House Education and Labor Committee June 1 reported a clean bill (HR 7300) authorizing $2.5 billion in grants to the states for school construction and teachers' salaries. In the meantime, Catholics, with the help of House Majority Leader John W. McCormack (D Mass.), a Catholic, and the acquiescence of HEW officials, were seeking assurances that the NDEA bill with its provisions for loans to private schools would be brought to the House floor together with the public school bill. They feared that Congress would pass the public school bill and then kill the private school loan section of the NDEA. Their fears were not unjustified, for several Southern and border-state Congressmen who favored public school aid represented strongly Protestant constituencies which opposed aid to Catholic schools. Two Catholic Rules Committee members who ordinarily supported the Administration—James J. Delaney (D N.Y.) and Thomas P. O'Neill (D Mass.)—voted with the Committee's five Republicans and two Southern Democrats—Smith and Colmer—to withhold House floor action on the public school bill until the NDEA bill was reported to it.

The House Education and Labor Committee promptly reported the NDEA bill (HR 7904), extending and amending the Act, with a provision for $275 million in longterm, low-interest loans to private schools for classroom construction for the specified subjects. Nevertheless, the Rules Committee July 18 tabled (killed) ensemble the public school bill, the NDEA bill and the college aid bill (authorizing both grants and loans for classroom construction, plus college scholarships) which had also been reported. Voting to table the bills were all five Republicans, and three Democrats—Smith, Colmer and Delaney. Although attention focused on Delaney's vote, three other Committee Southerners—Carl Elliott (D Ala.), Homer Thornberry (D Texas) and James W. Trimble (D Ark.)—were ready to table the NDEA bill had it come to a separate vote. Had this happened, there was little doubt—now that the lines of the controversy had hardened—that the public school bill could not have survived.

A final attempt to get some school bill through the House was made in late August, when Powell called up a one-year, $325 million, construction-only bill (HR 8890), introduced by Rep. Frank Thompson Jr. (D N.J.), which also extended the impacted areas programs. Powell brought the bill up under the seldom-used and, difficult parliamentary procedure of Calendar Wednesday; the effort swiftly came to naught. Powell Aug. 30 moved consideration of the bill and the House without debate refused, by a roll-call vote of 170-242 (D 164-82; R 6-160). The compromise bill had pleased few. Some Catholics called it discriminatory; the NEA called it "woefully inadequate"; and the House Republican party conference opposed it, saying they resented "the whole manner in which this thing has been handled."

A new college aid bill, dropping the scholarships, was sent to the Rules Committee and remained there for the rest of the session.

Impacted Areas School Aid, NDEA. When all else had failed in the House, leaders decided to go ahead with extension of impacted areas and NDEA aid. Some Democratic House leaders wanted only a one-year extension, leaving them a lever for school aid moves in 1962, but the price of Minority Leader Halleck's support was a two-year bill. The House Sept. 6 passed a bill (HR 9000) on a 378-32 roll call extending both programs for two years. Despite a last-minute plea from President Kennedy for a one-year extension, the Senate went along. President Kennedy Oct. 3 signed the bill (PL 87-344) "with extreme reluctance."

1962

President Kennedy asked Congress for a broad program of federal aid to education, but none of his major proposals was enacted. The President requested passage of his 1961 bill for grants for public elementary and secondary school construction and teachers' salaries, but because of the intensity of the 1961 fight over this request, neither the administration nor members of Congress made a major attempt to push general school aid in 1962.

Kennedy's 1962 education program also included a number of new proposals: grants to improve the quality of teaching, a program to combat adult illiteracy and special training for handicapped children. In addition, the President requested passage of programs left over from 1961 for educational television, aid for medical and dental education, aid for education of migrant workers and their children, and establishment of a Federal Advisory Council on the Arts. Of all these proposals, only that for educational TV was enacted.

Most of the Administration's bills were reported to the House Rules Committee, but died there. Because of the House bottleneck, and the fact that Chairman Lister Hill (D Ala.) of the Senate Labor and Public Welfare Committee was up for re-election against a staunch conservative, the Senate Committee took little action on the education program. In addition, some members complained that the administration had sent up too many bills, without establishing priorities.

Educational Television. PL 87-447 authorized a five-year, $32 million program of federal aid to educational television facilities. However, a supplemental appropriation bill (HR 13290) providing funds for fiscal 1963, passed by both houses, failed to get to conference before Congress adjourned, so no funds were provided. Congress did appropriate funds for fiscal 1964.

College Aid. Both houses passed a bill (HR 8900) to provide federal aid to higher education, but the House Sept. 20, by a 214-186 (D 84-156; R 130-30) roll call, voted to recommit the conference report to committee, where it died. The Senate version of HR 8900 provided loans for construction of college academic facilities, plus a program of federal scholarships, while the House bill provided both loans and grants to public and private colleges. The provision for grants to private colleges embroiled the measure in the church-state issue, while that for federal scholarships instigated opposition by a majority of House Republicans.

Loyalty Oath. Congress enacted a bill (HR 8556—PL 87-835) eliminating the non-Communist disclaimer affidavit requirements from the National Science Foundation Act of 1950 (PL 81-507) and the NDEA. Instead, the bill made it a criminal offense for any member of an organization ordered to register under the Subversive Activities Control Act of 1950 to apply for or use scholarships, loans or fellowships under either program. The bill continued the requirement in both Acts that applicants take a loyalty oath.

1963

In a turnabout from the previous year, Congress enacted bills which together authorized more than $2 billion for federal aid to education, a record which prompted President Johnson to refer to the "Education Congress of 1963." The measures constituted a large part of the broad education program, consisting of 25 specific proposals, requested in January by President Kennedy in an omnibus draft bill. However, the House and Senate committees considering the single administration bill divided it into several parts, a number of these —including those most directly affected by the church-state controversy—were not enacted.

Among the programs which the President requested but Congress did not pass were general public school aid, federal insurance of commercial student loans, establishment of a study group to assess the need for federal scholarships, programs to combat adult illiteracy, grants to improve teacher training and research, additional funds for public libraries and grants to expand university extension courses.

Congress did pass two programs related to education which had been requested by the administration but were not included in the President's education message. These provided aid to medical and dental schools and assistance for adult basic education as part of amendments to the Manpower Development and Training Act.

College Aid. HR 6143 (PL 88-204), the Higher Education Facilities Act of 1963, was passed Aug. 14 by the House on a 287-113 (D 180-57; R 107-56) roll-call vote and Oct. 21 by the Senate, 60-19 (D 41-11; R 19-8). The Act authorized a five-year program of federal grants and loans for construction or improvement of public and private higher education academic facilities, and authorized for the first three years of the program, beginning with fiscal 1964, appropriations of $1,195,000,000 as follows: annual appropriations of $230 million for matching grants to the states for construction, rehabilitation and improvement of undergraduate academic facilities; $25 million in fiscal 1964 and $60 million in each of fiscal years 1965 and 1966 for construction grants to graduate schools or cooperative graduate centers; and $120 million annually for loans to institutions for construction, rehabilitation or improvement of both undergraduate and graduate academic facilities.

Impacted Areas, NDEA. HR 4955 (PL 88-210) included three requests made by President Kennedy: A one-year extension, through June 30, 1965, of NDEA, with an increased authorization for student loans (from the existing $90 million to $125 million in fiscal 1964, $135 million in fiscal 1965, and such sums as were required in fiscal 1966-69); a two-year extension, through June 30, 1965, of expired impacted areas school aid laws; and an extensive vocational education measure. The bill was passed Aug. 6 by the House on a 378-21 roll-call vote and Oct. 8 amended, by the Senate on an 80-4 roll call. The conference report was agreed to Dec. 12 by the House by a 301-65 roll call and Dec. 13 by the Senate, 82-4 and the bill was signed into law Dec. 18.

1964

Congress added significantly to the major accomplishments of 1963 by enacting new education programs and extending and expanding several existing ones. Education legislation included a three-year extension of the NDEA and expansion of the program into important new academic subjects; a one-year extension of school aid programs to federally impacted areas; and enactment of a library services bill. These measures had been re-

quested by President Kennedy as part of his 1963 omnibus education bill. Other 1963 requests by Kennedy for an adult education literacy program and a work-study program providing part-time work for college students were incorporated into the Johnson Administration's anti-poverty bill.

In his Jan. 21, 1964, Budget message, President Johnson made seven other education requests, asking for: (1) increased educational opportunities for graduate students; (2) improved teacher training; (3) a program of library services and construction; (4) grants to raise teachers' salaries; (5) grants to construct classrooms; (6) a program of federally guaranteed student loans; and (7) a program of university extension services for adults. The first two requests were included in the NDEA amendments, as enacted, and the third was signed into law as a separate bill. The others did not reach the floor in either chamber.

NDEA, Impacted Areas. Extension and amendment of the NDEA and the impacted areas programs were combined into one bill (S 3060—PL 88-665) passed Aug. 1, 1964, by the Senate and Aug. 14 by the House by voice votes (PL 88-665). As enacted, the bill extended NDEA to June 30, 1968, and impacted areas to June 30, 1966. Impacted areas was broadened to cover the District of Columbia for the first time. Under the NDEA amendments, funds for teaching equipment and for teacher training institutes were expanded to include aid for new subjects—history, geography, civics and English— and the annual authorization for equipment was increased from $70 million to $90 million. The bill also raised NDEA student loans from the existing $135 million to $195 million by fiscal 1968, and fellowships from the current 1,500 annually to 7,500 by 1968; extended the provisions for cancellation of 50 percent of loans to college students who became public school teachers to include those who became private school or college teachers; extended stipends to private school teachers, as well as public school teachers, attending training institutes; raised grant authorizations for guidance, counseling and testing to $30 million a year by fiscal 1966-68, and for language development centers and institutes to $18 million by fiscal 1968; and provided a new authorization of $32,750,000 a year in fiscal 1965-67 for teacher training institutes for elementary and secondary school teachers.

Civil Rights. Title IV of the Civil Rights Act of 1964 authorized the Attorney General, under set conditions, to file suits for the desegregation of public schools and colleges. The Title also authorized the U.S. Office of Education to give technical and financial assistance of various types to local public school systems planning or going through the process of desegregation. Within the Office of Education, a $6 million budget was requested both for fiscal 1965 and for fiscal 1966 to finance training institutes and grant and assistance programs under Title IV. Under Title VI of the Act, school districts and institutions of learning which practiced segregation became ineligible for federal aid money. Education programs affected included college facilities construction, college dormitory construction, research grants and equipment, surplus materials distribution, national defense education activities, impacted areas funds, school lunch and school milk programs, vocational education, anti-poverty programs and loans to college students.

CHRONOLOGY OF EDUCATION LEGISLATION, 1965-72

The concept and dimension of federal aid to education expanded vastly during the administrations of Lyndon B. Johnson and Richard M. Nixon.

Congress in 1965 finally approved the nation's first general aid to education bill, the Elementary and Secondary Education Act (PL 89-10), which provided for more than $1-billion in aid to children in the nation's elementary and secondary schools. The bulk of the aid was authorized under Title I of the law, designed to aid school districts with large numbers of children from impoverished, or disadvantaged, homes. This aid-to-the-child approach skirted the question of aid to private and parochial schools, which had provoked heated controversy in Congress over school aid in previous years.

Congress in 1966 expanded the 1965 law to increase the number of disadvantaged students receiving aid. In 1967 Congress authorized extension of the programs through fiscal 1970 at a funding level of over $9-billion.

In 1970 Congress extended the programs for another three years, authorizing a total of $24.6-billion and again expanding the number of disadvantaged children eligible for aid under Title I.

Congress enacted another "first" in education aid in 1965, authorizing the first program of federal scholarships (grants) for college students as part of the eight-title $840-million Higher Education Act.

In 1968 Congress extended various programs of aid to higher education through fiscal 1971 (PL 90-575) after lengthy debate concerning proposals to penalize students who participated in campus disruptions.

And in 1972 Congress adopted the once-controversial assumption that every qualified student who needed aid to take advantage of the opportunity for post-secondary education should receive such aid, as a matter of right, from the federal government. In addition, in the sweeping 1972 Education Amendments (PL 92-318) Congress approved the first general aid to institutions, approving a program under which institutions of higher education would receive a certain amount in federal funds to be used for educating its federally aided students.

1965

Congress in 1965 authorized over $2 billion for revolutionary new education programs to help students and schools at the elementary, secondary, college and graduate levels. Although the first session of the 88th Congress in 1963 (labeled by President Johnson the "Education Congress") and the second session in 1964 had produced important new education legislation, the 89th Congress outdid its predecessor by enacting controversial programs that had been voted on and rejected for 20 years.

For the first time, Congress approved a general aid to education bill, the Elementary and Secondary Education Act, providing an initial $1.3 billion for the nation's elementary and secondary schools. Different versions of a general school aid program had been before Congress since World War II. Also enacted for the first time was a program of federal scholarships for college students. In the past, both of these programs had bogged down in bitter controversies, religious, racial and partisan.

The scholarships were part of numerous new programs authorized in the Higher Education Act. Included in the act were guaranteed loans to college students, grants for library books and materials and for university extension programs to combat urban problems, and funds to help small colleges.

Teachers, too, were singled out for special help. The act contained a graduate fellowship program for experienced and future teachers, and authorized a national Teacher Corps to improve classes in impoverished schools. As in the past, when conservatives regarded direct aid to teachers as a possible instrument for federal control of education, House Republicans opposed the Teacher Corps. The Corps was the only part of the entire education program which was blocked; though authorized for two years, it received no appropriations in 1965.

Later in the year, with presidential endorsement, Congress established the National Foundation on the Arts and the Humanities, providing federal grants to these fields of cultural and educational interest.

Poverty Theme. Passage of the Elementary and Secondary Education Act was attributed to the power of the large Democratic majority in Congress and the skill with which the administration and congressional leaders skirted the controversy over disbursing federal aid to parochial schools. Supporters of the bill successfully avoided the religious issue by emphasizing that aid would go to school children in needy areas and not to schools. The administration's hand was also strengthened by the absence of the racial issue which had provoked additional opposition in the past. This issue had been settled by passage of the 1964 Civil Rights Act, which forbade federal aid to schools that practiced racial discrimination.

Much of the credit for this achievement went to the "teacher who became President." President Johnson built his education program around the theme of poverty, drawing support from public concern over the problem of the poor in an affluent society. "Poverty has many roots," the President said in his education message, "but the taproot is ignorance."

The major share of funds under the elementary-secondary bill was to be distributed according to the numbers of impoverished pupils in school districts (although 95 percent of the nation's counties were eligible). The college scholarship program was for exceptionally needy students. The pre-school Project Head Start was actually part of the antipoverty program, enacted in 1964. The Teacher Corps was aimed at improving schools in impoverished areas. The aid program for small colleges was directed principally at impoverished Negro colleges.

Appropriations for the Office of Education in fiscal 1966 doubled the fiscal 1965 sum, rising from $1.5 billion to $3 billion.

ELEMENTARY AND SECONDARY EDUCATION

Elementary and Secondary Education Act. Congress and the President in 1965 broke through the impasse that had long stymied legislation to provide federal aid to elementary and secondary schools. The Elementary and Secondary Education Act that resulted (HR 2362—PL 89-10) authorized the first general school aid in the nation's history.

The President's victory was made possible after he abandoned the traditional proposals—across-the-board aid for school construction and teachers' salaries for all of the public school systems—in favor of general aid to districts with many children from low-income families. Furthermore, private schools were permitted to share in some of the federally aided services through special programs such as shared-time projects and educational television.

By using the "aid-to-children" approach and by providing some help to private school children, the bill avoided much of the crossfire over aid to church-related schools that had helped to kill past bills. The heavy Democratic majorities in Congress were able to overcome traditional Republican opposition to federal aid to education.

The ideas for the administration bill were contained in a report by a presidential task force headed by John W. Gardner, then president of the Carnegie Corporation and later in the year appointed secretary of HEW. Before the bill was sent to Congress, administration officials held many meetings with representatives for the National Education Association, which for years had opposed any aid to private schools while seeking broad federal support for public schools, and with Catholic and other interested groups. The administration aim was to win their prior approval of the bill so that it might go smoothly through Congress.

The President requested enactment of the bill in an education message Jan. 12. Acting swiftly, the House Education and Labor Committee held hearings and reported the bill favorably March 8, with minority views by all but two of the Republican members.

The House passed the bill March 26 by a 263-153 roll-call vote. It was opposed by the majority of Republicans and Southern Democrats but the large Northern Democratic contingent prevailed.

Within two weeks, the Senate Labor and Public Welfare Committee reported the bill without amendment, and three days later the Senate passed it and sent it to President Johnson for signature. The Senate vote April 9 was 73-18, with all three political groups supporting passage despite defeat of a number of Republican and Southern Democratic amendments.

Major Provisions—As enacted, the Elementary and Secondary Education Act (ESEA) contained five major titles. Total first-year cost of the bill was estimated at $1.4 billion. Of this, an estimated $1.1 billion was to be spent under Title I, which was designed to aid school districts with impoverished children. (It was expected that this would affect 95 percent of the nation's counties.) The program provided federal grants to the states (which would in turn distribute the funds to school districts) on the basis of the number of children from low-income (under $2,000 a year) families times 50 percent of each state's average expenditure per school child. The school districts could spend the funds in any way approved by state and federal educational agencies, but they had to take into account the needs of children who attended non-public schools.

The other four titles of HR 2362: authorized grants to states for purchases of textbooks and other library materials under which such books could be loaned to private schools; authorized grants for supplementary community-wide educational centers to provide services that individual schools could not provide; expanded the 1954 Cooperative Research Act to authorize grants for new research, training and research centers; and authorized grants to strengthen state departments of education.

The groundwork for enactment of the bill had been laid so well that congressional debate focused on the formula for providing aid rather than on the broad issue of providing federal aid for the first time. The major controversy was over the formula in Title I.

Throughout the legislative action, opponents said the administration method of multiplying half of a state's average expenditure per school child times the number of "low-income" pupils discriminated against the poorer states. They said it would be particularly hard on Southern school districts, which needed the most aid. Supporters of the administration formula responded that it provided for larger percentage increases in Southern school budgets, and that because it was much more expensive to educate a child in the North such a formula was necessary to aid school children in northern slums. Opponents in both chambers offered floor amendments to substitute a straight $200 grant for each impoverished child. In the House this was defeated on a 149-267 roll-call vote, and in the Senate it lost on a vote of 38-53.

Impacted Area Laws, Disaster Aid. ESEA technically was an amendment to the 1950 law (PL 81-874) that provided federal aid for school operations and maintenance in school districts "impacted" by the presence of federal installations and their employees and families. *(1950 law, p. 60)*

The least controversial section of the Elementary and Secondary Education Act law extended PL 874 for two years, through June 30, 1968. A related law (PL 81-815, authorizing funds for school construction) was scheduled to expire in 1966.

Late in 1965, Congress enacted the School Disaster Aid Act (HR 9022—PL 89-313), which included a major amendment of the impacted area laws. The amendment made a number of large cities eligible for funds by removing the requirement that school agencies with enrollments of more than 35,000 had to have 6 percent of their children "federally connected" to qualify for impact aid. Agencies with fewer than 35,000 students could qualify with 3 percent federally connected children, and PL 89-313 applied this percentage to all school districts. Among the cities that qualified under this provision were Boston, Baltimore, St. Louis, New Orleans and Los Angeles.

The disaster provisions of the law authorized federal funds to repair or rebuild public schools damaged in a federally recognized major disaster. Funds to help operate the schools for up to five years also were authorized. The program covered disasters between Aug. 30, 1965 and July 1, 1967.

Teacher Corps. Part B of Title V of the Higher Education Act of 1965, the Teacher Corps was the most controversial part of the new higher education bill *(see below)*. The idea of a corps of skilled teachers and young teachers-in-training who could be assigned to improve

White House Conference on Education, 1965

The need for better quality teaching in American schools, a shakeup of hidebound methods and a closer link between educational programs and social problems were the major themes of the 1965 White House Conference on Education, held July 20-21 in Washington, D.C.

The conference, the first in 10 years, was attended by 650 delegates from throughout the nation. Its chairman was John W. Gardner, president of the Carnegie Corp., who was named by President Johnson one week later as secretary of Health, Education and Welfare.

By design of its organizers, the conference was set up to preclude it from formally adopting any policy resolutions. President Johnson told the delegates the purpose of the meeting was to "stimulate some fresh thinking, not just talk about old ideas." Mr. Johnson said the chief problem in American education was "not merely more classrooms and more teachers, although we need them and we are going to have them," but "a fundamental improvement in the quality of American education....We are far too easily satisfied when we know that a child has a desk in a classroom with a teacher to instruct him. But it is what happens inside that classroom that really counts, and this is finally what is really important. And far too often what does happen is sadly unequal to what we have a right to expect."

During panel discussions, there was relatively wide agreement that education in the United States, to a far greater extent than could be considered acceptable, suffered from lack of imagination, lack of innovation and failure to develop new methods and approaches to meet emerging social problems. Many of the panelists agreed that the hidebound, unimaginative quality of much of American education left educators incapable of coping effectively with some of the most urgent problems of the day. The schools were said to be providing little leadership, in the North and South, in racial integration; they lacked both money and developed techniques for educating underprivileged and culturally deprived children, and were not doing enough for either gifted or handicapped students.

Some observers of the conference reported that the delegates were markedly more optimistic in their assessment of possible improvements than delegates to the 1955 conference had been.

---

education in slum schools was first advanced by Senators Edward M. Kennedy (D Mass.) and Gaylord Nelson (D Wis.). It was picked up by President Johnson, who incorporated it in his July 17 program to upgrade the training of elementary and secondary school teachers by federally financed fellowships.

Provisions for a Teacher Corps were added to the House-passed higher education bill (HR 9567) by the Senate. When the Corps was accepted by Democratic House conferees, the Republican House conferees refused to sign the conference report. They said the Corps would enable the government to exercise control over local schools.

During floor debate on the conference report, Rep. Albert H. Quie (R Minn.) moved to send the bill back to the conference committee with instructions to delete the Teacher Corps. The motion was defeated Oct. 20 by a 152-226 roll-call vote, with Republicans supporting the motion 111-7 and all but 41 Democrats opposing it.

When appropriations for the programs in the Higher Education Act were considered late in 1965, the Senate included $13.2 million for the Teacher Corps. The House conferees on the supplemental appropriations bill refused consent for any funds for the Corps and the bill was enacted without money for the Corps.

HIGHER EDUCATION

Higher Education Act. Featuring extensive aid for poor and middle-class students who wished to attend college, and new programs of graduate study for public school teachers, the Higher Education Act of 1965 was an eight-title $840-million bill. It embodied numerous requests of President Johnson, including the Teacher Corps he endorsed, and two programs initiated by Congress, raising funds authorized in 1963 for construction of college classrooms and granting financial aid to colleges for the purchase of classroom equipment.

The student-aid provisions authorized: federal scholarships of up to $800 a year for exceptionally needy students (the scholarships were called educational opportunity grants); funds to encourage state and private insurance programs for loans to students made by commercial lenders, with the students' interest costs subsidized by the government if their family income was less than $15,000 a year; transferred the work-study program for college students from the Office of Economic Opportunity to the Office of Education and removed the requirement that participating students must come from low-income families.

The teacher-aid provisions authorized federal fellowships for graduate study below the Ph.D. level for teachers, prospective teachers and other school personnel, including librarians, social workers and guidance specialists, among others. The number of fellowships was to begin at 4,500 a year and move up to 10,000 a year. To strengthen the universities' teacher education programs, the act provided payments to the institution of $2,500 per student, less fees charged him.

Other sections of the act authorized funds for: community service programs focusing on urban problems, to be conducted by colleges and universities; grants to improve college libraries and train librarians; a program to raise the academic quality of developing institutions—mainly small Negro colleges and semi-professional technical institutions—through federal grants and faculty exchanges with well-established colleges and universities; and equipment grants to improve classroom instruction in the sciences, humanities, arts and education.

NDEA. Included in the Higher Education Act were provisions amending the National Defense Education Act. The student loan section was amended to permit cancellation of loan repayments ("forgiveness") by students who taught in public or private schools eligible for federal aid under Title I of ESEA (schools with many children from low-income families). Fifteen percent of a loan could be forgiven for each year the student taught in such schools. Another amendment increased authorized funds under Title III of NDEA (which authorized equipment grants to lower schools for the teaching of specified subjects) to a total of $100 million, and added economics as a qualifying subject.

A third major amendment increased funds for Title XI (financing advanced teacher-training institutes) to a total of $50 million and made teachers of economics, civics and industrial arts eligible for the institutes.

College Classrooms. Title VII of the Higher Education Act amended the Higher Education Facilities Act of 1963. It removed the categorical restrictions of that act which had made federal funds available for construction only of classrooms and libraries in which science, mathematics, modern foreign languages or engineering were taught or studied. It also permitted transfers of allotments between junior colleges and four-year colleges within a state (the original act set aside 22 percent of the appropriations for exclusive use of two-year institutions) and reduced the interest rate on future classroom loans to a maximum of 3 percent (the going rate was then 3-7/8 percent). In addition, Title VII doubled the fiscal 1966 authorizations for undergraduate and graduate facilities grants.

College Housing. The interest rate on loans for construction of college dormitories (as well as classrooms, *above*) also was set at a maximum of 3 percent, over the objections of the administration and the Bureau of the Budget. The dormitory provision was in the Housing and Urban Development Act of 1965 (PL 89-117), which also authorized annual increases of $300 million for the college housing loan fund through fiscal 1969. The reduction of the interest rate, formerly about 3-7/8 percent, encouraged state universities to use the program for the first time, as 3 percent was lower than the rate then paid on state bond issues.

Programs for the Deaf. Two new laws for the deaf were enacted: a National Technical Institute for the Deaf (PL 89-36) and a program providing new educational media for the deaf (PL 89-258). (PL 89-36 authorized funds for construction and operation of a college to prepare deaf students for jobs in industry and other fields where special skills are required. PL 89-258 expanded a loan program of captioned films for the deaf to include other educational media, such as educational television with captions.

Arts and Humanities. Congress established a National Foundation on the Arts and the Humanities in order to develop for the first time a national policy of support for these activities. The act (PL 89-209) provided $20 million in fiscal 1966 to be granted to organizations and individuals engaged in the creative and performing arts, and to be granted or loaned for scholarships or research in the humanities. Part of the money was to match private donations. Similar amounts were authorized for fiscal 1967 and 1968.

The foundation was a three-part body. A Federal Council on the Arts and the Humanities, composed of nine federal officials (headed by the Secretary of the Smithsonian Institution), was to advise the chairmen of the arts and humanities endowments (who were members of the council) and to coordinate their activities with other undertakings of the federal government.

The endowments were autonomous organizations, each headed by a chairman, with an advisory council to help him. The National Council on the Arts, which Congress had established as an advisory group in 1964, became the advisory council of the National Endowment for the Arts.

The legislation, which was similar to a bill passed by the Senate in the previous Congress, had the support of President Johnson and passed the Senate by voice vote in June. Considerable opposition to it developed in the House.

It was reported by the House Education and Labor Committee over the opposition of 8 of the 10 Committee Republicans. Their minority views suggested that direct federal subsidies to the arts would lower the nation's "cultural level" and possibly lead to "attempts at political control of culture." Furthermore, they described the foundation as "an impenetrable thicket of duplication and overlapping."

The bill was held up in the House Rules Committee from July until September, when it was brought to the floor under the 21-day rule then in force, which allowed a legislative committee to bring a bill up for debate by majority vote if the Rules Committee had not granted a rule for debate within 21 days. After sharp arguments on the merits of the bill, the House Sept. 15 rejected on a 128-251 roll-call vote on a motion by then-Rep. Robert P. Griffin (R Mich.) to recommit (or kill) the bill. The "conservative coalition" of Republicans and southern Democrats voted to kill the bill but northern Democrats voted overwhelmingly for it.

The Senate accepted the House version of the bill Sept. 16, and President Johnson signed it into law (PL 89-209) Sept. 29. The first appropriation for the foundation was $10.7 million, more than $7 million less than the amount requested by the President.

1966

Congress in 1966, at President Johnson's request, enacted a measure (PL 89-750) expanding the Elementary and Secondary Education Act of 1965. The Act's strongest supporters in Congress were disappointed at the administration's efforts to hold down education costs in view of the budgetary demands of the Vietnam war, and Congress went beyond the President's proposals in several instances. The major presidential request that Congress rebuffed was an effort to cut in half the authorization for funds under the two 1950 programs (PL 81-815, 874) providing federal aid for schools in "impacted" areas. The administration sought $206 million for the program in fiscal 1967; Congress appropriated $439 million.

Late in the session, Congress enacted a $3.6-billion measure (PL 89-752) designed to increase aid for construction of college facilities, strengthen "developing institutions" and enlarge student loan programs. The Higher Education Amendments of 1966 corresponded closely to the President's proposals, except that Congress turned down his request to move away from direct federal funds for student loans.

The first funds for the Teacher Corps were appropriated.

ELEMENTARY AND SECONDARY EDUCATION

ESEA. The most important changes made by the 1966 legislation in Title I or ESEA expanded the scope of the program and made it more costly. In view of Vietnam costs, however, the changed formula was not to take effect for one year—in fiscal 1968. (Actually, only a part of the more generous formula, that helping the 15 poorest states, did take effect. *(See 1967 chronology.)*

One of the major changes in the 1966 amendments permitted any state to use the national average per pupil expenditure, if the national average were higher. This benefited the poorer states, which had sought a similar privilege when the act first was before Congress. It was expected to provide $343 million more to the poorer states in fiscal 1968. The second major change, the one that did not take effect, expanded the Title I program to include children whose families earned up to $3,000, rather than the existing limit of $2,000 a year. Unlike the first change, this was requested by the President. It was expected to provide Title I funds for an additional 300,000 children.

The 1966 law also increased authorizations for the other titles of ESEA, established a new program to aid in the education of handicapped children, and transferred the adult education activities of the Office of Economic Opportunity to the Office of Education in HEW.

Other changes repealed the act's incentive grant program, which authorized additional funds to school districts which substantially increased their educational spending (repealed on the ground it was not related to the poverty-orientation of the act), and provided special programs for children of Indians and migratory workers.

Congress also expanded Title I by including inmates of homes for neglected and delinquent children and children in foster homes and by requiring that in fiscal 1967 the most recent data be used to determine the number of children in a district who were receiving assistance under the Aid to Families with Dependent Children welfare program.

The 1966 bill weathered a sharp debate on school desegregation in the House. Southerners used it as a vehicle to express their opposition to guidelines for the desegregation of schools that had been issued by Education Commissioner Harold Howe II. An amendment by Rep. L. H. Fountain (D N.C.) prohibiting the commissioner from deferring federal grants to a school district until he had held hearings and established the district's noncompliance with desegregation rules was adopted on a 220-116 roll-call vote. The House also adopted an "anti-busing" amendment to ban any federal requirement for transporting children to achieve racial balance in schools. The administration said it had no busing plans, that such decisions were entirely up to local communities.

In the House-Senate conference on the bill, the "anti-busing" amendment was accepted and the desegregation amendment was modified considerably. It authorized deferral of funds for 90 days while a school district's alleged segregation practices were investigated and a decision on compliance reached.

As enacted, PL 89-750 authorized fiscal 1967 appropriations of $1.9 billion, but Congress followed up by actually appropriating only $1.4 billion.

Impacted Area Laws. The ESEA Amendments (PL 89-750) further liberalized the impacted area school laws instead of cutting them back as the administration proposed. The changes made districts with 400 federally connected children eligible for federal support of school operations under PL 81-874, even though they might not meet the law's requirement that 3 percent of the district's children be federally connected.

Also, the PL 81-815 construction law was extended through fiscal 1967 and its eligibility standards eased.

President Johnson had proposed amendments to the two laws that would have cut authorizations to $206 million. Instead, Congress authorized $490 million and appropriated $439 million.

Teacher Corps. The Corps received its first appropriation—$9.5 million—in May of 1966, plus a second appropriation, $7.5 million, in November for the fiscal year that began July 1, 1966. In the six months between the two appropriations, the future of the Corps was in great doubt, and it did not get its first director, Richard A. Graham, until November, when its life seemed more assured.

The House Appropriations Committee, in approving the first funds for the Teacher Corps, put two restrictions on its operations which Congress went on to ratify: (1) schools requesting the services of Corps members must have the approval of the state's education agency; and (2) federal financing must not exceed 90 percent of Corpsmen's salaries, with the local or state agency paying the remaining 10 percent.

HIGHER EDUCATION

College Classrooms. The Higher Education Amendments of 1966 (PL 89-752) authorized expenditures for undergraduate and graduate facility grants and loans in fiscal 1967-69. By fiscal 1969, 24 percent of the undergraduate grants had to be allotted to two-year community colleges or technical institutes.

NDEA. President Johnson, in his 1966 education message, proposed that NDEA student loans, which were a direct charge on the budget, be replaced by the 1965 act's federal interest subsidies and guarantees for loans from private lenders. The House rejected this proposal, and the administration then offered a new plan, based on sale of participations in federal loans. Under this plan, funds from the sale of participation certificates to private investors were to be merged with funds for regular NDEA loans. This proposal was accepted by the Senate but dropped in conference, largely because sales of participations in government-held loans had been suspended for the remainder of 1966 because of high interest rates in the private market.

Dropping the revised loan program meant that the existing NDEA program, which financed college loans to students at 3-percent interest, continued unchanged. Existing law authorized appropriations of $190 million in fiscal 1967 for direct student loans and Congress appropriated the full amount. In addition, it authorized an increase in the fiscal 1968 authorization for loans, from $195 million to $225 million.

Another NDEA amendment in PL 89-752 permitted total "forgiveness" of loan repayments if the recipient became a full-time teacher of handicapped children. Still another amendment added industrial arts as a subject qualifying for federal aid under the equipment grant section (Title III) of NDEA.

Student Veterinarians. PL 89-709, enacted Nov. 2, made students of veterinary medicine eligible for student loans under the Health Professions Educational Assistance Act of 1963. Veterinary schools also were made eligible for construction grants.

OTHER BILLS

Higher Education Act. The 1966 Amendments (PL 89-752) extended the Developing Institutions section (Title III) of the 1965 act through fiscal 1968. Only $5 million had been appropriated for the title's first year, fiscal 1966; the new law authorized $85 million for the next two years.

Library Assistance. 1966 brought a five-year extension of the Library Services and Construction Act of 1964. It also increased the act's authorizations for matching federal grants for library services and construction and added new grant programs for cooperative library networks within states and regions and for state institutions other than colleges and libraries.

The 1964 act had made federal funds available for the first time for urban libraries and for construction in both rural and urban areas. The 1966 extension (PL 89-511) increased the authorizations for services and construction (for which $55 million was appropriated in fiscal 1966) to $75 million in fiscal 1967, with annual increases of $20 million until the sum of $155 million was reached in fiscal 1971. The new grant programs in the act were much smaller. They were to start at $13 million and reach $37 million in fiscal 1971.

Appropriations in the first three years of the 1966 act did not reach authorized levels. In fiscal 1969, for example, the appropriation was $65 million compared to the authorized $140 million.

International Education. Congress, in the International Education Act of 1966 (HR 14643—PL 89-698), voted a $131-million program to strengthen international studies at American colleges and universities. But the program was killed by the House Appropriations Committee, which refused to approve funds to institute it in 1967, although the Senate approved a small sum.

The act was proposed by President Johnson, who said it would increase American students' awareness of foreign nations and their interest in serving abroad. Grants were to help establish or improve graduate centers of international studies and develop new courses at the undergraduate level.

HR 14643 was passed by the House June 6 on a 195-90 roll-call vote after opponents contended it was an opening move in an attempt to erase illiteracy in foreign lands. The bill's sponsor, Rep. John Brademas (D Ind.), emphasized that it dealt only with domestic education programs. There was no opposition in the Senate, where it passed by voice vote.

President Johnson signed the bill into law Oct. 29 at a ceremony held at a university in Bangkok, Thailand. He described PL 89-698 as "the first step" toward extending the goals of "the Great Society" to the rest of the world.

Cold War GI Bill. After seven years of consideration, Congress enacted the Veterans' Readjustment Benefits Act (PL 89-358), known as the Cold War GI Bill. It authorized a permanent program of educational and other benefits for veterans who served in the armed forces after Jan. 31, 1955. By its third year, the act was providing more federal support of college students than all other programs combined.

1967

Elementary and secondary education became entangled in the question of state vs. local planning of education programs, with the federal government cast as the whipping boy. Republicans proposed that funds for ESEA's largest programs be allotted as "block grants" to state departments of education, rather than directly to local school agencies that applied to the federal Office of Education. After big-city school superintendents and Catholic spokesmen joined administration forces to defeat the original block grants amendment of Rep. Albert H. Quie (R Minn.), a compromise was agreed to that affected only the innovative programs of Title III.

Several new programs were added to the act, including aid to children whose native language is not English, and dropout prevention activities; appropriations one year in advance of the school year were allowed for future education budgets. The bill as enacted (PL 90-247) authorized appropriations of more than $9.2 billion over a two-year period, including funds for federally impacted areas. Appropriations, however, turned out to be only half of what was authorized.

With far less controversy, Congress extended the Teacher Corps and expanded existing programs for teacher education. The administration's proposals for phasing out NDEA student loans in favor of greater reliance on private loans did not get beyond the hearing stage. The controversial plan to grant tax credits for the cost of college education won approval by the Senate for the first time, only to be dropped when the provision got caught in a parliamentary tangle with other, unrelated matters.

ELEMENTARY AND SECONDARY EDUCATION

ESEA. Congress Dec. 15 cleared the largest school assistance bill in the nation's history, the administration's Elementary and Secondary Education Amendments of 1967 (HR 7819—PL 90-247). The bill authorized appropriation of a total of $9,249,860,644 for fiscal 1969 and 1970 and added $132,884,000 to existing authorizations for fiscal 1968. Final congressional action came, barely an hour before adjournment of the session, when the conference report was approved by both chambers.

The bulk of the funds authorized in HR 7819—an estimated $2.7 billion in fiscal 1969 and $2.9 billion in fiscal 1970—was for federal aid to disadvantaged children under Title I of ESEA. The bill also extended authority for a number of existing programs, such as adult education, school library assistance and aid to state school departments, and it created several new programs, including additional grants for special education of handicapped children and aid to districts with non-English-speaking children.

HR 7819 provided that appropriations under the act could be made a fiscal year in advance. Thus, it authorized Congress in 1968 to vote appropriations for fiscal 1970 as well as fiscal 1969. The advance funding provision was designed to meet the objections of local school agencies that the school year was usually well under way before they knew how much federal money they would receive.

The scope of the bill far exceeded the original administration requests. However, the administration supported most of the changes, and passage of HR 7819 was one of President Johnson's major legislative accomplishments in the 1st session of the 90th Congress.

The bill had a rocky path through Congress. It was delayed for weeks in both chambers while major controversies were resolved.

Controversies—In the House, HR 7819 became the vehicle for a Republican attempt to substitute block grants to the states for the traditional direct categorical grants to the localities. Led by Rep. Albert H. Quie (R Minn.), a member of the House Education and Labor Committee, the Republicans contended that state education departments were better able to determine the needs of local school children than was the U.S. Office of Education and that red tape could be eliminated by channeling money through the states. The Administration argued that state agencies were not sufficiently staffed to handle the massive grant programs and that these agencies were unlikely to give urban areas their fair share. Furthermore, they said local school agencies were in the best position to plan their programs.

The Republicans received support in their efforts from the Council of Chief State School Officers and the U.S. Chamber of Commerce. But administration forces were able to muster powerful support from big-city school officials, labor and civil rights organizations and—most importantly—church groups.

Defeat of the Quie block-grant amendment could be traced directly to the fact that it raised the specter of the church-state issue, the very issue which had delayed passage of an aid-to-education bill for more than a decade. Catholic church leaders feared that laws in many states prohibiting aid to church schools would keep parochial school pupils from benefiting from the federal-aid programs if the money were channeled through the states. Catholic organizations and the church hierarchy lobbied heavily against the Quie proposal.

Quie's block-grant amendment was rejected May 24 by a 168-197 nonrecord (teller) vote when the Republicans failed to pick up substantial support from southern Democrats. The amendment would have given money under Titles I, II (library and textbooks), III (supplemental centers) and V (strengthening state agencies) to the states, to be distributed by the state departments of education according to a statewide plan. Quie would have changed the apportionment of Title I funds by allocating 50 percent, instead of the law's 80 percent, to areas with concentrations of children from low-income families.

After defeat of Quie's amendment, Republicans got behind amendments by Rep. Edith Green (D Ore.) placing all control of Title III and Title V funds in the state education departments.

Group Stands on Quie Amendment

The Republican "block grant" amendment to the elementary school bill evoked comment from a wide range of interest groups and individuals. The administration conducted a strong campaign against the measure, which was offered by Rep. Albert H. Quie (R Minn.).

Generally, the Quie amendment was opposed by national education groups, civil rights and some religious organizations as well as by school officials of large cities.

Supporting the amendment were many state school officials and school superintendents from small and middle-sized towns.

OPPOSED TO QUIE AMENDMENT

National Education Assn. (NEA)

U.S. Catholic Conference, Msgr. James C. Donohue, head of the education department. (The presidents of the National Council of Churches and Synagogue Council of America joined Donohue in a telegram opposing the amendment.)

Education bodies of the Baptist, Evangelical United Brethren, Episcopal and United Presbyterian Churches and the United Church of Christ.

American Council on Education (because there had not been hearings on the proposal)

National Congress of Parents and Teachers (PTA)

AFL-CIO Executive Council and American Federation of Teachers.

Citizens for Educational Freedom (representing parents of private school children, a large percentage of them Catholic)

Leadership Conference on Civil Rights

National Assn. for the Advancement of Colored People (NAACP)

American Assn. of University Women

Americans for Democratic Action (ADA)

Two former HEW Secretaries in the Eisenhower Administration, Arthur S. Flemming and Marion B. Folsom

New York City Mayor John V. Lindsay

New York State Commissioner of Education

California State Board of Education

California Assn. of School Administrators

School superintendents of New York City, Chicago, Detroit, Baltimore, San Francisco, Cleveland, Minneapolis, Atlanta and other cities.

SUPPORTING QUIE AMENDMENT

Council of Chief State School Officers

U.S. Chamber of Commerce

Governors of California, Colorado, Massachusetts, Montana, Nevada, Minnesota, South Dakota, Washington and Wisconsin (all Republicans)

State school superintendents of Arkansas, Colorado, Florida, Indiana, Kansas, Maine, North Dakota and Pennsylvania.

President of the Minn. Assn. of School Administrators.

National Union of Christian Schools (representing 280 Protestant schools)

Numerous school officials of small and medium-sized towns.

Southern Democrats played a key role in the voting. They helped defeat the Quie amendment and a GOP recommittal motion, supported Mrs. Green's amendments, and won several other votes of direct interest to the South. The latter included amendments that prohibited the government from withholding new funds from school districts on segregation charges until after a hearing and a ruling of violation; changed the formula for Title I grants to impoverished school districts so that the poorer states would get more money; and directed that desegregation guidelines be applied uniformly in the North and South.

Anticipating that appropriations for Title I programs would be smaller than was authorized under the 1966 revision of the formula, the House May 24, by a 222-194 roll-call vote, adopted an amendment to the authorization bill that awarded more money to the 15 poorer states at the expense of the 35 richer states. The amendment, sponsored by Sam M. Gibbons (D Fla.) retained one part of the 1966 revision, overruling the Education and Labor Committee which had voted to delay both parts of the revision. Gibbons' amendment permitted state allotments for Title I funds to be computed on the basis of one-half the state average expenditure per pupil or one-half the national average, whichever was higher, multiplied by the number of pupils from families making less than $2,000 a year.

Thirty-five states, including Florida, were entitled to less money under the Gibbons amendment than they were under the committee bill. And six of them actually were to receive less appropriated money than they received in fiscal 1967.

However, the Labor-HEW appropriation bill (HR 10196), passed the next day, provided that no state was to be allotted less money than it received in fiscal 1967. Since the fiscal 1968 Title I appropriations in HR 10196 were $137.6 million more than fiscal 1967 funds, most states received a small increase over 1967 and most southern states received a substantial increase. The largest single increase in funds was in Mississippi, which received $23.5 million in funds in fiscal 1967 and $44.8 million in fiscal 1968.

Senate Action—On Nov. 6, more than five months after House passage, the Senate Labor and Public Welfare Committee reported the ESEA Amendments bill. The committee provided for advanced appropriations, reinstated a program of incentive grants to states that spent more than the national average for education and included a number of new programs, among them additional grants to aid handicapped children, school dropouts and children from non-English-speaking backgrounds. These later were accepted by the House.

The Senate committee watered down Mrs. Green's block grant amendment for Title III funds, which HEW Secretary John Gardner and Education Commissioner Harold Howe II had vigorously opposed. On the Senate floor, an effort by Sen. Strom Thurmond (R S.C.) to get the Green amendment adopted without change was narrowly defeated, 35-38. In conference with the House, the Senate accepted the amendment, effective in fiscal 1970.

The bill was delayed for one month in reaching the floor by a threatened filibuster to reinstate a House anti-desegregation amendment sponsored by Rep. Fountain (D N.C.) and a proposed anti-busing amendment

by Minority Leader Everett McKinley Dirksen (R Ill.). Eventually, both issues were compromised by agreement with the Administration.

Major Provisions—Amendments to Title I allowed states to use the national expenditure per pupil in determining their allotments; set out priorities if appropriations fell short of the full amount allowed under the formula (handicapped or migrant children and those in state institutions were to receive their full entitlements); and re-authorized incentive grants for states that spent above-average proportions of their revenues for education, effective in fiscal 1969.

Title III grants for supplementary centers were to be made according to state plans and, as of fiscal 1970, were to be entirely allotted by the state education agency. All but 5 percent of the funds under Title V were to be allocated by state agencies.

New programs established in the 1967 law authorized: a bilingual education project for children from non-English-speaking backgrounds, with additional fellowships awarded for teachers of these children; pilot projects to develop effective programs to prevent school dropouts; and technical assistance to rural schools that wished to apply for federal aid.

Other amendments to ESEA: authorized advance appropriations for programs under the Act; required that 15 percent of Title III funds be spent on programs for handicapped children; authorized a small number of service centers for children who were both deaf and blind; and continued indefinitely the federal government's 90 percent share of the cost of adult education projects.

Impacted Area Laws, Disaster Aid. The ESEA bill extended the two impacted area laws (PLs 81-815 and 874) and the disaster relief law (PL 89-313), with minor amendments, through fiscal 1970.

Teacher Corps, Fellowships. The House June 27 and the Senate June 28 passed, and the President signed into law the next day, an administration-backed bill (HR 10943—PL 90-35) extending the Teacher Corps through fiscal 1970. Called the Education Professions Development Act, the Act extended Title V of the Higher Education Act of 1965, including the Teacher Corps and a teacher fellowship program, and created four new teacher-training programs effective in fiscal 1969.

The rapid-fire action of House passage, Senate passage and the President's signature on successive days resulted from the urgency of authorizing the Teacher Corps before June 30, the end of fiscal 1967.

Congress May 25 had approved $3,823,700 for the Corps in the Second Supplemental Appropriations Act for fiscal 1967 (HR 9481). But HR 9481 specified that the funds would lapse if the Corps were not authorized for fiscal 1968 before June 30.

For the first time in its uncertain life, the Teacher Corps was supported by a majority of House Republicans. A key roll-call vote was taken on a motion that would have killed the Corps; the motion lost, 146-257, with Republicans divided 83-95. Committee amendments ensuring local control of the Corps played an important part in reducing opposition to the program, and inclusion of other teacher-training projects in the bill helped to gather support for it.

HR 10943 authorized $135 million for the Corps in the fiscal years 1968-70. In addition, it authorized $435 million in the fiscal years 1969-70 for the Higher Education Act's graduate fellowships for elementary and secondary school teachers and grants to colleges and universities to help them improve their graduate education facilities.

HR 10943 authorized also four new programs to begin in fiscal 1969: (1) grants to assist local education agencies, under a state plan, to carry out programs to attract and qualify teachers and teacher aides in areas that were short of teachers; (2) grants for preservice and in-service training of persons in elementary and secondary education; (3) fellowships and other training for college and university teachers and administrators and (4) a small program of grants for the purpose of attracting qualified persons into the field of education. With the exception of the first (teacher shortage) program, all of these programs were proposed by the administration. The teacher shortage program was added to the bill on the initiative of the House Special Subcommittee on Education.

Later in the year, in the annual appropriations bill for the Departments of Labor and HEW, Congress provided $13.5 million for the Teacher Corps in fiscal 1968. The House, which passed the appropriations bill before the Teacher Corps authorization had cleared Congress, provided no money. The Senate later voted $18.1 million, after narrowly defeating, on a 43-45 roll-call vote, an amendment to provide the full $33 million the Administration had requested. The compromise $13.5 million figure was arrived at by House-Senate conferees.

House Controversy—The Education Professions Development Act (HR 10943) was put together by a subcommittee headed by Rep. Edith Green (D Ore.), a past critic of the Teacher Corps but an ardent friend of the teaching profession. The bill included several provisions designed to "localize" control of the Corps.

When the bill was brought to the floor June 27, the House defeated, by a 62-108 teller vote, an amendment offered by Edward J. Gurney (R Fla.) eliminating the Teacher Corps provisions from the bill. Later it rejected, by a 146-257 roll-call vote, a Gurney motion to recommit the bill to the Education and Labor Committee with instructions to delete the Corps provisions. Gurney, a member of the committee, charged that Republicans had "helped put a dress of respectability" on the Teacher Corps, but it was still "the miniskirt and bikini bathing suit of the Great Society—in other words...a federally oriented elite group of teachers financed by federal money."

However, Gurney was opposed by a bipartisan majority. Rep. Albert H. Quie (R Minn.), a committee member, said he had opposed the Teacher Corps in the past because of the control over it held by the U.S. commissioner of education. But he could support it now, Quie said, because the bill shifted control to the states and local school districts.

Major Provisions—As enacted, PL 90-35 authorized $33 million in fiscal 1968, $46 million in fiscal 1969 and $56 million in fiscal 1970 for the Teacher Corps. Had the full funds been appropriated, this would have provided for 6,000 volunteers in fiscal 1968, 7,500 in fiscal 1969 and 9,600 in fiscal 1970.

The provisions designed to "localize" the Teacher Corps deleted "National" from the title; provided that local agencies, rather than the commissioner, were to "recruit, select and enroll" the volunteers; specified that local districts were to pay at least 10 percent of the Corps members' salaries; assured that no more volunteers than were requested would be sent into any state; required the approval of the state education agency before Corps members were sent to a local district; and set the salary for teacher interns at $75 a week plus $15 for each dependent, or the lowest rate paid a teacher in the school district, whichever was less (experienced teachers in the Corps received their regular salaries).

HIGHER EDUCATION

Tax Credit for College Costs. For the first time in three tries, the Senate in 1967 voted to allow a tax credit for expenses of a college education. Adopted by a 53-26 vote, the amendment was attached to an unrelated House bill that became so encumbered with Senate amendments that it was recommitted to committee and stripped of all extraneous amendments, including the tax credit. Thus the House had no opportunity to vote on the question.

For several years congressional Republicans had advocated a tax credit for college expenses. The party's 1964 platform pledged enactment of "tax credits for those burdened by the expenses of college education."

Democratic administrations opposed the idea, both for budgetary reasons and for its alleged discrimination in behalf of the more prosperous parents of students.

The House Ways and Means Committee never acted on tax credit bills, but the issue was voted on in the Senate in 1964, 1966 and 1967. Each time the chief sponsor was Sen. Abraham A. Ribicoff (D Conn.), who was President Kennedy's first secretary of Health, Education and Welfare (1961-62).

Ribicoff introduced his 1967 bill (S 835) Feb. 6, with 46 cosponsors. Realizing that its best chance of enactment would be by attachment to a House-passed bill wanted by the administration, Ribicoff April 14 offered it as an amendment to the House-passed bill (HR 6950) restoring the tax credit on business investments.

Ribicoff's amendment was agreed to by the Senate on a 53-26 roll-call vote. The party breakdown on the vote was: R 25-5; D 28-21 (ND 22-12; SD 6-9). It was the first time in three votes on the proposal that a majority of northern Democrats supported the tax credit. Republicans had overwhelmingly supported it each time and southern Democrats regularly opposed it. When the tax credit was first voted on, in 1964, it lost on a 45-48 vote. In 1966 the margin of defeat was larger, 37-47.

Under Ribicoff's bill, students, their parents or others who helped pay their way through college were entitled to deduct up to $325 a year from their income tax payments. The tax credit was on a sliding scale that allowed deduction of 75 percent of the first $200 of college expenses, 25 percent of the next $300 and 10 percent of the next $1,000. The credit was to be reduced by 1 percent of the taxpayer's adjusted income over $25,000 so that there would be no credit for persons with income over $57,500.

A substitute proposal by Sen. Winston L. Prouty (R Vt.) that would have given a proportionately greater credit to poorer taxpayers was defeated on a 16-63 vote.

Ribicoff's amendment was subsequently deleted from HR 6950. So many extraneous amendments had been attached to the bill that Senate Majority Leader Mike Mansfield (D Mont.) moved to send it back to committee with instructions that all amendments be stripped from it. The Senate agreed to Mansfield's motion April 25.

Views on College Tax Credit

Senate debate on Ribicoff's amendment brought out the following contentions:

Pros. Those in favor of a tax credit for college students argued it would be the most effective way to help meet college expenses. "Fairness demands that the Congress recognize the need to give a tax break to the ordinary American taxpayer who faces today's enormous cost of higher education," Ribicoff told the Senate April 14. He said opinion polls had shown the public overwhelmingly in favor of such legislation.

Ribicoff said the revenue loss in fiscal 1968 would be less than $600 million and "might rise to $1.3 billion" by 1970. He contended this money would be more than paid back to the government in years to come since the educated recipients could be expected to earn a higher income and thus pay higher taxes than they otherwise would pay.

The proponents said a tax credit would aid the institutions as well as the students by allowing the colleges to raise their tuition. They said it also would encourage persons not related to a student to help one through college since a tax credit could be claimed. Further, Ribicoff contended, it would free graduates of the indebtedness that causes many to take jobs on the basis of immediate pay and would encourage teachers and others to take graduate training.

Cons. The administration and its supporters opposed the tax credit on four grounds: (1) The Treasury estimated it would cost $1.1 billion in lost taxes in the first year and up to $1.5 billion by the third year. In the face of an expected budget deficit of nearly $10 billion in fiscal 1967 and $8 billion in fiscal 1968, the nation was said not to be able to afford the additional revenue loss. (2) The individual taxpayer would not be helped in the long run because institutions would immediately increase tuition charges beyond what they felt they currently could demand. (3) The Ribicoff bill amounted to "class legislation" because it applied only to those with sufficient means to pay taxes. (4) The $325 maximum would hardly make a dent in student expenses.

In the House, more than 60 college tax credit bills were referred to the Ways and Means Committee in 1967. Most of these were introduced by Republicans.

Library Services. A one-year extension of full federal financing of the three new library programs authorized in 1966 was provided in PL 90-154. The programs were for interlibrary cooperation, state institutional libraries and services for the physically handicapped.

The 1966 law had required the state and local governments to pay 50 percent of the costs of the programs after June 30, 1967. PL 90-154 extended the effective date to June 30, 1968. Committee reports noted that many states had not had time to complete plans for matching the federal contributions.

For fiscal 1968 Congress appropriated $5,815,000 for the three programs.

Work-Study Program. A stop-gap bill (PL 90-82) was enacted setting the federal share of the cost of college work-study grants for 1968-1970. Had the legislation not been enacted, the federal share would have dropped from 90 percent to 75 percent, beginning Aug. 20, 1967.

PL 90-82 set the federal share at 85 percent until Aug. 20, 1968, at 80 percent for the next year, and at 75 percent thereafter. (This was changed in 1968.) The bill also allowed some variation in students' work periods by setting the maximum as an average of 15 hours a week per semester.

1968

Concerned at the rising federal budget deficit, and outraged at violent disturbances on college campuses, Congress in 1968 zigged and zagged on education programs. It cut appropriations for assistance to underprivileged elementary, secondary and college students but went beyond the budget request for the popular "impacted area" programs. Then it barred the executive branch from reducing education expenditures to meet the over-all spending ceiling Congress imposed on the entire government.

Reacting to campus riots, Congress enacted three conflicting provisions forbidding federal aid to students who took part in disturbances. The resulting confusion left administrators in a quandary as to how the three laws should be enforced.

For the first time in four years, no new elementary or secondary school programs were enacted, but an extensive higher education bill was passed. Experimental programs to help handicapped children of pre-school age were authorized in a separate bill. Legislation on the National Science Foundation and arts and humanities also was enacted.

ELEMENTARY AND SECONDARY EDUCATION

ESEA Funds. Appropriations for Title I of ESEA, the key section aiding disadvantaged school children, dropped below the previous year's level. Congress had appropriated $1,191 million for Title I in fiscal 1968; for fiscal 1969 the total fell to $1,123 million, $77 million less than the budget request. For the entire ESEA appropriation Congress approved $1,477 million, a cut of $200 million below fiscal 1968 figures. Two programs authorized in 1967 received their first appropriations: bilingual education, $7.5 million, and dropout prevention, $5 million.

The advance appropriation for Title I, first authorized in the 1967 law, was carried in the fiscal 1969 appropriation bill (HR 18037—PL 90-557). The bill provided $1,010 million for fiscal 1970, in the expectation that more could be added the following year when the regular fiscal 1970 appropriations were considered.

School Desegregation—A serious attack on HEW's authority, under the Civil Rights Act, to withhold funds from school districts clinging to segregation was barely beaten off in the House. In the end, the House narrowly reversed its position on an amendment by Rep. Jamie L. Whitten (D Miss.) to protect southern "freedom of choice" plans from HEW efforts to require full desegregation of schools. On June 26 the House adopted Whitten's amendment by a 137-101 teller vote. After the Senate rejected the amendment, the House retreated from its position and on a key 167-156 roll-call vote, Oct. 3, accepted the

Senate's milder language. Congress, however, required HEW to assign as many desegregation investigators to northern states as it did to the 17 southern and border states.

Impacted Areas. Once again the President sought to reduce the burden of aid to schools in federally impacted areas. That aid, he said, failed to reach some of the neediest school districts while assisting some that least needed federal help. Johnson proposed an appropriation of $410 million, $120 million less than the fiscal 1968 figure; Congress appropriated $521 million.

Handicapped Children. In HR 18763—PL 90-538, Congress authorized experimental programs to help handicapped children of pre-school age. Committee reports said that funds for education of handicapped children as authorized in Title VI of ESEA were not used in many states, or could not be used under state laws, for children of pre-school age.

PL 90-538, the Handicapped Children's Early Education Assistance Act, authorized the U.S. commissioner of education to make contracts with public or private non-profit agencies for experimental programs. The federal government would pay 90 percent of the costs of each project. The law authorized appropriations of $1 million in fiscal 1969, $10 million in fiscal 1970 and $12 million the next year.

HIGHER EDUCATION

Higher Education Amendments. Late in the year, Congress cleared the Higher Education Amendments of 1968 (S 3769—PL 90-575), which extended through fiscal 1971 the various titles of the Higher Education Act, the National Defense Education Act (NDEA) and the Higher Education Facilities Act. There was little controversy over the bill; proposals to penalize riotous students consumed most of the debate.

Earlier in the year a stop-gap bill (PL 90-460) extended the guaranteed loan program for students, which was due to expire June 30. It also raised the maximum interest on guaranteed loans to 7 percent. These provisions were continued in the three-year Higher Education Amendments bill (PL 90-575).

Higher Education Act—All titles of the act were extended and four new titles were added: Networks for Knowledge, encouraging colleges to share their educational facilities and equipment (Title VIII); Education for the Public Service, graduate training for governmental jobs (Title IX); Improvement of Graduate Programs, encouraging training at the Ph.D. level (Title X); and Law School Clinical Experience, to train more trial lawyers (Title XI).

In addition, a new program was added to Title IV of the act, the student assistance section. The new program provided grants to encourage colleges to establish cooperative education programs. These were defined as programs providing for alternate periods of full-time study and full-time employment so that students could earn money to continue their education and gain job experience at the same time.

Other amendments to Title IV: raised the maximum educational opportunity grant (federal scholarship) to $1,000 and removed the $200 bonus allowed students who placed high in their class; set the federal share of work-study grants at 80 percent; transferred the Upward Bound

program from the Office of Economic Opportunity to the Office of Education, effective July 1, 1969; authorized grants to colleges to provide special services (such as tutoring) to help disadvantaged students stay in college, and consolidated the two programs with the Office of Education's Talent Search program, which encouraged disadvantaged youths to attend college or take other post-high-school training.

The insured loan program in Title IV also was amended. The permissible interest rate was raised to 7 percent, the federal subsidy allowed to students after they completed college was removed, and a new federal guarantee program to cover 80 percent of any losses on student loans insured by nonfederal agencies was authorized.

In amendments to other titles of the act, PL 90-575 raised the federal share of community service projects (Title I) to two-thirds of the cost instead of one-half, and authorized grants to retired professors who wished to teach at small developing institutions (Title III).

NDEA—The NDEA student loan program, equipment grants, guidance and testing, and language development programs were extended with minor changes. The fellowship program's cost-of-education grants to universities were raised to a maximum $3,500 per fellowship to correspond to payments allowed under the Higher Education Act.

A large new equipment grant program was added to Title III. This was earmarked for schools with large concentrations of poor children, those eligible for aid under Title I of ESEA. This program was authorized for only two years, through fiscal 1970.

Title VII of NDEA, grants for educational media, was allowed to expire.

College Classrooms—The grant and loan provisions of the Higher Education Facilities Act were extended until fiscal 1971 and a new program of federally subsidized interest on private loans for construction was authorized. For the grant programs the federal share of costs was raised to 50 percent (it was previously 40 percent for junior colleges and 33-1/3 percent for four-year colleges).

International Education—PL 90-575 extended the International Education Act of 1966, which had never been funded, through fiscal 1971, at $90 million annually.

Other Provisions—The 1968 Amendments also carried three general provisions of importance. They:

• Called for a presidential report on the feasibility of making post-secondary education available to all who were qualified and wanted it.

• Permitted higher education funds to be appropriated one year in advance of the fiscal year in which they would be used.

• Required colleges and universities to deny federal aid to students who engaged in substantial disruption of the institution. *(See section below for a discussion of conflicting anti-riot provisions in other bills.)*

College Housing. The Housing and Urban Development Act of 1968 (PL 90-448) authorized a new program to relieve the government of the growing demand for federal loans for college housing. It authorized annual grants subsidizing the difference between interest on a loan secured from private sources and the 3 percent rate charged on direct federal loans. The HUD Department could sign contracts for up to $10 million annually with colleges and universities for interest subsidies in fiscal 1969 and 1970, subject to limits set in appropriation bills.

Higher Education Appropriations, Teacher Corps.
In appropriating almost $1 billion for higher education
programs in fiscal 1969 Congress followed the President's
lead in cutting back funds from the fiscal 1968 level. Although the total was $282 million less than the previous
year's, a few programs were given increased funds. One
was the Teacher Corps, which went up from $13.5 million
to $20.9 million. The President had requested $31,235,000.

Educational opportunity grants (federal scholarships)
received a severe cut. Of the $159.6 million requested by
the President, Congress appropriated only $124.6 million.
This meant a cut of 75 percent in the number of freshmen
who could receive federal grants in the next school year,
because the appropriation had to cover the second, third
and fourth years of college for those who already had
received grants. The number of freshmen receiving grants
was expected to go down from 144,600 to 31,300.

National Science Foundation. The Senate in 1968
passed with minor changes a bill (HR 5404) which the
House had passed the previous year. It became law (PL
90-407) July 18.

The bill clarified the organizational structure of the
NSF, expanded the scope of its activities, and required
that each year Congress pass an authorization bill for the
agency before appropriating funds for it. This practice was
followed for other scientific agencies, such as the Atomic
Energy Commission and the space agency, NASA.

PL 90-407 allowed the NSF to support applied—as
well as basic—research, and research in the social sciences
as well as the natural sciences. The foundation was
directed to keep track of the whereabouts of all federal
funds allocated for scientific research and to make an
annual report.

The director of the foundation was given authority
over all management and operations of the NSF, with the
foundation board relieved of its authority over operations
but kept responsible for overseeing broad policies.

PL 90-407 authorized appropriations of $525 million
for the NSF in fiscal 1969. However, the Independent
Offices appropriation bill (HR 17023—PL 90-550) allowed
the agency only $400 million, which was $100 million less
than the President's request.

Arts and Humanities. The House Education and
Labor Committee tried in 1968 to give the National Foundation on the Arts and the Humanities a large increase in
funds, but the final result was a two-year extension at
about the funding level of previous years (HR 11308—PL
90-348).

The House committee's bill authorized federal grants
of $135 million for the two fiscal years 1969 and 1970, but
the authorization was decimated on the House floor. By a
118-65 teller vote, the House accepted an amendment
reducing the authorization to $11.2 million for one year.
There was little opposition to the Foundation's activities;
it was the economy issue that carried the day.

The Senate raised the authorization to $34 million
for a two-year period, and the House agreed to this figure
on a 194-166 roll-call vote June 5. In addition, the bill
authorized the government to match up to $13.5 million
in private gifts to the foundation.

The appropriation for the foundation in fiscal 1969,
carried in the Interior Department and Related Agencies
bill (PL 90-425), was $11.5 million, half of what the Presi-
dent had requested before passage of HR 11308.

A related program, authorizing HEW grants for
equipment to be used in the study of the arts and humanities, was extended for three years at an annual authorization of $500,000. The provision was in the Higher Educa-
tion Amendments (PL 90-575).

RESTRAINTS ON STUDENTS

Congress in 1968 enacted five measures designed to
cut off federal aid to students engaging in crimes or other
activities which disrupted the operations of institutions of
higher learning. Three of the laws had conflicting provisions.

The action came in response to a number of disorders
on university campuses, notably at Columbia University.
The sentiment in Congress apparently overwhelmingly
favored condemnation of the student demonstrators; but
there was less agreement on what to do about it.

Conservatives adopted a hard line and sought to enact provisions requiring the cutting off of federal aid to
students engaged in the prohibited activities. Liberals
tended to give academic institutions some discretion in
determining when aid should be withheld. The Senate
leaned more toward the liberal view on that issue and the
House leaned more toward the conservative view.

Another point at issue was whether the institution or
the federal agency administering the aid program should
oversee administration of the aid cut-off provisions. Still
another was whether a hearing should be afforded the
student before his aid was withheld.

As a consequence, Congress enacted various forms of
the aid cut-off provisions. Some measures provided for
hearings, others did not; some placed the burden of administration on the university, others on the federal agency;
some required that the student be convicted of a crime,
while others said he need be found only to have disobeyed
a lawful regulation or order of the university resulting in
disruption of its operations; and one measure, the NASA
authorization (PL 90-373), cut off funds to colleges prohibiting on-campus recruiting by armed forces representatives. Only one such college (Oberlin) appeared to have
such regulations.

Civil libertarians contended that constitutional issues
of academic freedom and free speech were raised by the
aid cut-off provisions. They said that the provisions were
unconstitutionally vague, failed to provide for due process
and delegated uncontrolled discretion to university officials. A number of university presidents spoke out in
opposition to the measures.

Student Unrest. From Berkeley in 1964 to Columbia
in 1968, students forcefully made their presence felt on
many college campuses across the country. They were
bothered by impersonalization at large institutions, angered
by American involvement in Vietnam and concerned about
racial problems in the cities. They also demanded a
greater voice in determining university policies.

Unruly demonstrations began on the Berkeley campus
of the University of California in 1964 when students protested campus restrictions on political activities. During
the next four years the student movement mushroomed,
and within the first two months of the 1967-68 academic
year, the National Student Association reported 71
student protests on campuses across the country. By the
end of the school year more than 100 demonstrations
had been held.

Possibly the worst eruption occurred at Columbia University where student occupation of buildings and a student strike kept the campus in turmoil most of the time from late April through May. Ostensibly the issue involved construction of a new gymnasium on the edge of a city park used by residents of nearby Harlem, but underlying it was the demand for more student participation in university policy decisions. Before the university quieted, 897 students were arrested and 216 students, faculty members and policemen were injured.

Conflicting Bills. Three bills enacted in 1968 had conflicting provisions on student rioters. They were the Independent Offices-HUD appropriations bill (PL 90-550), which carried funds for National Science Foundation grants, the Labor-HEW Departments appropriations bill (PL 90-557), which provided funds for college student loans and scholarships, and the Higher Education Amendments of 1968 (PL 90-575), extending student-aid programs for three years. In addition, the defense appropriations bill carried the same language as the Labor-HEW bill, and the NASA authorization, referred to above, was concerned with colleges that barred recruiters for the armed forces.

Action on the bills with conflicting provisions is described below.

NSF Funds—In fiscal 1968, more than 14,000 graduate students received grants, loans, scholarships or fellowships from the National Science Foundation.

When the House considered the Independent Offices-HUD appropriations bill, which carried funds for the NSF, Rep. Louis C. Wyman (R N.H.) won acceptance May 8 of an anti-rioter amendment. The amendment prohibited payment of NSF funds to any student "who willfully refuses to obey a lawful regulation of the university or college which he is attending."

In reporting the bill July 9, the Senate Appropriations Committee toned down the Wyman amendment by requiring that a hearing be afforded students before funds could be stopped. Also added were sections placing the burden of withholding funds on the university, rather than on the scholarship or loan funding agency, and stipulating that the student's actions must have been of a serious nature and must have contributed to the disruption of the administration of a university.

In September the Senate version was agreed to by both chambers.

Higher Education Amendments—The Senate Labor and Public Welfare Committee reported S 3769 July 11 with a provision urging universities to "take immediate and prompt action to apply disciplinary measures, whether by withholding financial aid offered through federal programs, by other measures, or by both." The report stated that the right to withhold funds and the duty of maintaining discipline should be vested in the college itself, not in the federal government.

In considering HR 15067 (S 3769), the House July 25 by a 260-146 roll-call vote accepted an amendment by William J. Scherle (R Iowa) requiring colleges to withhold funds, rather than giving them the option to cut off aid, from students disrupting campus activities. Other restrictions also were added by the House. An effort to delete the entire restrictive section was defeated by an 18-109 vote.

S 3769 was reported out of conference Sept. 25 and passed by both chambers with substantial changes soften-

Aid to College Students

Following are the major federal financial programs enabling students to attend college. This does *not* include the new programs authorized by the Education Amendments of 1972 (PL 92-318) which would not be in operation until the 1972-1973 school year at the earliest. All are administered by the Office of Education with the exception of the Cold War GI Bill, which is administered by the Veterans' Administration.

Cost figures are in millions of dollars.

	Fiscal 1968		Fiscal 1971	
	Students	Cost	Students	Cost
Educational opportunity grants	292,600	$131.4	290,500	$167.7
NDEA direct loans	429,000	181.8	560,400	243.0
Insured loans	515,408	39.9	1,087,000	143.2
Work-study grants	375,000	133.8	430,000	158.4
Special programs for disadvantaged students:				
Upward Bound	25,368 }	35.4	24,200 }	50.1
Talent Search	115,000 }		207,000 }	
Cold War GI Bill	471,696	428.7	917,000	1,068.0
TOTALS	2,224,072	$951.0	3,516,100	$1,830.4

SOURCE: Federal Budget, fiscal 1973, and H Report 92-99.

ing the House-imposed restrictions on student aid and on payments to employees of the institution. It provided that the burden of cutting off funds be placed on the university, rather than the federal government; that the university afford notice and opportunity for a hearing before aid was withheld; that the student or employee be convicted in court of a crime involving use of force, or be found to have disobeyed a lawful regulation or order of the institution, resulting in disruption of the university; and that funds be denied such a student or employee for a two-year period.

HEW Funds—Appropriations for all programs of the U.S. Office of Education and HEW health activities were carried in the Labor-HEW bill.

As reported by the Appropriations Committee and passed by the House June 26, it was specified that no funds appropriated by the bill could be used to aid any student convicted of using force to disrupt a college or university.

In Senate floor consideration of the bill Sept. 6, debate focused on where power should be vested for cutting off student aid funds. Jacob K. Javits (R N.Y.) and Wayne Morse (D Ore.) each sponsored amendments delegating power to the universities, rather than to the funding agency. The Javits amendment, defeated by a 25-35 roll-call vote, gave universities discretion in withholding funds, rather than requiring that they do so.

After defeat of the Javits amendment, Morse proposed acceptance of the language included in the Higher Education Amendments bill, which made the universities accountable to the federal government in cases of withholding aid. The Morse amendment was accepted on a close 28-26 roll call.

House-Senate conferees were unable to reconcile the differences between the two chambers' positions and reported the anti-riot section in disagreement. After a week of further disagreement, however, the Senate receded and accepted the House version Oct. 9.

In debate before final action, Javits pointed out that Congress had already enacted two different versions of anti-disturbance legislation (in the NSF and Higher Education bills) and urged that the Senate give serious thought before approving a third version. "I do not think it adds to our majesty when we are seen to be wandering all over the lot on three different bills," he said. "I do not see that our action builds up the confidence of the students in the fact that we in Congress know what we are doing."

1969

Congress failed to complete action on any major education measures in 1969. Even the bill (HR 13111) providing fiscal 1970 funds for education programs remained unfinished business to be considered again by Congress in 1970.

Also left for completion in the second session of the 91st Congress was a bill to extend the Elementary and Secondary Education Act (ESEA) and aid to federally impacted areas programs. The House in April passed a bill (HR 514) to extend ESEA programs for two years, through fiscal 1972, to consolidate several of its programs and to extend impact aid to cover children living in federally financed public housing.

The Senate Labor and Public Welfare Committee in December ordered reported its own version of the ESEA extension (HR 514). HR 514 as reported by the Senate committee would extend ESEA programs for four years and increase authorizations but would not consolidate programs. The Senate bill also contained provisions concerning programs for the education of disabled and gifted children. These programs had been approved by the House as separate bills.

Congress raised the effective interest rates on guaranteed loans for college students by voting to allow "special allowances" of up to 3 percent on top of the 7-percent interest ceiling available on government-backed loans to college students.

Congress also enacted four provisions attempting to deal with campus riots but killed several other efforts to take action against students or the institutions where disruptions occurred. Congressional committees conducted investigations of student violence.

Major battles over funding and desegregation were waged in connection with HR 13111, the appropriations bill for the Departments of Labor and Health, Education and Welfare. But final action on the bill itself was delayed until January 1970. The House had added more than $1 billion in education funds to the amount requested by the administration and provided, in the second continuing resolution for the year, that education spending could continue at that increased level set by the House version of HR 13111. The Senate approved both House actions in raising education spending levels.

ELEMENTARY AND SECONDARY EDUCATION

Elementary and Secondary Education Act. The House April 23 approved the administration's proposal to extend Elementary and Secondary Education Act programs for two years, through fiscal 1972, in place of the five-year extension recommended by the House Education and Labor Committee.

The Senate Labor and Public Welfare Committee Dec. 19 ordered reported its version of HR 514 to extend Elementary and Secondary Education Act programs for four years, through fiscal 1974. The report was to be filed after the beginning of the second session Jan. 19, 1970.

The House April 23 by a 400-17 roll-call vote passed an amended bill (HR 514), the Elementary and Secondary Education Amendments of 1969, extending the Elementary and Secondary Education Act (ESEA) programs for two years, through fiscal 1972, consolidating into a single package two ESEA programs (Title II—books and materials—and Title III—supplemental services) and two programs contained in the National Defense Education Act (NDEA) (Title III(a)—equipment—and V(a)—counseling) and extending the impacted areas aid program to children living in federal-aid public housing.

The major vote came just before passage, when a coalition of 227 Republicans and southern Democrats helped adopt, by a 235-184 roll-call vote, an amendment offered by Rep. Edith Green (D Ore.) rewriting the entire bill. The major change between the Green bill and the one reported by the Education and Labor Committee (H Rept 91-114) was the two-year extension sought by the Nixon administration rather than a five-year continuation favored by a majority of committee members.

The House action on the ESEA was the first vote on a major social welfare issue in the 91st Congress. It was considered a legislative victory for the Republican administration.

The bill as passed by the House would continue for two more years the fiscal 1970 authorizations, which amount to an estimated $5.3 billion for all ESEA programs and programs of aid to federally impacted areas. This amounted to $4,368,500,000 for all ESEA programs, $702,407,000 for existing impact aid programs and $235,-000,000 for the new public housing impact aid programs.

The Senate Labor and Public Welfare Subcommittee on Education held hearings in June and July on its ESEA extension proposal, but not until six months later did it report a bill. During the hearings, on June 11 Secretary of Health, Education and Welfare Robert H. Finch asked for a two-year extension of existing programs while the Nixon administration conducted a thorough review of all federal aid-to-education programs. By mid-1972, Finch said, 1970 census figures would be available for use in revising the formula for distribution of funds under ESEA Title I (aid to educationally deprived children, the largest program in the act).

The second major change requested by Finch would consolidate five state grant programs—the four already combined by the House plus the educational equipment program administered by the National Foundation on the Arts and Humanities. This would eliminate red tape, the secretary said, and would make available to students in non-public schools all the programs to be consolidated.

Finch opposed the public housing amendments enacted by the House.

The full committee Dec. 19 ordered reported an amended bill (HR 514) extending the Elementary and Secondary Education Act for four years, through fiscal 1974, and increasing authorization for its programs by more than 25 percent. The bill as ordered reported contained provisions expanding school aid to federally im-

Education-Aid Authorizations for Fiscal Years

	1968	1969	1970	1971	1972
Elementary and Secondary Education Act:					
Title I—Educationally deprived children	$2,563,067,584	$2,725,959,699	$2,862,175,945	$3,547,396,000	$3,642,835,000
Special incentive grants	—	50,000,000	50,000,000	50,000,000	50,000,000
Title II—Libraries and textbooks	154,500,000	167,375,000	206,000,000	200,000,000	210,000,000
Title III—Supplementary education	515,000,000	527,875,000	566,500,000	550,000,000	575,000,000
Title IV—Cooperative research [1]	—	—	—	—	—
Title V—State education departments	65,000,000	80,000,000	80,000,000	80,000,000	85,000,000
Title VI—Handicapped children	171,500,000	187,125,000	234,000,000	348,000,000	399,000,000
Title VII—Bilingual education	26,000,000	40,000,000	50,000,000	80,000,000	100,000,000
Title VIII—Dropout prevention, Rural Area Information, Demonstration Projects [2]	3,500,000	33,700,000	36,000,000	40,000,000	47,500,000
Adult Education Act	—	70,000,000	80,000,000	160,000,000	225,000,000
Impacted Areas:					
Construction	62,000,000	66,000,000	66,000,000	15,000,000	20,004,000
Operation-maintenance	477,384,000	510,000,000	545,000,000	536,068,000	592,580,000
TOTALS	$4,097,951,584	$4,458,034,699	$4,775,675,945	$5,606,464,000	$5,946,919,000

1 *Title IV—$100-million authorized for fiscal 1966 and available through fiscal 1974.*
2 *Title VIII—Authorization for fiscal 1968 was for the Rural Area Information program. Authorizations for fiscal 1968 were for Rural Area Information and Dropout*

Prevention. Fiscal 1970: Rural Area Information, Dropout Prevention and Demonstration Projects. Fiscal 1971 and 1972: Dropout Prevention and Demonstration Projects.

pacted areas to cover students living in federally financed public housing and providing programs for gifted children and children with learning disabilities. It did not consolidate existing library and counseling programs.

Special Education. The House passed and sent to the Senate in 1969 two bills (HR 13304, HR 13310) amending the Elementary and Secondary Education Act (ESEA) to provide programs for gifted and talented children with learning disabilities.

HR 13304, for gifted and talented children, authorized the U.S. commissioner of education to make grants to state educational agencies to provide services and assistance to local school districts for such programs. It also provided fellowships for teachers and required the commissioner to conduct studies of such programs.

No additional funds were authorized for the program, which was an amendment to Title V of ESEA.

The Senate Labor and Public Welfare Committee, which held hearings on a similar bill (S 718) in July, incorporated the provisions of S 718 in a bill (HR 514) to extend Elementary and Secondary Education Act programs. *(See above)*

HR 13310 amended Title VI of ESEA to provide programs for children with specific learning disabilities, authorizing grants for research, teacher training and model centers. Authorizations were $6 million for fiscal 1971, $12 million for fiscal 1972 and $18 million for fiscal 1973.

The Senate, Labor and Public Welfare Committee also incorporated its provisions into the bill (HR 514) to extend Elementary and Secondary Education Act programs.

HIGHER EDUCATION

Student Loans. The Emergency Insured Student Loan Act (HR 13194—PL 91-95), cleared by Congress Oct. 16 authorized the payment of "special allowances" by the federal government on guaranteed student loans under the insured student loan program of the Higher Education Act of 1965. The bill was made necessary by rising interest rates that were preventing thousands of students from obtaining loans for the school year beginning September 1969.

Under the existing student loan program, the federal government guaranteed student loans of up to $7,500 per student carrying a maximum interest rate of 7 percent. The special allowance provision in HR 13194 permitted the government to pay a direct interest subsidy of up to 3 percent to lending institutions providing loans under the guaranteed loan program.

The bill authorized $20 million for fiscal 1970, $40 million for fiscal 1971, and as much as needed thereafter to meet the cost of the special allowances on loans made before the expiration date of the law.

It also increased authorizations for the national defense student loan program by $50 million to $325 million in fiscal 1970 and by $75 million to $375 million in fiscal 1971; for the college work-study program by $25 million to $275 million in fiscal 1970 and by $35 million to $320 million in fiscal 1971; and for the educational opportunity grant program by $25 million to $125 million for fiscal 1970 and by $30 million to $170 million for fiscal 1971.

Campus Disorders. Widespread and violent campus disorders early in the year brought on strong reaction from Congress and the administration during 1969.

In Congress, a rash of bills was introduced to cut off federal aid to disruptive students; and anti-student riot provisions were included in three pieces of legislation. Both chambers held hearings on campus disturbances.

President Nixon said student disorders endangered academic freedom and that school officials should "have the backbone to stand up against" campus violence. Attorney General John N. Mitchell warned that "the time has come for an end to patience."

A bipartisan band of liberals, most of them members of the House Education and Labor Committee, joined forces three times to block action aimed at disruptive college students.

The first instance came in June and July, when liberals on the committee for four weeks used a variety of parliamentary tactics to prevent a campus disorders bill (HR 11941) from being reported to the full House.

The bill, as introduced by committee member Edith Green (D Ore.), required all colleges and universities receiving federal aid to file with the U.S. commissioner of education plans of action for dealing with campus upheavals and allowed schools to end virtually all forms of federal aid to students convicted in court or found by the university to have violated its rules in connection with student riots.

Mrs. Green argued that HR 11941 would stall off more repressive action on the floor. However, the liberals, led by John Brademas (D Ind.) and Ogden R. Reid (R N.Y.), countered that the bill would be used on the floor as a vehicle for more repressive action.

The committee July 1 voted to send the bill to the Special Subcommittee on Education, thus in effect killing the measure.

On July 31, the same members were the leaders in a floor fight on a student unrest provision included in the appropriations bill (HR 13111) for the Departments of Labor and Health, Education and Welfare (HEW). Again using parliamentary strategy, they knocked out the section of the bill, although the House added another amendment, generally considered to be weaker.

And in mid-August, committee liberals agreed to report an emergency college student loan bill (HR 13194) only on the condition that no floor amendments such as an anti-student riot amendment could be added by the full House.

Provisions to cut off federal aid to students who participated in campus disturbances were included in other bills, including the appropriations bill for the Departments of State, Justice and Commerce (HR 12964) and the authorization bills for the National Aeronautics and Space Administration (HR 11271) and the National Science Foundation (S 1857).

Other congressional action in this area centered on investigations by the Senate Government Operations Committee's Permanent Investigations Subcommittee and the House Internal Security Committee into activities of militant student groups such as the Students for a Democratic Society (SDS).

Throughout the session, House members were more concerned with taking action against students engaged in campus disruptions than were senators. For instance, House action on the student loan bill was held up for a month over a dispute about adding student rioting amendments, while in the Senate the issue never arose.

Smaller disputes centered about the Reserve Officers Training Corps (ROTC) and military recruitment on campus after anti-military demonstrations occurred on several campuses in the spring.

National Science Foundation. Congress approved an authorization of $477.6 million for the National Science Foundation (NSF) in fiscal 1970 (S 1857—PL 91-120). The bill contained a provision similar to one in the Higher Education Amendments of 1968 (PL 90-575) requiring that institutions receiving NSF funds deny for two years aid from those funds to students or employees found to have been convicted of violent crimes against the institution or to have willfully refused to obey a regulation of the institution, provided that the student's action was of a serious nature and contributed to a substantial disruption of the administration of the institution.

1970

Congress in 1970 enacted the largest elementary and secondary education authorization bill in its history (HR 514—PL 91-230), and spent much energy in conflict with the White House over appropriations to carry out these education programs.

PL 91-230 extended for three years the 1965 Elementary and Secondary Education Act, aid to federally impacted areas and related education aid programs. Its total authorizations and entitlements for the three years amounted to $24.6-billion.

President Nixon in January vetoed the fiscal 1970 appropriations bill for the Departments of Labor and Health, Education and Welfare (HEW). Congress failed to override the veto and in March completed action on a compromise bill—just three months before the end of the fiscal year. Again in August education funds for fiscal 1971 were vetoed by the President, but Congress overrode that veto.

Desegregation replaced campus unrest as the chief education-related controversy especially during consideration of HR 514. This resulted in creation of a new Senate Select Committee on Equal Educational Opportunity, which immediately began a long series of hearings on the subject of educational opportunity. Congress failed to complete action on any revision of higher education programs, as requested by President Nixon, or on his proposed program of emergency federal aid to desegregating school districts.

EDUCATION FUNDS

First Veto. During a nationwide television and radio address, President Nixon Jan. 26, 1970, vetoed the $19.7-billion Labor-HEW appropriations bill (HR 13111) which contained $3,265,302,700 for the Office of Education. This amount was actually $207.5-million less than the budget request, but Congress had allocated funds differently than requested among the various programs. The administration asked $202.2-million for impact aid; Congress voted $600.2-million. The administration asked 404.6-million for elementary and secondary education (in addition to $1.01-billion already available); Congress voted $717-million.

The House Jan. 28 by a 226-191 roll call sustained the veto. The White House and congressional leaders negotiated a compromise on additional spending for education and health programs, on which was based the second labor-HEW appropriations bill for fiscal 1970, enacted March 5, 1970 (HR 15931—PL 91-204). It contained $3,005,219,700 for the Office of Education, which included $638.6-million for elementary and secondary education (in addition to the $1.01-billion already available) and $520.6-million for impact aid.

Second Veto. For fiscal 1971 education appropriations were separated from HEW appropriations into a separate appropriations bill. A $4,420,145,000 appropriations bill (HR 16916—PL 91-380) for the Office of Education was enacted into law Aug. 18 and passed over presidential veto. The $4.4-billion bill included $4,345,145,000 in appropriations for fiscal 1971 and $75-million in emergency school assistance for fiscal 1970. It exceeded the President's final budget request (including the $150-million request for fiscal 1970 for emergency school assistance) by $453,321,000, and it exceeded his requests for fiscal 1971 alone by $528,321,000.

Congress rejected, however, an administration request of $1,339,050,000 for advance funding for fiscal 1972 of Title I programs under the Elementary and Secondary Education Act.

Senate action enacted the bill into law Aug. 18 on a 77-16 roll-call vote.

The House Aug. 13 by a 289-114 roll-call vote overrode the veto—a margin of 20 more than the two-thirds majority needed to pass a bill over the President's objection.

The bill had been sent to the President for his signature July 28. On August 11, Nixon announced that he had vetoed the bill, "saying no to bigger spending and no to higher prices in the interest of all of the American people."

As enacted, the bill contained $1,846,968,000 for all elementary and secondary education programs and $551,068,000 for impact aid.

HR 16916 as passed also contained two controversial sections aimed at limiting the federal government's desegregation authority. Known as the Whitten amendments after their original sponsor, Rep. Jamie L. Whitten (D Miss.), the provisions stipulated that no funds in the bill could be used to force schools or school districts already considered "desegregated" under the 1964 Civil Rights Act to bus students, abolish schools or set attendance zones either against the choice of students' parents or as a prerequisite for obtaining federal funds. Federal officials repeatedly said that the Whitten amendments would serve to confuse the public but would not change enforcement of the administration's desegregation policy.

ELEMENTARY AND SECONDARY EDUCATION

Elementary and Secondary Education Act. The President April 13 signed into law (HR 514—PL 91-230) a three-year, $24.6-billion extension of the 1965 Elementary and Secondary Education Act, aid to federally impacted areas and other educational legislation.

Final congressional action came when the House April 7 adopted the conference report on HR 514 (J Rept 91-937).

Prior to final action, the Senate engaged in two major debates over equal enforcement throughout the nation of federal desegregation guidelines. The most heated Senate controversy on HR 514 centered around an amendment offered by John C. Stennis (D Miss.) and Abraham Ribicoff (D Conn.), which stated that federal guidelines on school desegregation must be applied equally to segregation in the North and South, whether *de jure* (the result of law) or *de facto* (the result of housing patterns).

Although the amendment passed the Senate, a House-Senate conference committee reinstated the distinction between *de jure* and *de facto* discrimination.

As cleared for the President's signature, HR 514 extended for three years, through fiscal 1973, the programs of the Elementary and Secondary Education Act (ESEA), the programs of aid to school districts "impacted" by tax-free federal property and numerous other elementary and secondary educational programs.

The most important change made by the 1970 legislation in Title I of ESEA—which provided per-pupil aid to school districts serving large numbers of poor children—expanded the program to include children whose families earned up to $4,000 rather than $3,000 a year. The law also stipulated that Title I funds could not be used in place of non-federal funds and that state and local funds in areas with Title I programs must be comparable to those available in other areas.

In addition it set authorization for the special incentive grant program for states exceeding the national effort for public education at $50-million annually and changed the distribution formula from a state-by-state allotment to an entitlement. The 1970 law set up a new program of grants for urban and rural school systems serving the largest concentrations of low-income families.

PL 91-230 increased authorizations for other titles of ESEA, consolidated Title III of ESEA (supplemental educational centers and services) and Title V(a) of NDEA (guidance, counseling and testing) and authorized programs under Titles III and V for gifted and talented children.

The 1970 law established new programs of grants for strengthening local education agencies, grants to aid planning and evaluation on local and state levels, of advisory councils on quality education, and of demonstration projects to improve nutrition and health services in public and nonpublic schools serving many poor children.

PL 91-230 also expanded the bilingual education program to cover Indian children living on reservations and attending Interior Department or tribal schools.

Impacted Area Laws. PL 91-230 amended the basic impact aid laws (PL 81-815 and PL 81-874) to cover children living in federally financed public housing.

House hearings on administration proposals to revise this aid program did not result in any action in Congress on the proposals to change criteria by which a district was judged eligible for this aid.

Other Programs. PL 91-230 also increased authorizations for programs under the Adult Education Act of 1966, extended loan forgiveness provisions in the direct student loan program to include forgiveness for military service, established a new program of aid for children with specific learning disabilities, authorized funds for education of the handicapped and extended vocational education programs, with increased authorizations, through fiscal 1972.

PL 91-230 also provided for an automatic one-year extension of authorization for any existing education program for which Congress had failed to complete action on an extension bill by the expiration date of the current authorization.

Authorization for the Teacher Corps was increased to $80-million for fiscal 1970 and $100-million for fiscal 1971; and a student Teacher Corps was established by PL 91-230.

HIGHER EDUCATION

President Nixon March 19, 1970, called for a shift in federal spending on college education to emphasize the needs of poor youths.

In a special message to Congress, Nixon proposed increasing grant-and-loan aid to students from low-income families so that they would have the same ability to pay as students from families earning at least $10,000.

Federally guaranteed loans would be available to every qualified student, regardless of family income level. But direct federal subsidies would go to the students who need them the most.

"Something is basically unequal about opportunity for higher education," the President said, "when a young person whose family earns more than $15,000 a year is nine times more likely to attend college than a young person whose family earns less than $3,000."

Under the President's proposed program, youths whose families have an annual income of $4,500 or less would be guaranteed a total of $1,300 each in grants and subsidized loans. The $1,300 could be supplemented by earnings, other scholarships and access to unsubsidized loans.

The President also recommended the creation of a National Student Loan Association to purchase student loan papers from banks and other financial institutions. Since the association would be privately financed, Nixon said, it would make more money available for the student loan program at no additional cost to the government.

Both House and Senate committees held hearings on the administration proposals and related bills, but took no further action on them in 1970.

In Congress during 1970, no major legislation involving campus unrest reached the floor of either chamber.

The Higher Education Act expired in mid-1971, so Congress was not under immediate pressure to act on a bill during 1970. Partly because of the press of other business—but in great measure in order to avoid a campus unrest fight in the Congress—the leadership in both chambers decided to put off higher education legislation until the 92nd Congress.

Campus unrest provisions restricting the spending of Federal funds were inserted in a number of bills. The Office of Education appropriations bill (HR 16916—PL 91-380) prohibited funds from being used for loans or salaries for students or school employees who had engaged in conduct involving the use or threat of force or seizure of property to interfere with school activities.

Other legislation with campus unrest clauses included the appropriations bills for the State, Justice and Commerce Departments and the Department of Defense and authorization bills covering military procurement and the National Science Foundation.

Veterans' Benefits. A bill enacted in 1970 (HR 11959—PL 91-219) boosted educational benefits by 34.6

percent for some 736,000 veterans who had served in the armed forces after Jan. 31, 1955. PL 91-219 increased to $175 a month the educational allowance for single veterans, to $205 a month for those with one dependent, and to $230 a month for those with two dependents.

National Science Foundation. Congress in 1970 approved a bill (HR 16595—PL 91-356) authorizing $537.7-million for the National Science Foundation for fiscal 1971. In addition Congress extended through 1973 (HR 11766—PL 91-349) the Sea Grant program established in 1966 to encourage "aquaculture" in the same way that the land grant aid system had encouraged agriculture.

DESEGREGATION AND EQUAL EDUCATION

A New Committee. The Senate Select Committee on Equal Educational Opportunity was established Feb. 19.

On Dec. 11, the Senate unanimously approved a resolution extending the life of the select committee for one year, setting Jan. 31, 1972, as the date for its final report. The date originally had been set at Jan. 31, 1971.

The resolution establishing the committee, cosponsored by Walter F. Mondale (D Minn.) and Jacob K. Javits (R N.Y.), was originally offered as an amendment to HR 514, the bill extending the Elementary and Secondary Education Act. Mondale and Javits both opposed the Stennis amendment to HR 514—introduced by John Stennis (D Miss.)—which attempted to eliminate the distinction between *de jure* and *de facto* school desegregation in Federal enforcement of desegregation.

The Mondale-Javits proposal was withdrawn as an amendment and enacted separately to avoid going to conference with the House or to the President for his signature. Traditionally, internal matters such as the establishment of a Senate committee are not subject to action by the House or the President.

The Committee, chaired by Mondale, was composed of 15 members: From the Labor and Public Welfare Committee, Democrats Jennings Randolph (W Va.), Mondale, and Harold E. Hughes (Iowa), and Republicans Javits and Peter H. Dominick (Colo.); from the Judiciary Committee, Democrats John L. McClellan (Ark.)—who served as the second ranking Democrat—Thomas J. Dodd (Conn.), and Birch Bayh (Ind.) and Republicans Roman L. Hruska (Neb.)—who was the Select Committee's ranking minority member—and Marlow W. Cook (Ky.); and from the Senate at large, Democrats Warren G. Magnuson (Wash.), Daniel K. Inouye (Hawaii), and William B. Spong Jr. (Va.) and Republicans Edward W. Brooke (Mass.) and Mark O. Hatfield (Ore.).

The committee was directed to study all aspects of school segregation, to make an interim report by Aug. 1, 1970, and a final report by Jan. 31, 1971 (which later was extended).

Announcing its hearings which continued through most of 1970, Mondale said that the committee would try to "reargue the case for integration."

Emergency School Aid. Congress did not complete action on a bill (HR 19446), the Emergency School Aid Act of 1970, which would have authorized $1.5-billion in Federal aid in fiscal 1971 and 1972 to school districts which were desegregating or attempting to overcome racial imbalance.

Following more than a year of controversy over his position, President Nixon issued a statement on March 24 which pledged that his administration would continue to move against school segregation required by law or established by official actions. In the statement, he promised to spend $1.5-billion in fiscal 1971 and 1972 for improving schools in "racially impacted areas" and for aiding school districts to overcome problems caused by court-ordered desegregation.

Specific legislation (HR 17846, S 3883) was sent to Congress on May 21. As written, the bill was aimed chiefly at approximately 1,400 school districts, the majority of them in the South, which were desegregating or had recently desegregated. It also was designed to aid *de facto* segregated schools, in which racial separation stemmed from neighborhood residence patterns and other factors, and large school districts in which minority students comprised over half the enrollment.

Each state would receive $100,000 initially under the administration bill. Remaining funds would be allocated in proportion to minority enrollments in each state. Students in the first category—districts under court order or HEW-approved plan—would be counted twice.

The House passed its version of the bill (HR 19446) Dec. 21, but opposition from both liberal and conservative members blocked Senate passage.

Conservatives criticized HR 19446 as a "busing bill"; they said it also was too lax in its requirements for Northern school districts.

Liberals opposed the House-passed bill as not stringent enough in the degree of desegregation required of recipients. As Congress adjourned, an alternative desegregation aid bill—awaiting action by the Senate Labor and Public Welfare Committee—also died. The alternative bill set stricter requirements for its recipients and stronger guidelines for use of authorized funds.

OTHER PROGRAMS

Congress in 1970 also enacted legislation (S 3318—PL 91-600) extending programs of federal aid to public libraries for five years, through fiscal 1976, and authorizing $1.14-billion during that time. It consolidated several programs of services and construction aid, set up new programs for poor people and metropolitan libraries.

A bill (HR 14252—PL 91-527) was also passed by Congress authorizing $58-million over fiscal years 1971-1973 for drug abuse education programs.

1971

Congress in 1971 failed to complete action on any aid-to-education bill beyond the bill providing appropriations in fiscal 1972. Most major programs of federal aid to higher education expired June 30, 1971, but the automatic one-year extension of all education programs by the language of PL 91-230 released Congress from the pressure of that deadline for enactment of extension legislation.

The administration's proposed revisions of aid to higher education and its program of emergency aid to desegregating school districts were linked late in the year when the House added the emergency school aid bill as a title of the by-then omnibus education bill re-

Desegregation Report

As members of Congress studied and argued about the extent and methods of school desegregation—and as the Supreme Court pondered crucial questions concerning the standards by which desegregation should be measured—the pace of desegregation in southern schools outstripped that of the rest of the country.

Statistics released by Elliot Richardson, Secretary of Health, Education and Welfare (HEW) Jan. 14—based on data collected in the fall of 1970—showed that the number of black pupils attending majority white public schools in the South doubled from the fall of 1968 to the fall of 1970.

More than one of every three black pupils in the South attended a majority white school in 1970, according to the HEW figures, a sharp increase over the fewer than one in every five who did so two years earlier.

But there was little comparable change outside the South. *(Table below)*

In the South, the percentage of black students in all-black schools decreased dramatically from 68 percent in 1968 to 18.4 percent in 1970. Outside the South, this percentage showed only minimal change, from 12.3 percent to 11.9 percent.

In revealing the figures, Secretary Richardson said that the Administration's commitment to desegregation was to "more than a numbers game." He declared that the real goal was "equal educational opportunity and (that the Administration was) committed to a uniform effort throughout the country to achieve it."

The HEW statistics showed that nationwide, there had been substantial progress in desegregation—from approximately one of every four black children attending majority white schools in 1968 to approximately one of every three doing so in 1970. Here is a summary of the report:

| | *PERCENT OF NEGRO PUPILS ATTENDING: | | |
Geographical Area	0-49.9% Minority Schools	80-100% Minority Schools**	100% Minority Schools
CONTINENTAL U.S. 1968	23.4	68.0	39.7
1970 est.	32.8	50.2	16.0
(1) 32 NORTH & WEST			
1968	27.6	57.4	12.3
1970 est.	27.7	57.4	11.9
(2) 11 SOUTH			
1968	18.4	78.8	68.0
1970 est.	38.1	41.7	18.4
(3) 6 BORDER +D.C.			
1968	28.4	63.8	25.2
1970 est.	29.6	60.3	22.0

(1) Alaska, Ariz., Calif., Colo., Conn., Idaho, Ill., Ind., Iowa, Kan., Maine, Mass., Mich., Minn., Mont., Neb., Nev., N.H., N.J., N.M., N.Y., N.D., Ohio, Ore., Pa., R.I., S.D., Utah, Vt., Wash., Wis., Wyo.
(2) Ala., Ark., Fla., Ga., La., Miss., N.C., S.C., Tenn., Texas, Va.
(3) Del., D.C., Ky., Md., Mo., Okla., W.Va.
* Districts with fewer than 300 pupils are not included in the survey. 1970 figures are estimates based on latest available data and are subject to variation upon final compilation.
** Percentage figure includes percentage shown in 100% minority schools.

vising programs of aid to college students. Further loaded down with antibusing provisions, the bill was before a Senate committee for reconsideration at the end of the year.

Education Funds. Congress passed, and the President signed, a bill (HR 7016—PL 92-48) providing $5,146,-311,000 for the Office of Education in fiscal 1972. The total included $612.6-million for impact aid; $1,993,-278,000 for elementary and secondary education; and $1,341,784,000 for higher education.

HIGHER EDUCATION

In its deliberations on financing of higher education in 1971, Congress considered several aspects of the issue and in the end combined several different bills into one omnibus measure.

The measure (S 659), after being passed by the Senate and the House, was reconsidered by the Senate Labor and Public Welfare Committee because of the major alterations made in the Senate-passed bill in the House.

As originally passed by the Senate just before the August congressional recess, S 659 was already the most sweeping aid-to-education bill ever considered by Congress. The product of two years' work in the Senate Labor and Public Welfare Committee, it extended existing programs of federal aid to colleges and students and established new ones—including a new basic grant program for students and a cost-of-instruction payment program for institutions attended by federally aided students—at a cost of $19-billion for the following four years.

The House revised provisions of the bill to extend existing programs for five years, to expand the existing student grant program, to provide a new program of general federal aid to colleges and universities, and to provide a new program of federal aid to occupational education. It also added the contents of a major bill providing aid to desegregate school districts. The bill (S 1557—HR 2266) had passed the Senate in April and been reported by the House Education and Labor Committee but was refused clearance for floor consideration by the House Rules Committee.

In an attempt to bypass the Rules Committee floor managers of the desegregation bill sought to get House consideration under suspension of the rules, a maneuver usually reserved for noncontroversial bills which requires a two-thirds majority of the House. The House on Nov. 1, however, refused to consider the measure under such circumstances. It did agree (three days later) to add the desegregation aid provisions, accompanied by anti-busing amendments, to S 659. The total amount authorized by the bill had risen to $24-billion.

The measure was then referred back to the Senate Labor and Public Welfare Committee. That committee ordered S 659 reported Dec. 3 with amendments which included the provisions of S 659 and S 1557 as approved by the Senate, the provisions of an Indian education bill (S 2482) already approved by the Senate and provisions creating a foreign service scholarship program.

Mr. Nixon on Feb. 22, 1971, again asked Congress to equalize the opportunity for a higher education by directing most federal aid to students from low-income

---

Supreme Court Decisions, 1969-1972

In decisions affecting schools and colleges, the Supreme Court in 1969 ruled:

• That a public school could not constitutionally bar the wearing of black arm bands in protest of the Vietnam War—when such protest did not substantially disrupt school activities. *(Tinker v. Des Moines Independent Community School District).*

• That a federal district judge could direct a desegregating school board to desegregate faculties and school staff personnel according to a specific mathematical ratio *(U.S. v. Montgomery County Board of Education).*

• That a "monkey law"—forbidding public school teachers to teach the Darwinian theory of man's evolution—was an unconstitutional violation of the 1st Amendment *(Epperson v. Arkansas).*

• That the time for "all deliberate speed" in school desegregation was past and that schools should desegregate immediately *(Alexander v. Holmes County Board of Education).*

In decisions affecting schools and colleges in 1971, the Supreme Court ruled that:

• Busing of school children was a permissible interim method of desegregating still-segregated schools *(Swann v. Charlotte-Mecklenburg Board of Education).*

• A state could require teachers to take an oath to uphold the state and federal constitutions, but could not dismiss, without a hearing, a teacher who refused to swear that he did not believe in forcible overthrow of the government *(Connell v. Higginbotham).*

• That the 1st Amendment bars state laws allowing the state to reimburse nonpublic schools for the cost of teachers' salaries, books, and other instructional materials in certain secular subjects and state laws authorizing supplementary salary grants to nonpublic elementary school teachers of secular subjects *(Lemon v. Kurtzman, Earley v. DiCenso, Robinson v. DiCenso).*

• That the 1st Amendment does not bar federal construction grants (under the Higher Education Facilities Act of 1963) to church-related colleges or universities so long as the buildings constructed are to be used exclusively for secular educational purposes *(Tilton v. Richardson).*

In education-related decisions in 1972, the Supreme Court held that:

• Federal courts could intervene to halt state or local action to create a new school district with the effect of impeding desegregation *(Wright v. Emporia City Council).*

• Children of members of the Amish sect were exempt under the 1st Amendment from state compulsory attendance laws *(Wisconsin v. Yoder).*

---

families and to shift the financing of student loans entirely to the private money market.

Democratic-sponsored counter proposals would extend and expand existing aid programs, and some added a new program under which eligible students were

Federal Spending on Education and Manpower Programs

(in millions, by fiscal year)

	1959	1965	1966	1968	1971	1972*
Elementary and secondary education	$259	$ 478	$1,646	$2,430	$3,164	$ 3,383
Higher education	225	413	701	1,392	1,429	1,442
Vocational education	38	132	136	265	415	531
Manpower training	4	336	731	1,263	2,602	3,643
Science education and basic research	106	309	368	449	522	538
Other education and manpower aids	451	850	925	1,227	757	957
Veterans readjustment benefits	864	50	211	673	1,659	2,240
Deductions for offsetting receipts	—3	—9	—11	—16	—12	—29
TOTALS	$1,944	$2,559	$4,707	$7,683	$10,536	$12,705

* Estimated

SOURCE: Bureau of the Budget

entitled—as a matter of right—to a certain basic federal grant. A separate cost-of-education payment would to to institutions for each federally aided student in attendance.

Nixon renewed his request that Congress authorize creation of a national foundation for higher education and a national institute of education.

Critics of the administration's proposals in Congress and in the education community said that the Nixon plan would substantially reduce aid to students from middle-income families and that the proposed shift to the private money market would cut the amount of aid available through loans.

One million additional low-income students would receive aid under the administration plan, said U.S. Commissioner of Education Sidney P. Marland. The higher education community reacted with alarm at the prospect.

Colleges and universities were already stretched to their financial breaking point, a panel of educators told the Senate Education Subcommittee in March. The push for institutional aid—general federal aid to colleges and universities to help them meet general operating expenses—gained momentum in 1971.

The administration opposed general formula institutional aid, but pressure from members of Congress and the education community did bring forth a mid-year endorsement for federal payments to meet the costs of educating federally aided students.

National Science Foundation. Congress approved authorization of $655.5-million for the National Science Foundation in fiscal 1972 (HR 7960—PL 92-86).

Education Revenue-Sharing. President Nixon April 6, 1971, sent Congress the sixth of his special revenue-sharing plans—one to consolidate into one program 33 existing categories of federal aid to elementary and secondary education. He had included $2.8-billion in the fiscal 1972 budget for the combined programs.

Nixon proposed including an additional $200-million for the first year of the plan's operation. The total amount would be apportioned among the states on the basis of a formula taking into account the total school-age population in each state, the number of students from low-income families and the number of students whose families reside or work on federal property.

No state would receive less under the new plan, Nixon said, than under the existing structure. Funds would be used in five broad areas: education of the disadvantaged, education of handicapped children, vocational education, impact aid and supporting materials and services.

Education interest groups were unenthusiastic about the proposal because it would erase existing categorical programs, which they considered effective, while providing only a small amount of additional funds. Senate hearings were the only congressional action on the proposal in 1971.

Desegregation and Equal Education. For the second year in a row Congress failed to complete action on a $1.5-billion program to aid the desegregation of the nation's public schools.

The plan, originally proposed by the Nixon administration in 1970, would have channeled the funds to school districts which were desegregating or attempting to overcome racial imbalance.

In 1971 a compromise version of the administration bill (S 1557) was passed by the Senate in April but a similar bill (HR 2266) stalled in the House when the Rules Committee refused to grant a rule for floor consideration.

The House in November agreed to incorporate similar desegregation aid provisions into the major aid-to-education bill (S 659) then being considered in the House. That bill was then returned to the Senate Labor and Public Welfare Committee which further amended it and had not reported it out by the end of the session.

School Prayer. The House Nov. 8 rejected an attempt to amend the Constitution to add language stating that voluntary prayer or meditation, by persons lawfully assembled in a public building, was not unconstitutional. The proposed amendment (H J Res 191) failed by 28 votes to win the necessary approval of two-thirds of the members present and voting. *(Story p. 37)*

Indian Education. The Senate approved a bill (S 2482) amending existing programs of aid to education to improve the educational opportunity available to Indian children and adults. The provisions of the bill were added to the omnibus education bill (S 659) by the Senate Labor and Public Welfare Committee late in the year.

1972

Congress completed action on the $21-billion Education Amendments of 1972 (PL 92-318), which extended existing programs of aid to postsecondary education through fiscal 1975 at a total level of $19-billion and which authorized a new program of $2-billion in aid to desegregating school districts. The new education act also contained several provisions restricting the use of federal funds for busing and delaying the effective date of federal court orders requiring busing.

Congress moved with more deliberation on two other anti-busing measures proposed by President Nixon in March. As of July 31, neither his equal educational opportunity bill with its strict guidelines for busing nor his student transportation moratorium bill appeared likely to receive floor action in the 92nd Congress.

Education Funds. Congress again, under threat of yet a third veto of education funds, added large amounts of money to the administration's request for education programs in the Labor-HEW appropriations bill (HR 15417) for fiscal 1973. The Senate provided $5,283,-043,000, almost $950-million more than requested; the House provided $3,999,885,000. Neither version of the bill contained funds for higher education programs, because at the time of consideration by the committees, the education amendments authorizing that aid had not been enacted. House-Senate conferees agreed on a bill containing a total of $30.5-billion in appropriations.

President Nixon Aug. 16 vetoed the bill and the House sustained the veto, necessitating congressional action on a new Labor-HEW bill.

Higher Education. President Nixon June 23 signed into law PL 92-318, the Education Amendments of 1972. PL 92-318 extended through fiscal 1975 existing programs of federal aid to postsecondary education, consolidating the various federal laws authorizing the programs into one basic statute—the Higher Education Act of 1965.

In addition, PL 92-318 established two new basic programs of federal aid—a program of basic educational opportunity grants to which every qualified student in need of aid was entitled and a program of federal cost-of-education payments to which every institution attended by federally-aided students was entitled.

PL 92-318 also authorized expanded aid to programs of career education, Indian education, and a new program of federal aid to desegregating or racially-impacted school districts. *(Detailed provisions, story p. 90)*

National Science Foundation. Congress in 1972 approved a bill (HR 14108—PL 92-372) authorizing $703.9-million for the National Science Foundation in fiscal 1973.

Desegregation and Equal Education. President Nixon March 17 asked Congress to enact his Equal Educational Opportunities Act which would establish that busing was strictly a last-resort remedy for segregation to be used only in certain circumstances and to target $2.5-billion in federal aid (authorized under other law) upon areas with the greatest need for improving their schools. Congress moved deliberately on this proposal (HR 13915, S 3395) in 1972; both houses held hearings and the House committee in late July reported out a bill which reduced the targeted aid to $1-billion. The House Aug. 18 passed HR 13915 with stronger restrictions on busing than requested by the President.

President Nixon also March 17 asked Congress to approve his Student Transportation Moratorium Act which would halt all new busing until July 1, 1973 or until passage of the equal opportunities bill. House hearings on the moratorium proposal (HR 13916, S 3388) were the only action on this proposal by midyear.

Education Revenue-Sharing. The House held hearings in early 1972 on the President's proposal for special revenue-sharing for education, but no further action appeared likely in 1972.

Veterans' Benefits. The House in March and the Senate in August passed the Vietnam Veterans' Readjustment Assistance Act of 1972. The Senate version of HR 12828 amended the 1966 Act and raised education benefits for single qualifying veterans about 43 percent, with proportionate increases for veterans with dependents. The House bill authorized increases of about 14 percent. A compromise measure was expected to clear Congress before the 92nd Congress adjourned. *(1966 act, p. 73)*

1972 EDUCATION ACT: $21-BILLION IN AID, BUSING CURBS

Congress June 8 completed action on an omnibus bill, the Education Amendments of 1972 (S 659—PL 92-318), which authorized $19-billion in aid to post-secondary education, $2-billion in aid to desegregating school districts and contained strong curbs on the use of busing for desegregation.

The busing amendments were only a small part of the omnibus higher education measure, which was two years in the making. The bill authorized $19-billion for higher education through fiscal 1975, incorporated a comprehensive restructuring of federal higher education programs and established a new program of direct federal assistance to needy students who qualified for college or vocational schools and to the institutions themselves. The conference report also provided $2-billion in emergency school aid for school desegregation.

The anti-busing provisions were a compromise between stringent language approved by the House in 1971 and more moderate language approved by the Senate March 1. Although the House, in an unusual procedure, twice instructed its conferees on the measure to insist on the House-approved anti-busing amendments, it accepted the conference version of the bill June 8, on a 218-180 roll-call vote.

The Senate had approved the conference report May 24 by a 63-15 roll call after defeating an attempt to strengthen the anti-busing provisions.

As approved by the conferees—after more than 20 meetings, including an all-night session—and accepted by the House and Senate, the bill's anti-busing provisions:

• Postponed until all appeals had been ruled on, or the time for them had expired, the effective date of all federal district court orders requiring the transfer or transportation of students to achieve racial balance. This provision expired Jan. 1, 1974.

• Limited the use of federal funds for busing (1) intended to overcome racial imbalance or (2) to desegregate a school system to instances when local officials requested federal funds for this use; barred busing where it would risk the health of the children or require that a student attend a school educationally inferior to the school he had formerly attended.

• Prohibited federal pressure on local school boards to induce them to undertake busing "unless constitutionally required."

PROVISIONS. As signed by the President June 23, the Education Amendments of 1972 (S 659—PL 92-318), contained the following provisions.

Title I—Higher Education

PL 92-318 extended, through fiscal 1975, the authorization for programs established by the Higher Education Act of 1965, the National Defense Education Act of 1958, the Higher Education Facilities Act and the International Education Act. Certain provisions of the other laws were incorporated by PL 92-318 into the 1965 Act which, thereby amended, became the basic federal-aid-to-higher-education law. Authorization levels for the various individual programs, unless otherwise noted,

were the same as those authorized in fiscal 1971. Programs extended and amended included:

• Aid to colleges and universities for community service programs and continuing education—$10-million for fiscal 1972; $30-million, 1973; $40-million, 1974; $50-million, 1975. PL 92-318 also authorized the commissioner of education, beginning in fiscal year 1973, to reserve up to 10 percent of the appropriation for this category for grants and contracts for special programs designed to seek solutions to national and regional problems relating to technological and social changes and environmental pollution.

• Aid to colleges and universities for the acquisition of library resources, library research and the training of librarians—$30-million for fiscal 1972; $75-million, 1973; $85-million, 1974; $100-million, 1975. PL 92-318 also extended federal aid for cataloguing operations by the Library of Congress at $9-million for fiscal 1972; $12-million, 1973; $15-million, 1974, and $9-million, 1975.

• Aid to developing institutions—$91-million for fiscal 1972 and $120-million annually for 1973-75.

• Emergency grants to institutions in serious financial distress at a total of $40-million to be available through fiscal 1974.

• A new program of basic educational opportunity grants under which any college student in good standing was entitled to a basic grant of $1,400 minus the amount his family reasonably could be expected to contribute toward his educational expenses. The grant would not ex-

---

Nixon's Views

President Nixon June 23 signed S 659 into law (PL 92-318). Calling the anti-busing provisions "inadequate, misleading and entirely unsatisfactory," Nixon said: "Not in the course of this administration has there been a more manifest congressional retreat from an urgent call for responsibility."

John Ehrlichman, presidential adviser for domestic affairs, told a news conference June 23 that if Congress did not take action on the President's anti-busing proposals, Nixon would "go to the country" during the presidential campaign to build support for a constitutional amendment regarding busing.

Nixon's anti-busing proposals called for:

• Imposing a moratorium on all new busing orders by federal courts.

• Directing "over $2.5-billion in the next year... toward improving the education of children from poor families" and imposing permanent restraints on the use of busing for desegregation of schools.

Nixon announced his proposals in a nationwide television address March 16—two days after the Florida primary in which 74 percent of the voters said they favored a constitutional amendment to prohibit forced busing of school children to achieve racial balance. (Busing moratorium and proposed constitutional amendment, p. 32; equal education opportunities, p. 89)

Integration Defined

The difficulty of defining the term "integrated school" was illustrated by the fact that PL 92-318 contained two definitions. The first read that the term "means a school with an enrollment in which a substantial proportion of the children is from educationally advantaged backgrounds, *in which the proportion of minority group children is at least 50 per centum of the proportion of minority group children enrolled in all schools of the local educational agencies within the standard metropolitan statistical area,* and which has a faculty and administrative staff with substantial representation of minority group persons."

The second definition read that the term "integrated school" meant "a school with 1) an enrollment in which a substantial proportion of the children is from educationally advantaged backgrounds, and *in which the assistant secretary (of education) determines that the number of non-minority group children constitutes that proportion of the enrollment which will achieve stability, in no event more than 65 per centum thereof,* and 2) a faculty which is representative of the minority group and non-minority group population of the larger community in which it is located, or whenever the assistant secretary determines that the local educational agency concerned is attempting to increase the proportions of minority group teachers, supervisors and administrators in its employ, a faculty which is representative of the minority group and non-minority group faculty employed by the local educational agency." *(Italics added)*

ceed the difference between the expected family share and the actual cost of attending the school. If appropriations were insufficient (less than 75 percent) to provide each student the full amount he needed, the individual grant would be limited to one-half the student's need; if the appropriation was 75 percent of the total required, the individual grant could be 60 percent of the student's need.

PL 92-318 contained language barring the award of any new grants under the program in any year in which appropriations for supplemental educational grants were less than $130,093,000, appropriations for work-study programs were less than $237.4-million, or appropriations for student loans were less than $286-million.

• Supplemental educational opportunity grants (the existing grant program) for students who needed aid beyond the basic grant or for students whose family contributions made them ineligible for the basic grant yet were still in need of some aid—$170-million for fiscal 1972 and $200-million annually for 1973-75.

PL 92-318 raised to $1,500 from $1,000 the maximum annual grant and provided that no undergraduate could receive an aggregate of more than $4,000 in grants (or $5,000 for an undergraduate whose normal course of study required five years). Half-time students were made eligible.

• State scholarship incentive payments for states to provide incentive grants to eligible college students. Funds were to be allotted among the states on the basis of the relative number of students attending institutions of higher education within the state. Individual annual grants could not exceed $1,500.

• Special programs for students from disadvantaged backgrounds (Talent Search, Upward Bound and special services) at $96-million for fiscal 1972, and $100-million annually for fiscal 1973-75.

• Insured student loan program allowing federal insurance of new loans amounting to $1.4-billion in fiscal 1972; $1.6-billion, 1973; $1.8-billion, 1974 and $2-billion, 1975.

PL 92-318 raised to $2,500 from $1,500 the maximum annual insured loan but retained the aggregate limitation of $7,500. The commissioner of education was authorized to waive these ceilings with respect to students in specialized training resulting in exceptionally high education costs. It also allowed students from families with adjusted incomes of more than $15,000 in some cases to receive federally subsidized loans (on which the federal government paid part of the interest).

PL 92-318 required the commissioner of education to publish a list of state agencies which were authorities on public post-secondary vocational education in their state and which could determine the eligibility of various programs for federal student aid.

• A student loan marketing association, backed by the federal government until July 1, 1982, which would provide a secondary market and warehouse for student loans in order to release money tied up in such loans for additional loans.

The new association would buy loans from schools and banks, and it would "warehouse" loans by lending to the lending institutions funds up to 80 percent of the face value of the insured loans involved. Funds advanced to a lender in this way could only be reinvested in other student loans. An appropriation of $5-million was authorized for use in establishing the association.

• The Emergency Insured Student Loan Act—extended through fiscal 1974—which authorized special payments to lenders in times of high interest rates.

• Work-study programs—$330-million for fiscal 1972; $360-million, 1973; $390-million, 1974; $420-million, 1975. PL 92-318 also permitted participation in this program by half-time students, emphasized that students "with the greatest financial need" would be given preference in participating in the program and established a new work-study program for community service learning designed specifically for veterans returning to school.

• Cooperative education.

• Direct student loans at a level of $375-million for fiscal 1972 and $400-million annually for 1973-75. PL 92-318 set a $2,500 aggregate limit on direct loans to an undergraduate student during his first two years of study (replacing a $1,000 per year ceiling), retained an overall aggregate of $5,000 for an undergraduate and $10,000 for a graduate student, and eliminated the annual ceilings of $2,500 for graduate students.

PL 92-318 narrowed the provisions allowing forgiveness for a portion of a direct loan for undertaking certain types of public service by eliminating forgiveness for teachers, except those teaching handicapped children, those teaching in Head Start pre-school programs and those teaching in schools with high concentrations of disadvantaged children, and by restricting forgiveness for military service to service in areas of hostilities.

• A National Commission on the Financing of Post-secondary Education to study the financial crisis in higher education and report to Congress by April 30, 1973.

• Education professions development—$200-million for fiscal 1973; $300-million, 1974; $450-million, 1975.

• Instructional equipment grants.

• Undergraduate facilities grants—$50-million for fiscal 1972; $200-million, 1973; $300-million, 1974; $300-lion, 1975.

• Graduate facilities grants—$20-million for fiscal 1972; $40-million, 1973; $60-million, 1974; $80-million, 1975.

• Loans for construction of academic facilities—at $50-million for fiscal 1972; $100-million, 1973; $150-million, 1974; $200-million, 1975.

• A new program of federal insurance for academic facilities loans to nonprofit private institutions.

• Construction assistance in major disaster areas.

• Networks for Knowledge—$5-million for fiscal 1972; $10-million, 1973; $15-million, 1974; $15-million, 1975.

• Grants for the improvement of graduate programs and for public service education—$30-million for fiscal 1973; $40-million, 1974; $50-million, 1975.

• Graduate fellowships for careers in post-secondary education and in public service.

• Fellowships for mineral resource conservation.

• Grants for area studies, language instruction and development—$50-million for fiscal 1973; $75-million for each of 1974-75.

• International Education Act—$20-million for fiscal 1973; $30-million, 1974; $40-million, 1975.

• A new program of grants for the statewide planning, establishment, expansion and improvement of community college programs—$15.7-million for planning grants to be available over fiscal 1973-74; and for grants to community colleges, $50-million for fiscal 1973; $75-million, 1974; $150-million, 1975.

• A new program of aid for occupational education—$100-million for fiscal 1973; $250-million, 1974; $500-million, 1975—80 percent of the funds for fiscal 1973 would be used for administration, planning grants and initial programs and 20 percent for technical assistance; in the succeeding years, 85 percent would be allocated to the states for improving occupational preparation, counseling and placement in elementary and secondary schools and for improving post-secondary occupational education.

• Creation of a Bureau of Occupational and Adult Education in the Office of Education to administer vocational education aid programs.

• Creation of a community college unit in the Office of Education to coordinate all office programs affecting junior colleges.

• Law school clinical experience aid—$1-million for fiscal 1972; $5-million, 1973; $7.5-million for each of 1974-75. *(Box on authorization levels p. 103)*

Title II—Vocational Education

PL 92-318 extended, through fiscal 1975, authorizations for already established programs of aid to vocational education, which included:

• Special vocational education programs for the disadvantaged at the fiscal 1972 authorization level of $60-million.

• Exemplary programs and projects at the fiscal 1972 level of $75-million.

• Residential vocational schools at annual levels of $75-million for demonstration schools and $15-million for residential vocational facilities.

• Consumer and homemaking education at the fiscal 1972 level of $50-million annually.

• Cooperative vocational education at the 1972 level of $75-million annually.

• Work-study programs for vocational students at the 1972 level of $45-million annually.

• Curriculum development at the 1972 level of $10-million annually.

• National Advisory Council on Vocational Education.

Title III—Administration of Education Programs

PL 92-318 established an Education Division within the Department of Health, Education and Welfare (HEW), headed by an assistant secretary of education who could not also serve as commissioner of education or as director of the National Institute of Education. The new division was to be composed of the existing Office of Education and a newly created National Institute of Education.

Title III also:

• Authorized $10-million for fiscal 1973; $50-million, 1974; $75-million, 1975 for grants for innovation and reform in post-secondary education.

• Established the National Institute of Education to provide leadership in the conduct and support of scientific inquiry into the educational process. At least 90 percent of the institute's funds were to be expended in grants or contracts with agencies and individuals for this research.

• Authorized an aggregate of $550-million for the institute to be available in fiscal 1973-75.

• Extended the Cooperative Research Act through fiscal 1975 with authorizations for the research functions, which would remain in the Office of Education, at $58-million for fiscal 1973; $68-million, 1974; $78-million, 1975.

Title IV—Indian Education

PL 92-318 authorized expanded programs of aid to improve the quality of education for Indian children attending public schools. It:

• Amended the law (PL 81-874) authorizing federal aid to federally impacted school districts to provide for increased aid to schools attended by Indian children to meet their special needs.

• Amended the Elementary and Secondary Education Act (ESEA) to authorize grants for projects and programs to improve the educational opportunity for Indian children. PL 92-318 authorized $25-million for fiscal 1973; $35-million for each of 1974-75.

• Amended the Adult Education Act to authorize grants for pilot and demonstration projects, research, evaluation and operation of adult education programs for Indians. PL 92-318 authorized $5-million for fiscal 1973, $8-million for each of 1974-75.

• Created a bureau-level Office of Indian Education within the Office of Education.

• Created a National Advisory Council on Indian Education.

Title V—Related Programs

PL 92-318 also:

• Extended through fiscal 1975 authorization for federal aid to local educational agencies for the acquisition of equipment.

(Continued on p. 94)

Higher Education Projections from 1969 to 1980

Enrollment

	Fall 1969	Fall 1979
Total, all institutions	**7,917,000**	**12,258,000**
Public	5,840,000	9,806,000
Private	2,078,000	2,451,000
Degree-credit	7,299,000	11,075,000
Public	5,260,000	8,671,000
Private	2,040,000	2,403,000
4-year	5,902,000	8,629,000
2-year	1,397,000	2,446,000
Men	4,317,000	6,251,000
Women	2,982,000	4,823,000
Full-time	5,198,000	7,669,000
Part-time	2,101,000	3,405,000
Undergraduate	6,411,000	9,435,000
Graduate	889,000	1,640,000
Non-degree-credit	618,000	1,183,000

Staff

	1969-70	1979-80
Total, professional staff	**872,000**	**1,221,000**
Instructional staff	700,000	986,000
Resident degree-credit	578,000	801,000
Other instruction	122,000	185,000
Other professional staff	172,000	235,000
Administration, services	91,000	124,000
Organized research	80,000	112,000
Public	589,000	906,000
Private	282,400	316,000
4-year	749,000	1,011,000
2-year	122,400	211,000

Expenditures

(in billions of 1969-70 dollars)

	1969-70	1979-80
Total expenditures from current funds	**$21.8**	**$40.0**
Public institutions	13.8	26.8
Student education	8.6	16.9
Organized research	1.8	2.8
Related activities	0.8	1.8
Auxiliary, student aid	2.6	5.3
Private institutions	8.0	13.2
Student education	4.1	6.5
Organized research	1.7	2.9
Related activities	0.4	0.6
Auxiliary, student aid	1.8	3.2
Capital outlay from current funds	**0.5**	**0.5**

Student Charges

(tuition, room, and board in 1969-70 dollars)

	1969-70	1979-80
All public institutions	**$1,198**	**$1,367**
Universities	1,342	1,578
Other 4-year	1,147	1,380
2-year	957	1,166
All private institutions	**$2,520**	**$3,162**
Universities	2,905	3,651
Other 4-year	2,435	3,118
2-year	2,064	2,839

Earned Degrees

	1969-70	1979-80
Bachelor's and 1st prof.	**784,000**	**1,133,000**
Natural sciences	176,880	239,130
Mathematics, statistics	29,740	52,980
Engineering	41,090	50,410
Physical sciences	21,090	18,070
Biological sciences	37,180	62,990
Agriculture, forestry	11,070	9,390
Health professions	33,600	41,970
General science	3,110	3,320
Social sci., humanities	607,120	893,870
Fine arts	52,250	77,860
English, journalism	62,840	116,840
Foreign languages	23,790	57,150
Psychology	31,360	60,740
Social sciences	149,500	273,190
Education	120,460	114,170
Library science	1,000	1,580
Social work	3,190	4,100
Accounting	20,780	29,780
Other bus. & commerce	81,870	91,920
Other	60,080	66,540
Master's	**219,200**	**432,500**
Natural sciences	46,080	88,580
Mathematics, statistics	7,950	23,290
Engineering	16,900	30,750
Physical sciences	6,300	6,210
Biological sciences	6,580	15,060
Agriculture, forestry	2,680	3,030
Health professions	4,570	7,940
General science	1,100	2,300
Social sci., humanities	173,120	343,920
Fine arts	13,850	27,120
English, journalism	10,890	28,420
Foreign languages	6,390	22,180
Psychology	4,700	12,910
Social sciences	20,970	51,100
Education	71,130	90,160
Library science	7,190	19,280
Social work	5,960	17,700
Accounting	1,490	2,980
Other bus. & commerce	22,950	61,750
Other	7,600	10,320
Doctor's (except 1st prof.)	**29,300**	**62,500**
Natural sciences	14,100	32,120
Mathematics, statistics	1,350	3,970
Engineering	3,980	12,650
Physical sciences	4,220	6,870
Biological sciences	3,410	7,310
Agriculture, forestry	800	730
Health professions	310	510
General science	30	80
Social sci., humanities	15,200	30,380
Fine arts	990	1,330
English, journalism	1,310	2,880
Foreign languages	860	2,210
Psychology	1,720	3,470
Social sciences	3,550	6,990
Education	5,030	10,350
Library science	20	40
Social work	100	220
Accounting	50	100
Other bus. & commerce	620	1,710
Other	950	1,080

SOURCE: U.S. Office of Education

(Continued from p. 92)

• Authorized grants for the creation of ethnic heritage studies programs; established a National Advisory Council on Ethnic Heritage Studies; authorized $15-million for fiscal 1973.

• Provided for a director of consumer education in the Office of Education and grants for consumer education programs—$20-million for fiscal 1973; $25-million, 1974; $35-million, 1975.

• Authorized endowment grants of $3-million each to the College of the Virgin Islands and the University of Guam, and granted each the status of a land grant institution.

Title VI—Youth Camp Safety

PL 92-318 required the secretary of HEW to investigate the need for federal safety standards for youth camps and to report to Congress by March 1, 1973.

Title VII—Emergency School Aid

PL 92-318 contained authorizations for a new program of aid to desegregating and racially impacted school districts. Its specific provisions:

• Authorized $1-billion for each of fiscal 1973-74 to provide financial aid to meet the special needs incident to desegregation, to encourage voluntary integration and to aid school children in overcoming the educational disadvantages of minority group isolation.

• Declared it federal policy that the desegregation guidelines and criteria established in Title VII and in related federal laws be applied uniformly in all regions of the nation in dealing with segregation in public schools, whether *de jure* or *de facto*.

• Earmarked annually from the total appropriated for this aid program:

1) Five percent for grants for metropolitan area projects—such as establishing and maintaining integrated schools, developing a multi-district plan to reduce minority group isolation, or planning and constructing education parks. *(Box for definition of integrated school, p. 91)*

2) Four percent for bilingual education programs.

3) Three percent for educational television.

4) Six percent for special programs and projects.

5) Fifteen percent for pilot compensatory programs to overcome the adverse effects of minority group isolation by improving the academic achievement of minority group children.

6) Eight percent for grants to private groups or public agencies other than school boards.

• Provided that the unreserved funds should be allocated among the states with each state receiving at least $100,000—under a formula which added to a basic grant of $75,000 a sum based upon the number of minority group children between the ages of 5 years and 17 years in each state compared to the national total of minority group children between those ages.

• Specified that eligible school boards were those which were:

1) Implementing a desegregation plan undertaken after a final court order, an order from a state agency or official, or with the approval of the secretary of HEW.

2) Voluntarily implementing complete desegregation plans.

3) Implementing, or willing to implement with this federal assistance, plans to eliminate, reduce or prevent minority group isolation.

4) Voluntarily implementing, or willing to do so with federal aid, a plan to enroll in the schools non-resident children whose enrollment would significantly reduce minority group isolation either in the district they had formerly attended or in the one to which they had come.

5) Enrolling more than 50 percent minority group children and receiving at least an equal sum in compensatory education funds under PL 92-318. (To receive compensatory education funds, a district had to have more than 50 percent of its enrollment, or at least 15,000 students, from minority groups.)

• Prohibited award of funds under Title VII to school boards which had, after June 23, 1972:

1) Aided, by transfer of property or services, any private segregated school.

2) Demoted or dismissed a disproportionate number of minority group teachers or personnel.

3) Separated by classes or within classes minority and non-minority group children for a substantial part of the school day (except for *bona fide* ability grouping as a standard practice).

4) Restricted activities or participation in order to avoid participation of minority group students.

• Allowed districts barred under the above provision from receiving aid to apply to the secretary of HEW for a waiver of ineligibility if such practices had ceased and there was satisfactory assurance that they would not reoccur.

• Authorized use of the funds for activities (aside from those for which funds were earmarked) such as remedial services, additional staff members and staff training and retraining, recruiting and training of teacher aides, in-service teacher training, guidance and counseling, new curricula and instructional methods, shared facilities programs, innovative inter-racial educational programs or projects, community activities, administrative and auxiliary services, planning, evaluation, repair or minor remodeling.

• Established a National Advisory Council on Equality of Educational Opportunity to report on the program to Congress by Dec. 1, 1973.

• Authorized award, at the discretion of the court, of a reasonable attorney's fee, to a plaintiff other than the federal government winning a final order in a suit against a local school board, a state, or the United States government to bring compliance with federal civil rights law.

• Stated that nothing in Title VII should be read to require any school board assigning students to school on the basis of geographic attendance areas drawn on a racially non-discriminatory basis to adopt any other method of pupil assignment.

Title VIII—Busing

PL 92-318 provided that it should not be read to require the assignment or transportation of students or teachers to overcome racial imbalance, and also:

• Prohibited the use of federal education funds for busing students to overcome racial imbalance or to desegregate schools, except on the express written, voluntary request of local school officials. PL 92-318 also barred the use of federal education funds for busing when the time or distance involved was so great as to risk the health of the children or to impinge significantly on the educational process, or when the school to which a student was to be bused was an inferior school to that to which the student would otherwise be assigned under a non-discriminatory geographic zone assignment system.

• Prohibited federal pressure on local school boards to use state or local funds for busing of students, unless constitutionally required. PL 92-318 also barred federal pressure on any school board to bus students when the time or distance involved was so great as to risk the health, or educational opportunity of the children or when busing would mean that the children would be bused to a school substantially inferior to that to which they would otherwise be assigned under a non-discriminatory geographic zone assignment system.

• Postponed the effective date of any federal district court order requiring the transfer or transportation of any student for the purpose of achieving a balance among students with respect to race, sex, religion or socio-economic status until all appeals of the order had been exhausted or until the time for them had expired. Provision was to expire Jan. 1, 1974.

• Authorized the parent or guardian of a child bused under a court order to seek to reopen or intervene in the further implementation of such court order if the time or distance involved in the busing risked the health of the student or significantly impinged on the educational process.

• Provided that the rules of evidence required to prove that state or local authorities were practicing racial discrimination in student assignment must be uniform throughout the United States.

Title IX—Sex Discrimination

PL 92-318 forbade any education program receiving federal funds from discriminating on the basis of sex, with the exception of admissions to private undergraduate institutions, of educational institutions controlled by religious organizations in which such a policy would conflict with the institution's tenets, of the military and merchant marine academies of the United States and of admissions to any public institution of undergraduate education with a traditional one-sex policy, and provided that federal aid to any program or institution refusing to comply with Title IX could be terminated.

Title X—Institutional Aid

PL 92-318 authorized a program of direct federal aid on an annual basis to institutions of post-secondary education, under which:

• Each institution would be entitled to an annual cost-of-education payment—45 percent of the funds available for which would be allocated on the basis of:

1) $500 for each basic federal grant recipient in attendance at an institution with enrollment of up to 1,000; $500 for each of the first 100 basic grant recipients at larger institutions.

2) $400 for each recipient over the first 100 at an institution with enrollment of up to 2,500; $400 for each of the next 150 recipients over the first 100 at larger institutions.

3) $300 for each recipient over the first 250 at an institution with enrollment of up to 5,000; $300 for each of the second 250 recipients at larger institutions.

4) $200 for each recipient over the first 500 at an institution with enrollment of up to 10,000; $200 for each of the second 500 recipients at larger institutions.

5) $100 for each recipient after the first 1,000 at institutions enrolling over 10,000 students.

• To this cost-of-education payment would be added— from the second 45 percent of the available funds and based on the aggregate amount of supplemental educational opportunity grants, work-study payments and direct loans paid each year to students at each individual institution, a payment equal to:

1) 50 percent of the aggregate for institutions with up to 1,000 students.

2) 46 percent for those with 1,001 to 3,000 students.

3) 42 percent for those with 3,001 to 10,000 students.

4) 38 percent for larger institutions.

• The remaining 10 percent of funds available for institutional aid would be allocated to schools on the basis of the number of graduate students in attendance at a $200 per capita rate.

• A cost-of-education payment would also be made to each institution, increasing substantially the number of veterans in attendance, amounting to $300 for every veteran receiving vocational rehabilitation or GI bill educational benefits.

• Limited to $1,000,000,000 the total payments under the new program in any fiscal year.

Background

S 659 as originally approved by the Senate in August 1971 contained only higher education provisions, with authorizations of $19-billion in federal aid for post-secondary education in fiscal years 1972-75.

Two months later, in November, the House approved its own higher education bill, with authorizations of $22.5-billion in federal aid for post-secondary education in fiscal years 1972-76, and added a desegregation aid measure authorizing $1.5-billion to aid desegregating school districts in fiscal 1972-73.

The House also added three strong anti-busing provisions forbidding the use of federal education funds for busing, forbidding federal pressure for the expenditure of state or local funds for busing and delaying the effect of a court order requiring busing until all appeals of that order were exhausted.

When the House version, which now carried the Senate bill number, was returned to the Senate it was again referred to the Labor and Public Welfare Committee. Early in December 1971 the committee voted to substitute for the House provisions the provisions of the Senate-approved bills plus a mild statement that busing was not required by the bill.

References. *Busing moratorium and proposed constitutional amendment, p. 32; equal educational opportunities, p. 89; education funds, p. 89.*

Senate Committee Action

The Senate Labor and Public Welfare Committee Feb. 7 reported an omnibus education bill, the Education Amendments of 1972 (S 659—S Rept 92-604).

The committee unanimously recommended that the amended bill be adopted by the Senate as a substitute for the House version of the bill.

Provisions. As reported by the committee, the amended version of S 659 contained provisions:

• Authorizing revision and extension through fiscal 1975 of most federal programs of aid to higher education, incorporating them all into one federal law, the Higher Education Act of 1965; providing a new basic student aid program of educational opportunity grants and new aid through cost-of-instruction allowances to the colleges attended by basic grant recipients.

● Authorizing appropriations for three years, through fiscal 1975, for programs of vocational education and creating a bureau of occupational, career and adult education within the Office of Education.

● Establishing a National Foundation for Post-secondary Education and a National Institute of Education.

(All the above provisions were part of S 659 as originally approved by the Senate.)

● Authorizing expanded and new programs to improve the quality of education for Indian children attending public schools. (These provisions were approved by the Senate Oct. 8, 1971, as the Indian Education Act of 1971, S 2482.) *(p. 89)*

● Authorizing $1.5-billion for emergency assistance to desegregating schools and for support of quality integrated schools in fiscal 1972 and 1973. (This provision was approved by the Senate April 26, 1971, as S 1557.) *(p. 88)*

● Authorizing a foreign service scholarship program. (This provision had been ordered reported as S 390, favorably in 1971 by this committee and unfavorably by the Foreign Relations Committee.)

● Providing that no part of S 659 should be interpreted to require the assignment or transportation of students or teachers in order to overcome racial imbalance. (This provision had not been contained in any of the measures previously approved by the Senate.)

Committee Views. For its views on the measures incorporated into the omnibus bill, the committee referred back to the reports it had filed in 1971 on the various measures.

Concerning the anti-busing provision—added by the committee in December—the committee stated its belief that the question of transportation should be decided at the local level. The provision it added clarified federal policy on that question, the committee report said.

The new amendment would allow financial assistance—through federal funds—for school desegregation including transportation undertaken following desegregation plans under a federal court order, the 1964 Civil Rights Act, state law or state court orders or a voluntary plan initiated by the local school board.

The committee stated that it felt a ban against federal aid to meet the cost of desegregation-related transportation (such as contained in the House version of S 659) would result in additional taxes at the local level or cutbacks in vital education services.

Cost. The committee estimated that new obligational authority of $576.3-million would be needed to carry out S 659 in fiscal 1972, plus additional budget authority totalling $155-million for use during fiscal 1972 and 1973.

New obligational authority of $800-million would be needed for the new national foundation and national institute for fiscal years 1973-1975.

New budget authority for all other programs included in S 659 would reach $7-billion in fiscal 1973, $6.3-billion in fiscal 1974 and $6.7-billion in fiscal 1975, the committee estimated.

Senate Floor Action

The Senate, after eight days of debate devoted primarily to consideration of a variety of anti-busing amendments, approved language only moderately restricting the future use of busing for desegregation of schools.

On March 1 the Senate by a roll-call vote of 88-6 approved an amended bill (S 659), the Omnibus Education Amendments of 1972, to which the anti-busing language was attached, and sent it back to the House.

The compromise language on the busing issue in S 659 as passed by the Senate was proposed by Majority Leader Mike Mansfield (D Mont.) and Minority Leader Hugh Scott (R Pa.). It:

● Forbade the use of federal education funds for busing to overcome racial imbalance or to desegregate a school system "except on the written request of local school officials;" forbade any court or federal official to order local school officials to make such a request; barred use of funds for busing when the time or distance involved was so great as to risk the health of children involved or to impinge on the educational process.

● Forbade any federal pressure on local school boards: 1) to induce them to use state or local funds for busing "unless constitutionally required" or 2) to undertake busing which would risk the health of the children, impinge on the educational process or require that a student attend a school educationally inferior to that which he would otherwise, under a non-discriminatory pupil assignment system, attend.

● Postponed, until all appeals were exhausted, the effective date of any federal court order requiring busing of students between school districts or the consolidation of two or more school districts. This postponement was to expire June 30, 1973.

Busing Amendments

On Feb. 24, Walter F. Mondale (D Minn.) proposed that the Senate amend S 659 to make clear that its desegregation requirements were to be applied uniformly across the nation, whether the segregation in question was the result of law *(de jure)* or other factors such as neighborhood housing patterns *(de facto)*.

To the Mondale amendment the Senate Feb. 24 added the three parts of the Mansfield-Scott compromise by votes of 51-37, 50-38 and 79-9.

The following day (Feb. 25) the Senate adopted far stronger anti-busing language through an amendment proposed by Robert P. Griffin (R Mich.). The amendment:

● Withdrew from the federal courts the jurisdiction to issue orders or make decisions requiring busing on the basis of race, color, religion or national origin.

● Forbade any federal agency or employee to withhold federal aid, or threaten to withhold federal aid, in order to induce school officials to implement busing plans. (The Civil Rights Act of 1964 provided the Department of Health, Education and Welfare and other federal agencies with the authority to enforce non-discrimination requirements by suspending and terminating federal education aid to school districts—and other recipients of federal aid—which refused to comply.) From 1965 through 1968 this enforcement power was the most often-used federal means of enforcing school desegregation.

The Nixon administration had used this power sparingly, preferring to rely on suits brought in federal court to enforce desegregation requirements. *(Congress and the Nation Vol. I, p. 1639; CQ paperback, Civil Rights: Progress Report 1970, p. 49-52)*

• Postponed the effective date of any court order requiring busing between school districts or the consolidation of two or more school districts until all appeals of the order were exhausted.

The Griffin amendment was adopted by a 43-40 roll-call vote.

But on Feb. 29—after several absent senators campaigning for the Democratic nomination for President returned to Washington—the Senate undid its anti-busing actions of the previous week by rejecting, 48-49, the Mondale amendment which by then included both the compromise Mansfield-Scott and the stronger Griffin amendments. This vote nullified the earlier adoption of both amendments.

The Senate then reaffirmed its decision on the Griffin amendment by rejecting it again, when offered as an amendment to another amendment, by a 47-50 vote, and re-adopted the Scott-Mansfield amendment, 63-34.

No other anti-busing amendments were approved during debate on S 659; the Senate rejected five others which:

• Postponed the effective date of all federal district court orders requiring busing until all appeals of the order had been exhausted. The Senate Feb. 29 rejected, 43-49, the amendment proposed by Howard H. Baker Jr. (R Tenn.).

• Postponed the effective date of all court-ordered busing until desegregation plans were adopted uniformly across the country. The Senate rejected the amendment proposed by David H. Gambrell (D Ga.) Feb. 29, 29-62.

• Barred any federal action denying a student the right to attend his neighborhood school. The Senate rejected the amendment proposed by Sam J. Ervin Jr. (D N.C.) March 1 by a 26-67 vote.

• Barred any federal action interfering with freedom-of-choice school attendance plans. The Senate rejected this Ervin amendment March 1, 31-63.

• Forbade that any public school student be required to attend or barred from attending a particular school because of his race, creed, color or economic class. The Senate rejected this Ervin amendment March 2 by voice vote.

Before the final 88-6 vote passing S 659, the Senate again rejected, 47-48, the Griffin amendment presented in modified form by Robert Dole (R Kan.).

Other Major Amendments

The Senate voted on a variety of other amendments on desegregation and education programs. The Senate:

• Specifically authorized the commissioner of education to undertake programs of educational renewal with existing federal education funds. The program had already been begun without congressional approval.

• Prohibited sex discrimination in almost all education programs at all levels receiving federal aid; excepted the admissions policies of private institutions of higher education.

• Expressed the sense of the Congress that students should be represented on the governing boards of colleges and universities.

• Deleted provisions establishing a foreign service scholarship program.

• Rejected a massive $20-billion program of nationwide metropolitan-area school desegregation proposed by Abraham Ribicoff (D Conn.). In April 1971, the Senate had rejected the same amendment by a vote of 35-51: R 7-32; D 28-19 (ND 21-13; SD 7-6); the 1972 vote, 29-65, was more lopsided, reflecting erosion in the ranks of northern senators: R 4-40; D 25-25 (ND 17-16; SD 8-9).

Debate

Almost all the debate on S 659 dealt with desegregation. Even before debate began Feb. 22, Mondale, chairman of the Select Committee on Equal Educational Opportunity, Feb. 18 opposed any anti-busing proposal:

"Every reasonable effort must be made to overcome the results of officially approved school segregation.... And reasonable transportation will be required where necessary to defeat the results of racially discriminatory student assignment policies....

"Quality integrated education—sensibly achieved and with community support—is one of the best hopes for the education of our children and the future of divided communities throughout this nation," he continued.

"We have only two choices. We can assume our share of the burden...(and) ask...how we can best work to assure that school integration is conducted in a sensible, educationally beneficial manner.... Or we can stand in the schoolhouse door."

The House amendments, Mondale said, were senseless and divisive, abandoning every school district which was desegregating. Busing had not increased as a result of school desegregation; most school children outside of cities were bused to school, and for 65 percent of them the reason for busing was not desegregation, he said.

Debate officially began Feb. 22 with Ribicoff sharply criticizing "the rush of politicians stumbling over each other to oppose busing.... The arguments we rejected for years, when raised by southerners...are now embraced by liberals throughout the north."

"We have an obligation to confront the problem of segregation squarely and develop solutions.... Some are talking now of compromises on the question of busing, perhaps resulting in an amendment introduced by liberals that would appear to be against busing without really ending it.... This may be fine for our conscience ...but it hardly qualifies as constructive leadership."

Barring the use of federal funds for busing was no answer, said Ribicoff, noting that southern school officials were watching with dismay as their representatives voted to deny them this financial aid in carrying out court-ordered busing plans.

Explaining his compromise amendment, Scott Feb. 23 said it emphasized voluntary desegregation and voluntary use of busing. It was in keeping with the Supreme Court's April 1971 decision which noted that there might be some validity to objections to busing based on a risk to the health or education of the children concerned.

Ribicoff Feb. 24 criticized the amendment as "a step on the road backward toward separate but equal schools...public notice that we have given up the struggle to end discrimination." James B. Allen (D Ala.) criticized the amendment as a "pro-busing" measure.

Griffin Feb. 23, in introducing his amendment, said it was an exercise of the constitutional power granted Congress to delineate the jurisdiction of the federal court system. He said that although he had introduced a constitutional amendment to bar busing, he would prefer to deal with the problem through legislation. *(Proposed constitutional amendment, p. 32)*

Congress had exercised this power over judicial jurisdiction before, Griffin said, citing a 1932 action withdrawing from the federal courts the power to issue injunctions in labor disputes. This extreme action in the case of busing was now needed, he said, because the courts and bureaucrats had lost sight of the fundamental purpose and meaning of the Supreme Court's decision of 1954—that government at all levels should be colorblind. Griffin said that his amendment would in no way impair the power of the courts to use other methods, such as redistricting, to encourage desegregation.

Howard H. Baker Jr. (R Tenn.) argued Feb. 25 that busing had been shown to be unworkable and not in the best interests of the educational opportunity of American children. "Busing visited upon...children to satisfy some numerical equality and...judicially decreed proportion ...is also inherently unequal and...creates the same lack of opportunity cited in the (1954) court decision."

Allen said Feb. 29 that adoption of the Mansfield-Scott amendment made a constitutional amendment barring busing necessary. The amendment adopted by the Senate, he said, would not stop massive forced busing, did not repudiate the "hideous racist doctrine" of racial balance in schools and would not save a single neighborhood school.

Amendments Accepted. Feb. 24—Hugh Scott (R Pa.)-Mike Mansfield (D Mont.) amendment to rejected Mondale (D Minn.) amendment *(below)*—Forbid the use of federal education funds for busing to overcome racial imbalance or to desegregate schools except on written request of local school officials; forbid any federal court or official to order local school officials to make this request; forbid the use of federal funds for busing when the time or distance involved risked the health of the children or significantly affected the educational process. Roll-call vote, 51-37. (Adoption of the amendment later nullified by rejection of the Mondale amendment.)

Scott-Mansfield amendment to rejected Mondale amendment *(below)*—Forbid any federal official to pressure a local school board to use state or local funds for busing, unless constitutionally required, or to undertake busing which would risk the health of the children, impinge on the educational process or require that a child attend a school educationally inferior to that which he would attend under a non-discriminatory pupil assignment policy. Roll call, 50-38.

Scott-Mansfield amendment to rejected Mondale amendment *(below)*—Postpone, until all appeals were exhausted, the effective date of any federal court order requiring busing of students between school districts or consolidation of two or more school districts. The postponement would expire June 30, 1973. Roll call, 79-9.

Feb. 25—Robert P. Griffin (R Mich.) amendment to rejected Mondale amendment *(below)*—Withdraw from all federal courts the jurisdiction to make any decision or issue any order which effectively required that pupils be

bused to schools on the basis of race, color, religion or national origin; forbid any federal agency or employee empowered to extend federal education aid to withhold aid in order to induce the implementation of any busing plan; postpone the effectiveness of any court order requiring busing between two school districts or the consolidation of two or more school districts in order to achieve a racial or religious balance until all appeals had been exhausted. Roll call, 43-40. A motion to reconsider was tabled by a 44-41 roll call.

Hiram L. Fong (R Hawaii)—Make the Pacific Trust Territory eligible for federal aid for construction of higher education facilities. Voice vote.

Feb. 28—J. Glenn Beall Jr. (R Md.)—Provide that the program of emergency aid to institutions of higher education be available through fiscal 1974, rather than through fiscal 1973 as provided in S 659. Voice.

Alan Cranston (D Calif.)—Authorize use of federal education funds by the commissioner of education for programs of educational renewal. Voice.

Cranston—Provide for cost-of-instruction grants to institutions of higher education on the basis of the number of veterans attending each institution with GI bill educational aid or vocational rehabilitation assistance. Voice.

Lloyd Bentsen (D Texas)—Amendment to Bayh (D Ind.) amendment *(below)*—Exempt the admissions policies of public one-sex institutions of undergraduate higher education. Voice.

Birch Bayh (D Ind.)—As modified by Bentsen amendment *(above)*—Prohibit sex discrimination in any education programs receiving federal education aid, with the exception of the admissions policies of private institutions of higher education. Voice.

Walter F. Mondale (D Minn.)—Allow certain state agencies to be designated authorities for the purpose of determining the eligibility of institutions of vocational education to receive federal aid. Voice.

Henry Bellmon (R Okla.)—Include Indians in Oklahoma, Alaska and California who did not live on reservations among those (living on or near reservations) for whom special educational programs were provided. Voice.

Thomas F. Eagleton (D Mo.)—Provide locally elected school officials a voice on the Advisory Commission on Intergovernmental Relations. Voice.

Feb. 29—Fred R. Harris (D Okla.)—Declare it the sense of the Congress that there be student representation on the governing boards of colleges and universities. Roll call, 66-28.

Scott-Mansfield amendment in the nature of a substitute for adopted Allen amendment *(below)*—Forbid the use of federal education funds for busing except on request of local officials; forbid federal pressure on local school boards to use state or local funds for busing unless constitutionally required or to undertake busing at the risk of the health or education of the child or to require that a child attend a school educationally inferior to that which he would otherwise attend under a non-discriminatory pupil assignment policy; postpone until all appeals were exhausted the effect of any federal court order requiring busing between school districts or the consolidation of school districts. Roll call, 63-34. (For previous votes on amendment section-by-section, *see above*.)

James B. Allen (D Ala.)—As modified by adoption of Scott-Mansfield substitute *(above)*—Forbid the use of federal education funds for busing except on request of local officials; forbid federal pressure for busing using state or local funds; forbid busing which risked the health or education of the child or forced a child to go to a school educationally inferior to one he would otherwise attend under a non-discriminatory assignment policy; postpone the effectiveness of court orders consolidating districts or requiring busing between districts until all appeals were exhausted. (The Allen amendment originally provided that nothing in the act should be interpreted as requiring the assignment or busing of students or teachers in order to racially balance any school.) Roll call, 66-29.

Lawton Chiles (D Fla.)—Modify provision in S 659 barring federal desegregation aid to public school districts which had given aid to segregated private schools by clarifying the language so that it made clear that it applied only when the district knew that the property was going to a private school. Voice.

Sam J. Ervin Jr. (D N.C.)—Provide that uniform rules of evidence be used in determining discrimination in school desegregation cases across the nation. Voice.

J.W. Fulbright (D Ark.)—Delete section creating Foreign Service Scholarship Program. Roll call, 48-42.

Jack Miller (R Iowa)—Provide that persons taking part in the program of Interns for Political Leadership should not take part in partisan political or campaign activities. Voice.

March 1—Ervin—Provide that provisions of the Civil Rights Act of 1964 barring federally ordered busing for racial balance apply to all public schools. Roll call, 92-0.

Herman E. Talmadge (D Ga.)—Allow parents or guardians of children bused to a public school in accord with a court order to seek to intervene in the implementation of the court order if the time or distance of travel involved is so great as to risk the health of the students or if the effect of the order was alleged to impinge significantly on the quality of the student's education. Roll call, 89-5.

Claiborne Pell (D R.I.)—Provide that $500-million in desegregation aid be available from the date of enactment of S 659 through fiscal 1973, and that an additional $1-billion be available for use in fiscal 1974. (The bill as reported had made the funds available in fiscal 1972 and 1973 respectively.) Voice.

Amendments Rejected. Feb. 28—Lawton Chiles (D Fla.)— Provide special federal aid for schools in disadvantaged neighborhoods in order that they become high quality schools. Roll call, 14-65.

Feb. 29—Walter F. Mondale (D Minn.)—As amended by adopted Scott-Mansfield and Griffin amendments *(above)*—Provide for uniform application of desegregation requirements in S 659 to *de facto* and *de jure* segregation across the country; restrict the use of federal funds for busing; withdraw the jurisdiction of the federal courts to order busing and forbid the federal government to withhold aid to induce the use of busing. Roll call, 48-49.

Robert P. Griffin (R Mich.)—Amendment to adopted Allen (D Ala.) amendment *(above)*—Withdraw from federal courts the jurisdiction to require busing on the basis of race, color, religion or national origin; forbid withholding of federal aid to induce implementation of busing plans; postpone the effective date of court orders requiring busing between districts or consolidation of two districts. Roll call, 47-50.

Abraham Ribicoff (D Conn.)—Authorize $1-billion each for desegregation aid in fiscal 1974 and 1975; require by 1985 the desegregation of all metropolitan-area schools in the nation; authorize $20,050,000,000 for the period 1974-85 to aid in the planning and implementation of the desegregation. Roll call, 29-65.

Howard H. Baker Jr. (R Tenn.)—Postpone the effective date of all federal district court orders requiring busing until all appeals had been exhausted. Roll call, 43-49.

David H. Gambrell (D Ga.)—Amendment in the nature of a substitute for the Baker (R Tenn.) amendment *(above)*—Postpone the effective date of court-ordered busing plans until desegregation plans had been adopted uniformly across the country. Roll call, 29-62.

March 1—Sam J. Ervin Jr. (D N.C.)—Deny to any federal court, agency, department or officer the power to require that state or local school authorities deny to any student of any race, religion or national origin admission to the school nearest his home and operated for pupils of his age and ability. Roll call, 26-67.

Ervin—Deny to any federal court, department, agency or officer the power to require that state or local school authorities assign students of any race, religion or national origin to any schools other than those chosen by the students or their parents, so long as all the schools under the state or local jurisdiction were open to all students regardless of race, religion or national origin. Roll call, 31-63.

Gambrell—Require the attorney general and the secretary of health, education and welfare to report to Congress on the conditions of school segregation throughout the country and the policies and criteria used by the departments of justice and health, education and welfare in respect to desegregation; the report was to include certain specific information and comparisons. Roll call, 29-63.

Chiles—Allow districts desegregating under court order to be eligible, without meeting any other requirements, for desegregation aid provided by S 659. Roll call, 38-57.

Robert Dole (R Kan.)—Withdraw from federal courts the jurisdiction to require busing on the basis of race, color, religion or national origin; forbid withholding of federal aid to induce implementation of busing plans; postpone the effective date of court orders requiring busing until all appeals had been exhausted. Roll call, 47-48.

Ervin (D N.C.)-James B. Allen (D Ala.)—Provide that no public school student could be assigned to or required to attend, or forbidden to attend, a particular school because of his race, creed, color or economic class. Voice.

House Instructs Conferees

The House March 8 instructed its conferees on the omnibus education bill (S 659) to insist on its strongly worded anti-busing amendments and requested a conference with the Senate.

In an unusual action, the House agreed, 272-140, to a motion instructing the conferees to insist on the House-approved amendments which:

• Postponed the effective date of any federal district court order requiring the busing of students to achieve a racial, sex, religious or socio-economic balance in schools until all appeals of such order had been exhausted—or until the time for all appeals had expired.

• Prohibited the use of all federal education funds to bus students or teachers to overcome racial imbalance or to desegregate schools.

• Forbade any federal employee to pressure any local education agency or any private non-profit agency to use any state or local funds for any purpose—such as busing—for which federal funds could not be used.

The House traditionally resists such motions, preferring not to restrict its conferees' actions in this way. Motions to instruct are usually defeated by adoption of motions to table—killing the instructing motions. But on March 8, the House refused, 139-270, to adopt such a motion offered by Carl D. Perkins (D Ky.), chairman of the Education and Labor Committee which had jurisdiction over the bill.

The House then adopted the motion to instruct, which was offered by Earl B. Ruth (R N.C.), and asked for a conference with the Senate to iron out differences between House and Senate versions of the omnibus education bill to which the anti-busing amendments were added.

Two months later, on May 11, the House voted, 275-124, to instruct—for the second time—its conferees to insist on the House-approved anti-busing amendments. The motion, offered by Joe D. Waggonner Jr. (D La.), was opposed by Education and Labor Committee Chairman Carl D. Perkins (D Ky.) and ranking committee minority member Albert H. Quie (R Minn.).

Motions to Instruct Conferees. In 1971 the House took five votes on motions to instruct its conferees on certain issues. In all cases, the House refused to instruct conferees as follows:

• To accept a Senate amendment adding money for education programs to the education appropriations bill.

• To accept the Mansfield amendment calling for a total U.S. troop withdrawal from Vietnam—a motion to table was adopted twice in 1971 by the House.

• To accept a Senate amendment barring certain uses of funds appropriated for the Subversive Activities Control Board.

• Not to accept any non-germane Senate amendments—such as the Mansfield amendment—to the defense procurement bill.

Conference Action

Conferees filed their reports (S Rept 92-798, H Rept 92-1085) on S 659 May 22 and 23.

Major differences between the House and Senate versions of S 659 were resolved as follows.

Busing

House conferees agreed to:

• Senate language amending the House ban on use of federal education funds for busing to overcome racial imbalance in public schools by allowing use of the funds "on the express written voluntary request of appropriate local school officials."

• Senate language barring use of federal funds for busing—or federal pressure on local school boards to use state or local funds for busing—when the time or distance of travel involved was so great as to risk the health of the children, to impinge significantly on the educational

process or when busing required that students go to schools offering substantially inferior educational opportunities to those available to them at the schools to which they would otherwise be assigned under a nondiscriminatory pupil assignment policy.

• Senate language amending the ban on federal pressure on local school boards to induce them to use state or local funds for busing by allowing such pressure when busing was "constitutionally required."

• Senate language authorizing parents of children bused in accord with a court order to seek to intervene in the implementation of the order if the child's health or education was threatened by the busing.

• Senate language requiring that rules of evidence required to prove that state or local authorities were practicing racial discrimination in pupil assignment be uniform throughout the United States.

Senate conferees agreed to:

• House language postponing, until all appeals had been ruled upon or until the time for them had expired, the effective date of any federal court order requiring busing of students to achieve a balance in the schools as to sex, race, religion or socio-economic status. This provision would expire Jan. 1, 1974.

Conferees noted in their report that this section did not authorize the reopening of desegregation cases in which final orders had been entered but that it did apply to desegregation orders still on appeal or still eligible for appeal. They added the hope that "the judiciary will take such action as may be necessary to expedite the resolution of the issues subject to this section."

Higher Education

House conferees agreed to:

• The Senate approach to the higher education provisions, incorporating all major aid-to-higher-education programs under the Higher Education Act of 1965.

• The Senate language extending authority for most existing higher education aid programs through fiscal 1975, instead of through fiscal 1976 as the House version provided.

On other points of disagreement, conferees:

• Authorized aid to developing institutions at $91-million for fiscal 1972, as recommended by the Senate, and at $120-million per year for fiscal 1973-75, as recommended by the House.

• Reduced the authorization for a new program of emergency grants to institutions in serious financial distress (provided by the Senate and not the House) to $40-million from $150-million.

• Adopted Senate provisions establishing a new program of basic educational opportunity grants entitling any student in good standing at an institution of higher learning to a grant of $1,400 minus the amount his family could reasonably be expected to contribute toward his educational expenses.

Conferees agreed that such grants could not exceed the difference between the expected family contribution and the actual cost of attendance at the institution.

Conferees also specified how funds were to be used when appropriations were insufficient to pay all entitlements in full.

• Adopted a House provision increasing the maximum amount for an individual annual supplemental educational opportunity grant to $1,500 from $1,000.

• Agreed to extend the Emergency Insured Student Loan Act authorizing special payments to lenders in times of high interest rates through fiscal year 1974. The Senate had extended it through fiscal 1973; the House, through fiscal 1976.

• Agreed to House language increasing the individual annual limit for an insured student loan to $2,500 from $1,500 (the aggregate loan ceiling for an individual would remain at $7,500).

• Extended the work-study program through fiscal 1975 at the amounts authorized in the House bill; adopted House language allowing participation of half-time students, giving preference to students in great financial need; and established a new program of public service jobs primarily for veterans.

• Extended the direct student loan program through fiscal 1975 with authorization of $375-million for fiscal 1972 and $400-million for each of fiscal 1973-75.

• Adopted the House language setting an aggregate direct loan limit of $2,500 for the first two years of study leading to a bachelor's degree.

• Rejected several Senate amendments clarifying the status of the Teacher Corps within the Office of Education with the understanding "that the status of the Teacher Corps within the Office of Education should be the same as was originally intended with the enactment of the Higher Education Act of 1965:...independent of the regular bureaucratic structure of the office...and the director...is not intended to be subjected to the administrative direction of persons other than the commissioner of education."

• Dropped Senate language increasing to 33 percent from 24 percent the amount of the funds appropriated for undergraduate facility construction which was to be reserved for community colleges and technical institutes.

• Adopted House provisions authorizing a new program of federal mortgage insurance of academic facilities loans but limiting participation in the program to private non-profit institutions. The Senate had included public institutions as well.

• Deleted Senate language authorizing the Interns for Political Leadership program and House language creating a program of mineral conservation education.

• Consolidated into a single title Senate provisions creating a new program of federal grants for the establishment and improvement of community colleges and House provisions establishing a new program of federal aid to vocational education.

Education Division

• Agreed to Senate language establishing an Education Division within the Department of Health, Education and Welfare (HEW) under an assistant secretary for education. It would be composed of the Office of Education and the National Institute of Education.

• Dropped authorization for creation of a National Foundation for Post-secondary Education, but retained and granted to the secretary of HEW authority to make grants for improving postsecondary educational opportunities.

Related Programs

• Agreed to all the Senate provisions concerning Indian education.

• Agreed to a Senate provision authorizing grants for creation of ethnic heritage studies projects.

• Retained House language authorizing endowment grants of $3-million each for the College of the Virgin Islands and the University of Guam and Senate amendments granting those institutions the status of land grant institutions.

Youth Camp Safety

• Deleted Senate language establishing a youth camp safety program and retained House language requiring the secretary of HEW to report to Congress on the need for federal standards for camps.

Desegregation Aid

• Authorized $1-billion for each of fiscal 1973 (as provided in the House version) and fiscal 1974 (as provided in the Senate version).

• Adopted the House allocation of 6 percent of the funds for special programs and evaluation and the Senate allocation of 3 percent for educational television.

• Reduced the Senate allocations of 15 percent for metropolitan projects to 5 percent; of 15 percent for private groups to 8 percent, and of 22 percent for compensatory education to 15 percent.

• Provided that the unreserved funds were to be allocated among the states (as the Senate had provided) with every state receiving a minimum of $100,000.

• Retained House language making eligible for aid districts implementing desegregation plans under mandate from federal or state agency or court.

• Adopted a modified Senate provision allowing aid— to prevent resegregation—to schools with between 20 and 50 percent minority-group students.

• Dropped the Senate language requiring an eligible school district to establish at least one stable, quality integrated school and adopted a comprehensive district-wide plan for the elimination of minority-group isolation.

• Retained House language making eligible school districts voluntarily enrolling non-resident children and Senate language allowing grants for inter-district projects within metropolitan areas.

• Retained Senate language allowing districts applying for desegregation aid funds to receive funds for compensatory education if they had either 50 percent or 15,000 minority-group students.

• Retained Senate language barring aid to school districts which knowingly transferred property to private segregated schools; dropped Senate language barring aid to any school district which had a discriminatory policy against minority-group employees resulting in the disproportionate demotion or dismissal of such employees; retained Senate language allowing *bona fide* ability grouping.

• Retained the Senate list of authorized activities for which the desegregation aid funds could be used.

• Retained the House amendment requiring the consideration of only six factors before approving or disapproving an application for aid and barring less favorable consideration of an application of a voluntarily desegregating school district than that given a district required by a court to adopt such a plan.

Sex Discrimination

• Retained the Senate language exempting from the ban on sex discrimination (by any educational program receiving federal aid) only the undergraduate admissions policies of private institutions of higher education and public institutions of a traditional one-sex policy. (The House had exempted all undergraduate discrimination.)

Institutional Aid

- Provided that 45 percent of the funds appropriated for direct federal aid to institutions of higher education be paid on the basis of the amount of federal student aid (supplemental grants, work-study payments and direct loans) paid to students at each institution.
- Provided that another 45 percent of the funds be paid on the basis of the number of basic federal grant recipients attending each institution.
- Provided that the remaining 10 percent would go to institutions on the basis of the number of graduate students in attendance, at a rate of $200 per capita.
- Set a $1-billion limit on payments under the program.

Final Action

SENATE. The Senate May 24 upheld compromise school anti-busing provisions worked out by House-Senate conferees. Then it approved by a 63-15 roll-call vote the conference report on S 659, the Education Amendments of 1972.

Acceptance of the report (S Rept 92-798) came after two days of debate which focused on the compromise busing provisions.

Before accepting the conference report, the Senate May 23, in the key vote on the busing issue, rejected an attempt to restore the stronger anti-busing measures passed by the House. The attempt was made by Minority Whip Robert P. Griffin (R Mich.), who offered a motion to recommit the bill to conference with instructions to accept the House language on busing. Sen. Claiborne Pell (D R.I.), floor manager of S 659, moved to table (kill) Griffin's motion. The tabling motion was adopted, 44-26.

Pell, floor manager of the bill, said S 659 "is the fruit of many years work by many people....It is truly a landmark bill." Minority Leader Hugh Scott (R Pa.) said the bill "is probably the best major educational bill of its nature to be offered to Congress."

Debate May 23. Leading off the debate on the conference report, Griffin offered a motion to recommit the report to conference with instructions to accept the House position on anti-busing measures. During previous Senate consideration of S 659 in February, Griffin had proposed his own stronger anti-busing provision. The provision was first adopted and later rejected by the Senate.

Griffin's second attempt to strengthen the anti-busing provisions was defeated May 23 when the Senate voted 44-26 to table (kill) the motion.

Howard H. Baker Jr. (R Tenn.), who Feb. 29 had offered an amendment to delay busing, asked whether the conference provision would postpone busing in Nashville, where a district court order had been handed down but was being appealed. Pell said his interpretation of the compromise was that busing in Nashville would be postponed, whereupon Baker said he felt he could not support the Griffin motion to recommit.

Peter H. Dominick (R Colo.), a conferee on S 659, urged defeat of Griffin's motion, arguing that the busing issue should not "torpedo a bill as necessary, as promising and as comprehensive as this."

The two senators from Florida disagreed on the recommittal motion. Republican Edward J. Gurney said he strongly supported Griffin's move, while Democrat Lawton Chiles said he would vote to table the motion because he believed the busing issue would not be advanced by its passage.

The busing compromise was attacked by advocates as well as opponents of busing. Jacob K. Javits (R N.Y.) said: "The real battle comes upon the question of what to do about the really unrelated question of busing. Is it big enough to jettison the bill or, considering everything that is at stake in terms of proportion, shall those of us who feel as strongly as I do about equal educational opportunity and desegregation swallow hard and take the conference report?"

Abraham Ribicoff (D Conn.) said he would vote against the conference report: "The reforms contained in S 659 are needed—but not at the price the conferees ask us to pay," he said.

Debate May 24. Pell likened the anti-busing provisions to the "tip of an iceberg," and said: "Just as one cannot see the bulk of an iceberg, which is underwater, the broad new educational approaches in this bill have been submerged beneath the surface. But this tip, which is very obvious, causes the problem which makes its passage difficult. It is this tip that has caused the unholy alliance of the left and right in opposition to the bill."

Several senators who had voted against tabling Griffin's motion said they would vote for the conference report. Harry F. Byrd Jr. said that although he felt the busing provisions did not go far enough, he would vote for the conference report because it was a "highly important piece of legislation." The position of John C. Stennis (D Miss.) was similar. Stennis, who also voted against the motion to table, said: "On balance, considering all the factors...I think the needs for additional federal financial assistance for education at all levels are so great that I should support the conference report."

Final Vote. When the final vote came on the conference report, several senators who had urged stronger busing provisions voted to accept the compromise language. They noted that the provisions went further toward halting busing than any previous Senate action and that the higher education provisions should not be jeopardized by rejection of the report.

Voting against acceptance of the conference report were several members who said they supported the rest of S 659 but were opposed to the inclusion of any anti-busing provisions in the bill. Among them were Javits, Ribicoff, Lowell P. Weicker Jr. (R Conn.), Walter F. Mondale (D Minn.), Gaylord Nelson (D Wis.), Philip A. Hart (D Mich.) and Harold E. Hughes (D Iowa). Of the southern senators voting, only David H. Gambrell (D Ga.) voted against the conference report, stating that the busing provisions were not strong enough.

HOUSE. The House June 8, by a 218-180 roll-call vote, cleared for the President's signature the House-Senate compromise on S 659, which contained controversial school anti-busing provisions.

House approval of the conference report (H Rept 92-1085) was in doubt until the roll call was announced because of widespread dissatisfaction with the anti-busing provisions. Opponents of busing argued that conferees should have retained the stronger anti-busing measures originally passed by the House in November 1971. Other representatives, including members of the Black Caucus, voted against the bill on grounds that the busing provisions were unconstitutional and would prove a setback for school integration.

Following the final House action on S 659, Secretary of Health, Education and Welfare Elliot L. Richardson issued a statement praising the bill as "truly a landmark in the history of higher education."

Several members who voted for the bill said they did so in spite of dissatisfaction with the busing provisions to avoid jeopardizing more than two years' congressional work on the higher education programs. The vote breakdown was 89 Republicans in favor, 76 against; 129 Democrats for passage, 104 against.

At the outset of the debate, Rep. Joe D. Waggonner Jr. (D La.) raised three points of order against the conference report. All three were overruled. One of his objections was that conferees had "clearly violated" House instructions to retain the House anti-busing provisions.

Rep. Edith Green (D Ore.), second-ranking Democrat on the Education and Labor Committee, said she had "very strong objections" to many of the bill's educational provisions, which she said offered "false promises." She also opposed the busing compromise as providing only illusory relief from busing.

Urging passage of S 659, Rep. John Dellenback (R Ore.), a conferee, said: "We have here a bill that has had four subcommittees of the House...involved with it. This matter has gone on for more than three years, with 84 days of hearings, and there are more than 6,900 pages of testimony.... This bill would bring to higher education critically important increased stability...a stability that is absolutely imperative if we are to have any higher education."

Ranking Republican House conferee Albert H. Quie (R Minn.) said the conference report had not substantively altered the House busing provisions and that the bill, if passed, would be the first congressional measure to limit the actions of federal courts in the area of school desegregation.

Minority Leader Gerald R. Ford (R Mich.), who had not previously revealed how he would vote, said he had decided to vote against the bill because he felt the anti-busing provisions were not strong enough.

Declaring that the higher education provisions were "desperately needed," Rep. William D. Ford (D Mich.), said he was "shocked and somewhat amazed by the distinguished minority leader from Michigan, who...launched a wholly unwarranted and misleading attack on this legislation with respect to its effect on (busing)."

Rep. William S. Broomfield (R Mich.), author of one of the original House anti-busing amendments, supported the conference report.

"As long as we perpetuate unequal educational opportunities in elementary and secondary grades, the benefits and services which are provided in higher education...will widen still further the gap in education," said Rep. Augustus F. Hawkins (D Calif.), a member of the Black Caucus and an opponent of the conference measure. "The racially exclusionary implications in the anti-busing amendments of this report are deep and strong," he said.

"This is the best possible conference report that could possibly be obtained," said Rep. Carl D. Perkins (D Ky.), manager of the bill and chairman of the House Education and Labor Committee. "Any attempts to

Authorized Federal Aid to Colleges and Students

(in millions)

	Fiscal 1971	Fiscal 1972	Fiscal 1973
Higher Education Act			
Community services	$ 60	$ 10	$ 30
Library assistance	139	39	87
Developing institutions	91	91	120
Work-study grants	285	330	360
Supplemental education opportunity grants	140	170	200
Basic education opportunity grants [1]	—	*(Such sums as necessary)*	
Emergency aid to failing colleges [1]	*(40 to be available through fiscal 1974)*		
Aid to disadvantaged students	96	96	100
Educational Professions Development:			
Recruitment	5		
Teacher Corps	56		
Teacher upgrading	65		
Teacher fellowships	250	200	300
School personnel training	90		
College personnel training	36		
College equipment	70	70	70
Cooperative education	11	11	11
Networks for Knowledge	15	5	10
Public service education	13	13	30
Improved graduate programs	10	10	
Law school clinical experience	8	1	5
Community college development [1]	—	—	65.7
Occupational education [1]	—	—	100
Cost-of-education aid to institutions [1]	—	*(Such sums as necessary)*	
National Defense Education Act [2]			
Student loans	300	375	400
Equipment grants, loans	130	130	130
Language development	39	39	50
Higher Education Facilities Act [2]			
Undergraduate facilities grants	936	50	200
Graduate facilities grants	120	20	40
Academic facilities loans	400	50	100
Grants to reduce borrowing costs	25	39	51
International Education Act [2]	90	90	20

1 First authorized in 1972.
2 Consolidated into the Higher Education Act by PL 92-318.

SOURCE: House Report 1919, 90th Congress, and Senate Report 798, 92nd Congress.

further change or revise or add to what is before us at this very moment will fail."

"This legislation should command the support of every member of the House," Majority Leader Hale Boggs (D La.) said. "Our six million college students and the institutions they attend can wait no longer for Congress to take action in this important area."